BRAINPOWER
GAME PLAN™

Foods, Moves, and Games to
Clear Brain Fog, Boost Memory, and
Age-Proof Your Mind in 4 Weeks!

By Cynthia R. Green, PhD, and the Editors of *Prevention*
Foreword by Liz Vaccariello

 MELCHER
MEDIA

To all of you who seek a smarter way to stay healthy, vibrant, and happy!

The authors, editors, and publisher have made extensive efforts to ensure the accuracy of the information contained in this book. However, this book is intended as a reference volume only, not as a medical manual. The information given here is designed to help you make informed decisions about your health. It is not intended as a substitute for any treatment that may have been prescribed by your doctor. If you suspect that you have a medical problem, we urge you to seek competent medical help.

Mention of specific brand-name products, companies, organizations, or authorities in this book does not imply endorsement by the author or publisher, nor does mention of specific brand-name products, companies, organizations, or authorities imply that they endorse this book, its author, or the publisher. The brand-name products mentioned in this book are trademarks or registered trademarks of their respective companies.

Every effort has been made to contact the original copyright holders of all materials reproduced in the book. Any errors brought to the packager's attention will be corrected in future editions.

Internet addresses given in this book were accurate at the time it went to press.

Prevention® is a registered trademark of Rodale Inc.
Brainpower Game Plan™ and "What's Your Brain Q?"™ are trademarks of Rodale, Inc.

This book was produced by
 MELCHER MEDIA
melcher.com

Printed in the United States of America

Rodale Inc. makes every effort to use acid-free ♾, recycled paper ♻

Interior design by Cooper Graphic Design
Cover design by Jill Armus
Cover illustration © 2009 Michael Austin c/o theispot.com
Interior exercise photos by Patrik Rytikangas
Illustrations © Headcase Design / headcasedesign.com
Fitness training program by Sue Fleming
Nutritional plan by Willow Jarosh, MS, RD, and Stephanie Clarke, MS, RD

Library of Congress Cataloging-in-Publication Data
Brainpower game plan : sharpen your memory, improve your concentration, and age-proof your mind in just 4 weeks /
by the editors of prevention and Cynthia R. Green ; foreword by Liz Vaccariello.
    p. cm.
Includes index.
ISBN-13: 978-1-60529-900-6 (trade)
ISBN-10: 1-60529-900-6 (trade)
1. Mnemonics. I. Green, Cynthia R.
BF385.B783 2009
153.4—dc22
                                                                2009008088

2 4 6 8 10 9 7 5 3

 RODALE
LIVE YOUR WHOLE LIFE™

We inspire and enable people to improve their lives and the world around them
For more of our products visit **rodalestore.com** or call 800-848-4735

Contents

Age-Proof Your Mind

"I don't want to lose my mental edge. I want to stay sharp. I want to feel as with it in 30 years as I do today."

In my role as editor of *Prevention*, I hear comments like these from readers all the time. And if these comments sound familiar to you, I'm thrilled to offer some exciting news: you can protect your brain cells and improve your everyday memory by up to 78%! How? By following the Brainpower Game Plan, which we editors of *Prevention* have created with psychologist Cynthia R. Green, PhD.

What exactly do I mean by "brainpower"? Having solid brainpower means being able to think quickly and clearly in everyday situations, and taking the right steps to ensure that your brain stays healthy for many years to come.

At some point in your life you may have taken an IQ test, which measures intelligence. In a few pages, you are going to take a different type of test—which is available only in this book—that measures your brainpower, producing a number we call your Brain Q. You'll retake the test after finishing the Brainpower Game Plan. Follow the plan closely and rest assured— your Brain Q will soar.

What exactly will that mean? How will increasing your brainpower change your life? For starters, you'll have far fewer of those annoying brain cramps that can mess up your day. You know what I mean. Struggling to remember your mail carrier's name. Finding yourself losing focus during basic mental chores, like balancing your checkbook. Feeling like your life has slipped out of control because you can't get organized.

Increasing your Brain Q will also help disease-proof your brain. People sometimes joke that their minds are turning to mush if they forget why they entered a room or can't remember a simple set of directions. But the kidding around often masks genuine concerns. Am I just a little ditzy or is this a sign of something more serious? That's why virtually every issue of *Prevention* features new information about how to protect your mind and boost your brainpower. We talk to leading scientists who study the brain. We break down cutting-edge studies and tell you what they mean. We focus on brain health with the same intensity that we cover new research about the heart, weight loss, or any other health issue—because we know it matters to you.

And brain health does matter, of course. After all, the mind holds the essence of all that is you. But keeping your brain healthy does far more than preserve memories. Making sure your brain cells are well nourished and get regular exercise allows you to make quick decisions, multitask on busy days, and pay keen attention at critical moments.

At *Prevention* we saw clues that consumers are yearning for tools to get their minds in top shape. For instance, the "brain fitness" games are among the most popular destinations on our Web site (*prevention. com*). Users return again and again to play these fun "mind games" and improve their scores. Clearly, there is a growing need for a comprehensive source of facts and sound advice about cultivating and maintaining brain health.

That's why we asked psychologist Cynthia R. Green, PhD, to help us create the Brainpower Game Plan. One of the nation's leading authorities on brain fitness, Cynthia is an assistant clinical professor in the department of psychiatry at Mount Sinai School of Medicine in New York City, where she founded the renowned Memory Enhancement Program. But despite Cynthia's serious scientific credentials, don't expect a lot of dry talk and complex theories that have never left the lab. Like the team at *Prevention*, she knows that getting healthy should be fun. In fact, as you make your way through this book you will spend as much time *doing* as reading: Cynthia has designed an array of games, puzzles, and other mental workouts to challenge and strengthen your mental muscles, and will teach you all kinds of cool strategies that will kick your brainpower into overdrive.

What's more, we're going to show you how making the right changes at mealtime will help protect your memory. (Good news here, too: a lot of fabulous-tasting foods are highly brain-friendly.) And if you need extra inspiration to get up off the sofa and hit the gym, or take a brisk walk, you'll find it in these pages: breakthrough scientific discoveries show that a hearty bout of huffing and puffing breathes new life into brain cells.

The Brainpower Game Plan is a win-win proposition. Follow it closely and you'll slash your risk for dreaded diseases that strike later in life and rob the brain of its ability to perform basic functions. But you won't have to wait years to enjoy the fruits of your efforts, since I guarantee you will begin to experience substantial benefits right away. You'll feel more clearheaded and focused. You'll get more done every day. You might even lose a few pounds in the process!

How do I know? Because we asked a panel of volunteers to test-drive the game plan, and they consistently reported these and many other improvements. (You'll be hearing more about the members of our test panel soon.) I believe that a better, healthier brain is just days away for you, too.

With Cynthia as your guide, you're about to embark on an exciting journey of discovery. I learned a great deal from her about the remarkable science of brain health during the months we spent creating the Game Plan. I can say with confidence that you, and your brain, are in good hands.

LIZ VACCARIELLO
Editor-in-chief, *PREVENTION*

END BRAIN FOG IN JUST FOUR WEEKS

End Brain Fog in Just Four Weeks

Ready to recharge your brain's batteries? Tired of coping with the occasional mind meltdown? Then let's get started.

I'm going to help you sharpen your memory with a plan that will prevent your brain from short-circuiting. In my career as a psychologist and memory expert, I have pored over stacks and stacks of research studies in order to find out what measures have been proven to bulletproof the brain and perk up the mind. As a scientist, I am excited to know that my colleagues around the world are making breakthrough discoveries about brain health practically every day—discoveries that you will put to use immediately.

THE SCIENCE BEHIND THE BRAINPOWER GAME PLAN

The Brainpower Game Plan incorporates the three biggest keys to short- and long-term brain health: exercise, diet, and mentally challenging games, which I call brain training.

No matter how chaotic your schedule, you can probably find time for a short daily walk—which can pay big dividends in terms of brainpower. Harvard researchers followed nearly 19,000 women for 2 years and found that those who walked or got some type of moderate exercise for just 90 minutes a week—that's less than 13 minutes per day—lowered their risk of developing problems with memory and attention span by 20%.

Scientists have also determined that regular exercise boosts the levels of chemicals that feed and protect brain cells, as you will learn later on. What's more, fast-mounting evidence shows that exercising your brain—as you will with the daily workouts I've created—strengthens the mind too. A 2008 University of Michigan study, for example, found that men and women who played a mentally challenging game every day for several weeks improved not only their memories but also their scores on intelligence tests.

11

> **Studies show that vegetables, fruit, certain oils, nuts, curry, and even chocolate can affect your brainpower."**

I can't guarantee that the Brainpower Game Plan will bump up your IQ, but I am certain it will help you feel more clearheaded and productive—as though you added horsepower to your brain's engine. You will also be confident in the knowledge that you're taking important steps to safeguard your brain against disease. As part of my longtime affiliation with Mount Sinai Medical Center in New York City, I have been involved in research on Alzheimer's disease. As you may know, Alzheimer's is the most common form of dementia, which is the general term for severe loss of memory and other important brain skills. (As you will learn, there are several other forms of dementia.) More than 5 million Americans have Alzheimer's disease—and twice that number of baby boomers will develop the condition, according to the Alzheimer's Association.

It's a frightening disease, to be sure, so isn't it good to know that scientists are learning more all the time about how you can lower your risk? For example, I'm going to make a strong case in this book for why you should add fish to your diet if you don't already eat it regularly.

The research is persuasive: one 2006 study at Tufts University found that indulging three times a week in seafood—especially varieties such as salmon, which are high in all-important omega-3 fatty acids—reduced the risk of Alzheimer's disease by 39%. Fish lovers lowered the threat of other forms of dementia by nearly half. And there's more: studies show that vegetables, fruit, certain oils, nuts, curry, and even chocolate can improve your brain health.

THE BRAINPOWER GAME PLAN REALLY WORKS—HERE'S PROOF

I have a lot more exciting research to talk about, but here's what is truly different about the Brainpower Game Plan: we tested it—and we know it works. The editors at *Prevention* recruited a panel of readers who agreed to try out the 4-week plan. The panel consisted of participants (average age: 50) from all over the United States. Some work outside the home, some have kids or care for an older parent, all juggle many responsibilities every day.

More important, each member of our panel came to us concerned about his or her brain health. For most, the daily frustration of forgetting names or missing appointments had reached a critical level. Others told us that seeing their parents struggle with memory loss and other difficulties caused by dementia had been a wake-up call. "What can I do to avoid that fate?" they asked.

Before panel members started the Brainpower Game Plan, we asked them to take a quiz designed to evaluate their brain skills and lifestyle. This quiz produces a number we refer to as your Brain Q, as Liz explained.

After they followed the Brainpower Game Plan for 4 weeks, we re-administered the test to see how much the Brain Q of each panel member had improved.

The results were spectacular. On average, our panelists' Brain Q scores jumped 28%. But some soared even higher—78%, in one case. However, our panel members didn't need to see their score sheets to know that the Brainpower Game Plan really works. Take Diane Cox, 41, of Winston-Salem, North Carolina. Diane told us she had felt so scatterbrained that stopping on the street for a simple conversation with a friend became a nightmare—she was too worried about forgetting an appointment or critical errand. Diane credits the Brainpower Game Plan with helping her restore order in her life. "It has made a huge difference," she says.

Others said the benefits they took away from their 4 weeks on the Brainpower Game Plan will stay with them forever. "I've learned new things that I will carry with me for the rest of my life," says Marianne Seminoff, 51, of Littleton, Colorado. Barbara Capalbo, 52, of Yorktown Heights, New York, was even more to the point: "This plan saved my life."

Now it's your turn. First, you'll take a quiz to test your Brain Q. Then we'll describe all of the science that proves that your Brain Q can improve—a lot! Then we'll get you started on the Brainpower Game Plan. Our panelists improved their Brain Q scores significantly doing our easy and fun Brainpower Game Plan, and we're sure you will too.

> " The Brainpower Game Plan test panel had remarkable results. On average, panelists' Brain Q scores jumped 28%. But some soared even higher—78%, in one case."

What's Your Brain Q?

Your Brain Q is a bird's-eye view of the current state of your brainpower. It's a baseline measurement that you can improve with the Brainpower Game Plan.

The Brain Q quiz is designed to take stock of your current brain health: how sharp are the basic mental skills you rely on every day? And are you taking the right steps to keep your brain healthy as the years pass?

The Brain Q Quiz is divided into four sections.

The first will measure your Everyday Brain Skills: your overall memory, your ability to focus on a task, process information quickly, and think creatively. The purpose of the exercises is to challenge your brain's capacity to cope with real-life situations that you probably confront every day: remembering the names of new acquaintances, for instance, or recalling important details, dealing with numbers, and solving thorny problems at work.

This portion of the quiz is intentionally difficult, so don't worry if you struggle with parts of it—few people attain anything close to a perfect score the first time around. And it's important not to peek! Tempting though it might be to sneak back for another look, the only way to get an accurate Brain Q score is to follow the quiz's directions.

The next three sections will evaluate how well you practice lifestyle habits that have been proven to promote a healthy brain. I'll ask you questions about how much you Exercise, what your Diet looks like, and your level of Memory Fitness, Stress, and Socializing Skills. This portion of the quiz will examine how you feel about your memory function and the roles stress and socializing play in your life.

Be honest with yourself as you work through the questions. Don't be tempted to choose the answer that seems "right." The correct answer is always the one that best describes your current situation.

When you finish the quiz, I'll show you how to compute your baseline Brain Q. Then, after you complete the 4-week Brainpower Game Plan, you will retake the quiz. I guarantee that the second time around you will see—and feel—a striking improvement in your memory, focus, and all-around brain health.

Find a quiet spot where you won't be disturbed or distracted. Ready? Then turn the page and get started.

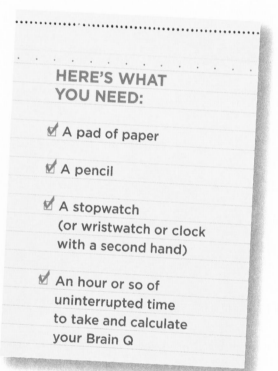

HERE'S WHAT YOU NEED:

☑ A pad of paper

☑ A pencil

☑ A stopwatch (or wristwatch or clock with a second hand)

☑ An hour or so of uninterrupted time to take and calculate your Brain Q

TAKE THE QUIZ ONLINE!

Want to enhance the day-to-day performance of your brain? Take the Brain Q Quiz online and you'll be one step closer! After you answer the questions online, we'll calculate the results for you. Whenever you're ready to test your brainpower again, you can retake this interactive quiz and see how your score has improved over time. Start now at *prevention.com/brainfitnessquiz*.

SECTION 1: Everyday Brain Skills

NO. 1

Set your stopwatch for 2 minutes and write down as many words that begin with C as you can. Do not repeat words and avoid using proper names. Stop when 2 minutes are up.

Fill in the blanks with the numbers or letters that come next in the sequences.

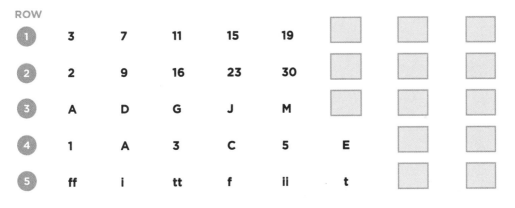

ROW								
1	3	7	11	15	19			
2	2	9	16	23	30			
3	A	D	G	J	M			
4	1	A	3	C	5	E		
5	ff	i	tt	f	ii	t		

Read the following paragraph. When you finish reading, turn the page.

Andrea Ingram takes the 7:30 AM train to work every weekday from Bloomfield Station, near her home in New Jersey. One morning, as the train passed through a deserted area just outside the town of Glen View, Andrea noticed a dog wandering near the tracks. She quickly alerted the conductor, Mr. Greenwood, who contacted the local authorities. The next morning, Andrea brought her three sons to the animal shelter where the dog had been taken. The dog, a poodle mix, was healthy and appeared to enjoy playing with the boys. Andrea's middle son, Henry, returned 2 days later and brought the dog a toy bone. After 1 month, the authorities had not found the dog's owners, so Andrea and her children adopted the dog. They named her Tracks.

Set your stopwatch for 2 minutes and write down as much of the story you just read as you can remember. Include all the details you can recall, in any order. No peeking—rely only on your memory. Stop when 2 minutes are up.

Set your stopwatch for 3 minutes and solve as many of the following math problems as you can. Feel free to use a separate sheet of paper for your calculations. Stop when 3 minutes are up.

ROW

1. $5 \times 3 =$ ___ $23 + 45 =$ ___ $123 - 78 =$ ___ $345 - 67 =$ ___

2. $121 \div 11 =$ ___ $4 \times 9 =$ ___ $43 \div 2 =$ ___ $144 \div 12 =$ ___

3. $23 + 9 =$ ___ $60 - 6 =$ ___ $12 \times 3 =$ ___ $76 - 34 =$ ___

4. $34 \div 2 =$ ___ $129 - 45 =$ ___ $14 \div 2 =$ ___ $34 - 6 =$ ___

5. $13 - 4 =$ ___ $89 \times 4 =$ ___ $44 \times 3 =$ ___ $12 - 9 =$ ___

6. $8 + 13 =$ ___ $23 \times 4 =$ ___ $45 \div 5 =$ ___ $401 - 32 =$ ___

7. $81 - 4 =$ ___ $12 - 9 =$ ___ $90 - 33 =$ ___ $103 - 42 =$ ___

8. $103 - 12 =$ ___ $42 \div 8 =$ ___ $46 + 23 =$ ___ $20 - 4 =$ ___

9. $23 + 45 =$ ___ $34 \div 2 =$ ___ $345 \times 10 =$ ___ $12 - 7 =$ ___

10. $21 + 7 =$ ___ $86 \times 8 =$ ___ $99 + 2 =$ ___ $6 + 21 =$ ___

11. $400 \div 4 =$ ___ $35 \div 7 =$ ___ $32 \div 8 =$ ___ $23 - 12 =$ ___

12. $370 - 43 =$ ___ $9 + 80 =$ ___ $72 \div 9 =$ ___ $502 \div 4 =$ ___

13. $37 - 5 =$ ___ $10 + 20 =$ ___

Read the following list. When you finish reading, turn the page.

Apples	Rice	Popcorn	Lettuce
Soap	Shampoo	Crackers	Chicken
Celery	Bagels	Peaches	Pears
Oatmeal	Salmon	Eggs	Pasta
Carrots	Butter	Blueberries	Tomatoes

NO. 5 | PART 2

Set your stopwatch for 2 minutes and write down as many items from the list as you can remember, in any order. Stop when 2 minutes are up.

_____ _____ _____ _____

_____ _____ _____ _____

_____ _____ _____ _____

_____ _____ _____ _____

_____ _____ _____ _____

NO. 6

At the beginning of this quiz, you read a brief story. Set your stopwatch for 2 minutes and write down as many details of that story as you can remember, in any order. Stop when 2 minutes are up.

_____

_____

_____

_____

_____

_____

_____

_____

_____

_____

Set your stopwatch for 2 minutes and examine this group of photographs, which feature 9 different people and their first and last names. When 2 minutes are up, turn the page.

CARLIE MONROE

TIM GRAY

WALTER CHIMURITTO

ALANA SANDERSTEN

SYBIL BROWERTON

MARK FOWLER

ANDREW GRISCOM

MARILYN CONE

ROBERT FERNANDEZ

Now look again at the photographs, this time not matched with names. Set your stopwatch for 2 minutes and fill in as many of the first and last names as you can remember. Stop when 2 minutes are up.

A short time ago you read a list of words. How well do you remember the list now? Set your stopwatch for 2 minutes and write down as many of the words as you can remember. Stop when 2 minutes are up.

_____	_____	_____	_____
_____	_____	_____	_____
_____	_____	_____	_____
_____	_____	_____	_____
_____	_____	_____	_____

NO. 9 | PART 1

Set your stopwatch for 1 minute and study the photograph below. When time is up, turn to the next page.

Write down as many objects as you can remember from the photograph you just studied.

_____   _____

_____   _____

_____   _____

_____   _____

_____   _____

_____   _____

_____   _____

_____   _____

A short time ago you studied a group of photographs of different people and their names. Set your stopwatch for 2 minutes and fill in as many first and last names as you can remember. Stop when 2 minutes are up.

SECTION 2: Diet

Read each statement and circle the answer that most accurately describes you.

1	I eat fish—especially fatty varieties, such as salmon.	never	rarely	sometimes	often	always
2	I eat at least three servings of vegetables a day.	never	rarely	sometimes	often	always
3	I eat breakfast.	never	rarely	sometimes	often	always
4	I watch my sodium intake.	never	rarely	sometimes	often	always
5	I eat at least one serving of fruit a day.	never	rarely	sometimes	often	always
6	I eat foods that are rich in vitamin E, such as avocados, olive oil, sunflower seeds, and nuts.	never	rarely	sometimes	often	always
7	I eat fast food.	never	rarely	sometimes	often	always
8	I wait until I'm starving to eat.	never	rarely	sometimes	often	always
9	I snack on candy and cookies when I'm hungry.	never	rarely	sometimes	often	always
10	I eat packaged foods such as crackers and cookies.	never	rarely	sometimes	often	always

SECTION 3: Exercise

Read each statement and circle the answer that most accurately describes you.

11	I take a brisk walk during the day.	never	rarely	sometimes	often	always
12	I dance—either in a class or just for fun.	never	rarely	sometimes	often	always
13	I exercise strenuously enough to work up a sweat.	never	rarely	sometimes	often	always
14	I practice yoga, tai chi, Pilates, or some other type of flexibility and form-specific training.	never	rarely	sometimes	often	always
15	When I'm feeling stressed out, I exercise to clear my mind.	never	rarely	sometimes	often	always
16	I include strength training in my workout.	never	rarely	sometimes	often	always
17	I incorporate a new exercise into my workout.	never	rarely	sometimes	often	always
18	I work out with friends or colleagues.	never	rarely	sometimes	often	always
19	Regular old walking is a part of my routine—that is, I walk to work, to school, or around the neighborhood.	never	rarely	sometimes	often	always
20	I would describe myself as a very active person.	never	rarely	sometimes	often	always

SECTION 4: Memory Fitness, Stress, and Socializing

Read each statement and circle the answer that most accurately describes you.

21	I feel burned out and overwhelmed.	never	rarely	sometimes	often	always
22	I feel really bored and unchallenged at work. I watch the clock.	never	rarely	sometimes	often	always
23	I worry that I am going to forget someone's name.	never	rarely	sometimes	often	always
24	I spend most of the day alone.	never	rarely	sometimes	often	always
25	I enter a room and forget what I went in there to do.	never	rarely	sometimes	often	always
26	I lose my train of thought in conversation.	never	rarely	sometimes	often	always
27	I have no trouble relaxing—I know how to unwind and put a chaotic day behind me.	never	rarely	sometimes	often	always
28	I go out with friends.	never	rarely	sometimes	often	always
29	I enjoy having a new experience, whether it's taking a class, traveling to a foreign country, or simply taking a different route to or from work.	never	rarely	sometimes	often	always
30	I enter my appointments into a calendar, day planner, or personal digital assistant (PDA). What would I do without it?	never	rarely	sometimes	often	always

YOU'RE FINISHED!

IMPROVEMENT
14%

Brain Q
AFTER
129

Brain Q
BEFORE
113

PANELIST: **Teresa McCoart**

AGE: **52**

Forgetting names—that was my biggie. There were other gaffes, though, like forgetting to pick up my 10-year-old daughter, Lauren, after cheerleading practice. That was embarrassing. Of more concern to me, though, was the knowledge that both of my parents had developed dementia. That made me realize how devastating memory loss is to an individual and the effect it has on their loved ones.

I noticed **after a few days on the Brainpower Game Plan that I felt less stressed out**, which translated to a better mood around the house. My husband said he could tell I was feeling better!

The snacks helped control my appetite, especially during the first days of the diet. And I put two of the Brainpower Game Plan's memory techniques to use right away—the "Resize It" (see page 109) technique was very helpful!—and I particularly enjoyed taking the Scent Walk (see page 151). I find great pleasure in outdoor scents, so I loved it. It was really relaxing for me. I plan to keep stretching my powers of imagination and creativity by rediscovering my interest in art and photography.

ANSWERS TO SECTION 1:
Everyday Brain Skills

NO. 1

If you wrote down:	Give yourself:
Zero words =	0
1-5 words =	1
6-10 words =	2
11-15 words =	3
16-20 words =	4
21+ words =	5
NO. 1 POINTS:	

NO. 2

Answers:

ROW 1 23, 27, 31

ROW 2 37, 44, 51

ROW 3 P, S, V

ROW 4 7, G

ROW 5 ff, i

If you wrote down:	Give yourself:
Zero correct =	0
1-3 correct =	1
4-6 correct =	2
7-9 correct =	3
10-12 correct =	4
13 correct =	5
NO. 2 POINTS:	

NO. 3

Here are all the phrases that you might have remembered after you read the story:

Andrea Ingram
7:30 AM
Train
Every weekday
Bloomfield Station
New Jersey
One morning
Deserted area
Just outside
Town of Glen View
Noticed
A dog
Wandering near the tracks
Quickly alerted
The conductor
Mr. Greenwood
Contacted
The local authorities
The next morning
Brought her three sons

Animal shelter
Where the dog had been taken
A poodle mix
Was healthy
Appeared to enjoy
Playing with the boys
Middle son
Henry
Returned
2 days later
Brought the dog
A toy bone
After 1 month
The authorities
Were unable to find
The dog's owners
Andrea and her children
Adopted the dog
They named Tracks

If you wrote down:	Give yourself:
Zero phrases =	0
1-8 phrases =	1
9-15 phrases =	2
16-23 phrases =	3
24-32 phrases =	4
33-40 phrases =	5
NO. 3 POINTS:	

NO. 4

Answers:

ROW **1** 15, 68, 45, 278

ROW **2** 11, 36, 21.5, 12

ROW **3** 32, 54, 36, 42

ROW **4** 17, 84, 7, 28

ROW **5** 9, 356, 132, 3

ROW **6** 21, 92, 9, 369

ROW **7** 77, 3, 57, 61

ROW **8** 91, 5.25, 69, 16

ROW **9** 68, 17, 3450, 5

ROW **10** 28, 688, 101, 27

ROW **11** 100, 5, 4, 11

ROW **12** 327, 89, 8, 125.5

ROW **13** 32, 30

If you got:	Give yourself:
Zero correct =	0
1–3 correct =	1
4–6 correct =	2
7–9 correct =	3
10–12 correct =	4
13+ correct =	5
NO. 4 POINTS:	

NO. 5

Remembering that list wasn't easy. Here's how to score yourself.

If you remembered:	Give yourself:
Zero words =	0
1–4 words =	1
5–8 words =	2
9–12 words =	3
13–16 words =	4
17–20 words =	5
NO. 5 POINTS:	

NO. 6

Refer to the phrases from No. 3.

If you remembered:	Give yourself:
Zero phrases =	0
1–8 phrases =	1
9–15 phrases =	2
16–23 phrases =	3
24–32 phrases =	4
33–40 phrases =	5
NO. 6 POINTS:	

Everyday Brain Skills

NO. 7

Faces and names can, for some, be the hardest thing to remember. How'd you do?

If you remembered:	Give yourself:
Zero names =	0
1–2 names =	1
3–4 names =	2
5–6 names =	3
7–8 names =	4
9 names =	5

NO. 7 POINTS:

NO. 8

Now you were asked to remember that list all over again.

If you remembered:	Give yourself:
Zero words =	0
1–4 words =	1
5–8 words =	2
9–12 words =	3
13–16 words =	4
17–20 words =	5

NO. 8 POINTS:

NO. 9

Here is a list of all the objects pictured.

- BIRDCAGE
- DRESS
- BLACK CASE
- RUG
- DRESS STAND
- LIFE PRESERVER
- SHIRT ON HANGER
- WINDOW
- HANGING ROBE
- SMALL GUITAR
- BIRD FEEDER
- WOODEN FOLDING CHAIRS
- LARGE WOODEN CHEST
- FRAMED PICTURE ON WALL
- MIRROR
- SMALL PITCHER
- LARGE GLASS BOTTLE
- COLORFUL TRAY ON GROUND
- ROCKING HORSE
- COLORFUL SCARVES

If you remembered:	Give yourself:
Zero objects =	0
1–4 objects =	1
5–8 objects =	2
9–12 objects =	3
13–16 objects =	4
17–20 objects =	5

NO. 9 POINTS:

NO. 10

Your final question in Part 1 asked you to remember a group of names and faces. Here's how to score yourself.

If you remembered:	Give yourself:
Zero names =	0
1–2 names =	1
3–4 names =	2
5–6 names =	3
7–8 names =	4
9 names =	5

NO. 10 POINTS:

ANSWERS TO SECTION 2:
Diet

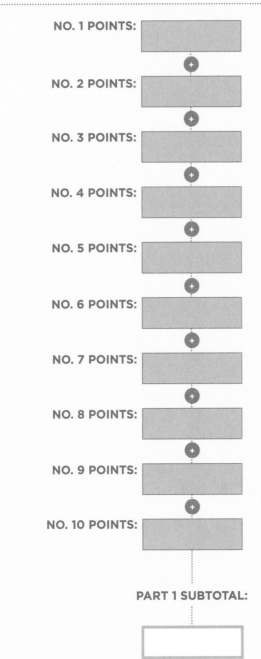

NO. 1 POINTS:

+

NO. 2 POINTS:

+

NO. 3 POINTS:

+

NO. 4 POINTS:

+

NO. 5 POINTS:

+

NO. 6 POINTS:

+

NO. 7 POINTS:

+

NO. 8 POINTS:

+

NO. 9 POINTS:

+

NO. 10 POINTS:

If you answered numbers 1–6:	Give yourself:
never =	1
rarely =	2
sometimes =	3
often =	4
always =	5

If you answered numbers 7–10:	Give yourself:
always =	1
often =	2
sometimes =	3
rarely =	4
never =	5

1 _____   6 _____
2 _____   7 _____
3 _____   8 _____
4 _____   9 _____
5 _____   10 _____

Add up the points you recorded above for questions 1 through 10 for your

PART 1 SUBTOTAL:

PART 2 SUBTOTAL:

ANSWERS TO SECTION 3:
Exercise

If you answered numbers 11–20:	Give yourself:
never =	1
rarely =	2
sometimes =	3
often =	4
always =	5

(11) _____   (16) _____

(12) _____   (17) _____

(13) _____   (18) _____

(14) _____   (19) _____

(15) _____   (20) _____

Add up the points you recorded above for questions (11) through (20) for your

PART 3 SUBTOTAL:

ANSWERS TO SECTION 4:
Memory Fitness, Stress, and Socializing

If you answered numbers 21–26:	Give yourself:
always =	1
often =	2
sometimes =	3
rarely =	4
never =	5

If you answered numbers 27–30:	Give yourself:
never =	1
rarely =	2
sometimes =	3
often =	4
always =	5

(21) _____   (26) _____

(22) _____   (27) _____

(23) _____   (28) _____

(24) _____   (29) _____

(25) _____   (30) _____

Add up the points you recorded above for questions (21) through (30) for your

PART 4 SUBTOTAL:

Total = Your Brain Q Score

HOW DID YOU DO IN EACH CATEGORY? Make note of where your score was the lowest out of the possible 50 points for each part. This way, you can focus throughout the Brainpower Game Plan on improving particularly in that department, whether it's needing to exercise more, making your diet more healthy, or sharpening your everyday memory.

Next, add your scores from all four parts. This number is your Brain Q.

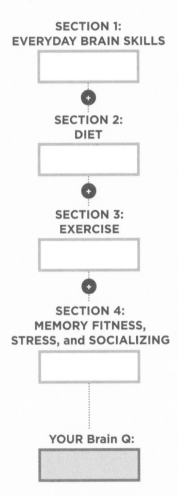

SECTION 1:
EVERYDAY BRAIN SKILLS

+

SECTION 2:
DIET

+

SECTION 3:
EXERCISE

+

SECTION 4:
MEMORY FITNESS,
STRESS, and SOCIALIZING

YOUR Brain Q:

THIS CUMULATIVE SCORE IS YOUR BRAIN Q. Don't attach too much significance to the number itself—it's merely your baseline score. This isn't the same type of test you would take at a doctor's office. What really matters is how much your Brain Q improves over the next 4 weeks. My prediction? You will be amazed how much it soars. **In fact, your Brain Q could double in just 1 month.**

CHAPTER 1
NOURISH YOUR BRAIN

The Science Behind the Strategies

Eat Well

Exercise

Play Brain Games

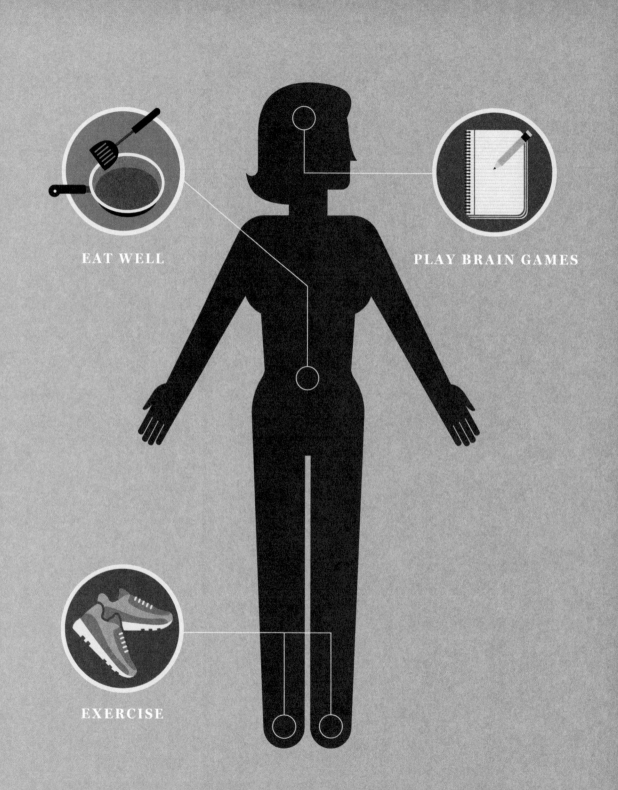

EAT WELL

PLAY BRAIN GAMES

EXERCISE

Nourish Your Brain

Before you start the Brainpower Game Plan I'm going to make a powerful scientific case for why each part of it works.

First, however, let's meet your brain. The typical adult brain weighs a little less than 3 pounds. It's made up mostly of water and fat, and its texture is similar to that of firm jelly. Viewed from above, the brain looks like an enormous walnut with a split down the middle. The two craggy-looking halves that form the brain are called *hemispheres*. The right hemisphere controls the left side of your body and the left hemisphere controls the right.

Your brain contains about 100 billion special cells called *neurons* or nerve cells.

All human activity—thoughts, movements, and the silent workings of your organs—occurs as a result of information that bounces from one neuron to another. The rest of the brain is made up of *glia cells*, which support neurons. Neurons are connected to one another by branch-like structures called *dendrites* and *axons*. Neurons communicate using chemical messengers called *neurotransmitters*, which travel through the branches by leaping across tiny gaps called *synapses*. The human brain may contain up to 100 trillion synapses.

> " Following the Brainpower Game Plan is like adding extra memory to your computer's hard drive: you'll get more done every day and feel better equipped to take on life's challenges."

Your brain is made up of many distinct regions, each with its own set of roles and responsibilities in controlling your thoughts and actions. The region that scientists believe is largely responsible for forming memories (making it essential for learning) is the *hippocampus*. Damage to the hippocampus can prevent a person from developing new memories or recalling the past. People who develop Alzheimer's disease may experience extensive shrinkage in the hippocampus.

Your brain receives oxygen- and nutrient-rich blood from the heart via four *arteries*. The arteries branch off into a dense network of *veins* and *capillaries* that deliver blood to every corner of the brain. Even though it makes up a tiny fraction of your body weight, your brain uses about 20% of your blood supply.

Scientists once believed that the adult human brain was incapable of producing new brain cells. We now know that your brain makes new neurons throughout your life, in a process called *neurogenesis*. One of the key players in neurogenesis is called Brain-Derived Neurotrophic Factor (BDNF). This protein promotes the growth and health of neurons. Certain activities—such as exercise—cause BDNF levels to soar.

Contrary to what many believe, your brain doesn't shed thousands of dead cells every day. In fact, a healthy person stands to lose only a small number of brain cells over his or her lifetime. However, neurons do shrink in size as you age. Overall, the brain shrinks 5 to 10% (by weight) between the ages of 20 and 90.

About 5 million Americans have Alzheimer's disease, which can kill brain cells on a massive scale. Scientists aren't sure how, but the brains of people who have the disease develop clumps called *plaques* made up of a protein called *beta-amyloid*. Plaques may block signals from traveling between neurons. The neurons of people with Alzheimer's disease develop twisted strands of fiber called *tangles*, which also appear to interfere with normal brain function.

Brain cells die if deprived of blood for any reason—by a stroke, for example. A major stroke can destroy enough brain cells to paralyze limbs or cause speech difficulties. However, "ministrokes" may produce only mild symptoms, such as dizziness, or even go unnoticed. Damage to brain tissue caused by ministrokes can lead to a condition called *vascular dementia*, which is characterized by memory loss, confusion, poor concentration and judgment, and other mental problems.

Throughout this chapter, you'll learn how you can improve your brain's health. Following the Brainpower Game Plan (which I created with several collaborators, whom you'll meet soon) is like adding extra memory to your computer's hard drive: you'll get more done every day and feel better equipped to take on life's challenges. At the same time, you'll be safeguarding the organ that holds your memories, personality, and sense of self. How's that for peace of mind?

READ A BRAINPOWER SUCCESS STORY

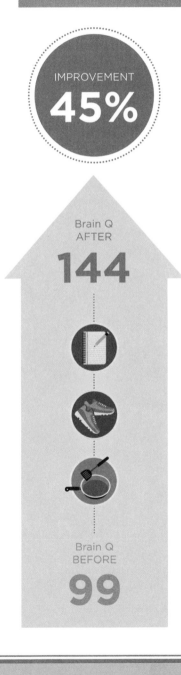

IMPROVEMENT
45%

Brain Q
AFTER
144

Brain Q
BEFORE
99

PANELIST: **Teresa Morales**

AGE: **53**

I felt frustrated by those blurry-brain moments that made me wonder: am I losing my mind? I was constantly losing track of my keys or handbag—or forgetting why I walked into a room. I wrote reminder notes to help me remember important errands and tasks—but I'd lose those, too!

Not only has the Brainpower Game Plan helped me feel more on the ball, but I'm getting back into good shape. I used to tell myself I'd start exercising tomorrow. And tomorrow would never come! This plan forces me to exercise regularly. Once you start, it feels natural. I've switched to healthier snacks, too, and let me tell you, it's made a huge difference: I've lost 5 pounds in 2 weeks and my clothes fit better.

Best of all, I feel more confident that I'm not going to forget things. I learned a lot from the plan. My husband even noticed the change—he suggested we repeat the plan together.

Eat Well

Eating the right foods—and limiting others—can boost brainpower and help fight Alzheimer's disease and other forms of dementia.

We all have memories of a special meal, whether it's a Thanksgiving feast with the whole family or a romantic dinner at an out-of-the-way bistro, perhaps overlooking a moonlit bay. My own memorable meal? I can still recall with perfect clarity the incredibly sweet figs my family and I had for dessert, surrounded by climbing vines and lovely flowers, at a restaurant in France 16 years ago.

We can't guarantee that every meal you eat on the Brainpower Game Plan will be as memorable, but your memory, attention span, and ability to learn will benefit from the healthful foods you will be choosing. Breakthrough research reveals that your diet has a huge influence on how much information you retain, how fast you can dig through your brain's database for names or other words, and how well you perform basic

day-to-day tasks that require mental sharpness, such as balancing your checkbook. At the same time, a healthy diet may protect your brain from the ravages of Alzheimer's disease and other forms of dementia.

When I began work in this field in the mid-1990s, scientists had practically no idea that your diet had a major impact on brain health. Yet today it seems like every week we hear about another study offering evidence that eating the right foods can protect and improve your brain's daily performance. We're also learning that cutting back on certain foods can help ward off diseases that interfere with mental clarity; it turns out that a bacon double cheeseburger is no friend to your brain or heart.

Don't worry, though: eating for a better, healthier brain doesn't mean you have to deprive your tastebuds. "I really liked the combination of foods in the Brainpower Game Plan," says Andrea Gaines, 47, of Jersey City, New Jersey. "I was surprised how much I enjoyed following it." Unlike many fad diets, the plan does not require you to eliminate entire categories of food. And splurges are definitely allowed—who knew that a little chocolate now and then could help preserve your neurons? Let's look at how what you eat affects the way you think.

TRIM DOWN TO SMARTEN UP

There's nothing wrong with wanting to look great at the beach or your high school reunion, but there are plenty of other good reasons to keep your weight under control. Fighting flab takes strain off your heart, helps prevent diabetes, and may even lessen the risk of some cancers. But did you know that losing excess body fat might protect your brain too?

That's what the science seems to say. For starters, flab triggers other unhealthy conditions that can spell trouble for brain health. We know, for example, that gaining weight makes a person more likely to develop high blood pressure, or hypertension. We have also known for more than a decade that people with hypertension have an increased risk of cognitive problems as they age. A 2004 study in China found that people with high blood pressure double their chances of developing Alzheimer's disease. Hypertension has also been linked to vascular dementia—the kind caused by clogged arteries that reduce blood flow to the brain.

Packing on too many pounds also makes a person more vulnerable to diabetes—another condition that can damage blood vessels, causing them to clog.

That may explain why a 2004 Swedish study found that people who develop diabetes are 2½ times more likely to develop vascular dementia. I've seen how these conditions threaten brain health many times in my own practice. I once treated an executive in his 50s who had both high blood pressure and diabetes. He became so immersed in his work and caught up in his crazy schedule that he neglected to see his physician regularly and take proper medication. His blood pressure ended up soaring out of control, which landed him in the hospital for several days.

When this man returned to work, he discovered something alarming: he felt completely scattered and unorganized.

"People with hypertension have double the chances of developing Alzheimer's disease."

He struggled to make simple decisions. The problem was so severe that he came to my clinic for an evaluation. We discovered through a series of tests that his episode of acute high blood pressure seemed to have taken a toll on his brain, permanently interfering with his ability to make sound judgments and jeopardizing his career.

Yet it's also becoming clear that excess body fat is bad for your brain even if you don't have hypertension, diabetes, or any other disease. That means there may be something about being overweight or obese that directly injures brain cells and causes cognitive chaos.

But what? Nobody knows for sure, though some clues have emerged. Research suggests that abdominal fat—the kind that forms unflattering rolls about the midsection—may be particularly dangerous for your overall well-being, including the health of your brain cells.

Your Belly and Your Brain

Far from being dead weight, ab fat is a highly active chemical factory that releases a stew of hormones and inflammatory cells into the body. Scientists believe that some of these naturally occurring chemicals may not only damage the heart and other organs but also be toxic to brain cells, causing changes that could lead to dementia.

A major 2008 study offers a good argument for banishing a potbelly. Researchers at Kaiser Permanente (an HMO) in California showed that people who maintain a healthy body weight are less likely to develop dementia than those who are obese and carry a lot of ab fat. The Kaiser Permanente team started by looking at medical records from the 1960s and '70s for a group of patients who were in their 40s at the time. They checked on the patients' health status 30 years later and found that slim people were about 3½ times less likely to have been diagnosed with dementia as they grew older than those who were obese and had large waistlines (an indicator of abdominal fat).

The connection between body fat and dementia is all the more worrisome when you consider that two-thirds of Americans are overweight or obese. Both conditions are bad for your overall health—including your

> " People who maintain a healthy body weight are less likely to develop dementia than those who are obese and carry a lot of belly fat."

READ A BRAINPOWER SUCCESS STORY

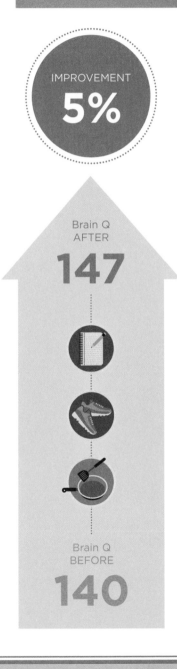

IMPROVEMENT
5%

Brain Q
AFTER
147

Brain Q
BEFORE
140

PANELIST: **Andrea Gaines**

AGE: **47**

It happened to me time after time: I would tell one of my girlfriends a piece of news only to hear, "Andrea, you told me that already—2 weeks ago!" The thing is, I have a selective memory and can easily recall important information that I need to know as a buyer for a clothing store. What I did yesterday, however, eluded me. I hoped to upgrade my memory when I embarked on the Brainpower Game Plan but I admit: I felt apprehensive at first. I wasn't sure what I had gotten myself into. **However, by the second week I began to notice some weight loss—I eventually dropped 5.5 pounds!—and my muscles were more toned.** I just felt great. I loved the diet, especially the eggplant mini-pizzas. In fact, my entire family enjoyed the meals. We're all eating healthy these days.

I really loved learning all the memory strategies. I use the one called "Link Up" to remember lists and, on the whole, I feel more aware and on top of things. It was a really terrific experience for me.

brain's well-being—but there is a difference. You are overweight if your body mass index is 25 to 29.9, according to the Centers for Disease Control and Prevention. You are obese if your BMI is 30 or higher.

The BMI is a number that describes your weight in proportion to your height. For example, a person who is 5-foot-4 and weighs between 145 and 173 pounds is overweight. A person of the same height whose weight exceeds 174 pounds is obese. You can calculate your BMI using the calculator at *prevention.com/BMI*.

Despite this mounting evidence, I find that most people—including many doctors—still aren't aware that flab is bad for your brain health. If weight is a problem for you, the Brainpower Game Plan will help you to trim your waistline while nourishing your mind.

FISH FEEDS YOUR BRAIN

At age 115, Henrikje van Andel-Schipper was the oldest person in the world at the time of her death in 2005. Scientists who interviewed the Dutch woman say she remained sharp-witted and just plain witty until her last days. Her secret? When asked, van Andel-Schipper quipped, "Pickled herring."

Then again, maybe she wasn't joking. Eating plenty of fish and shellfish can help keep your mind in top form and lower your risk of dementia, multiple studies suggest. What's so magical about seafood? Most scientists believe it's the dose of omega-3 fatty acids you get with every bite of tuna or trout.

Omega-3 fatty acids are powerful and versatile nutrients. Your body needs fatty acids of all different types, from various foods. One of the most important jobs for fatty acids is forming cell membranes. About 40% of the fatty acids in brain cell membranes are docosahexaenoic acid, or DHA, which is one of the main omega-3 fatty acids in fish oil. Experts believe that DHA is probably necessary for transmitting signals between brain cells. Another omega-3, known as eicosapentaenoic acid, or EPA, appears to be important for brain health, too.

Better Performance and Long-Term Brain Health

Some research hints that enjoying regular servings of broiled salmon or baked haddock may make your brain work more efficiently.

In a 2007 study, researchers at Wageningen University in the Netherlands analyzed blood samples from 807 men and women over 50 and found that those with the highest levels of omega-3 fatty acids scored 60 to 70% better on tests that measured reaction time and speed of processing complex information than people who had low omega-3 levels.

Other research suggests that eating fish helps bolster your defense shield against dementia. In a 2006 study involving 899 men and women, researchers at Tufts University found that people who ate fish three times a week and had the highest levels of DHA in their blood slashed their risk of Alzheimer's disease by 39% and other forms of dementia by 47%.

Fish has another important benefit for the brain: it helps prevent strokes. In a 2002 study in the *Journal of the American Medical Association (JAMA)*, researchers studied more than 43,000 men and found that those who ate fish one to three times per month were about half as likely to suffer these potentially devastating "brain attacks" as those who rarely ate fish.

Massive strokes can be fatal or leave victims paralyzed or plagued by other severe side effects. However, even "silent strokes"—which may occur unnoticed, without producing obvious symptoms—can cause cognitive problems, including memory loss. As many as one in 10 middle-aged adults has suffered a silent stroke and doesn't know it. Studies show that silent strokes more than double the risk of developing dementia.

Scientists have made some other discoveries that make the case for eating fish even more compelling. For example, lab rats fed diets rich in omega-3 fatty acids learn more quickly and have better memories than those fed diets high in unhealthy fats and sugar. Studies also show that feeding omega-3s to lab animals increases levels of BDNF, a protein that is needed for the growth and survival of brain cells. Other studies hint that DHA helps brain cells produce energy more efficiently and prevents the formation of cell damage called oxidative stress (which you'll read more about soon).

Eating seafood regularly will do much more than boost your Brain Q, of course. After all, studies show that people who eat fish just once a week cut in half the risk of sudden cardiac death, which kills more than 300,000 Americans each year. Eating fish also lowers levels of artery-clogging blood fats called triglycerides and confers a slight drop in blood pressure. Those changes alone could reduce your risk of heart disease and other conditions—including dementia—later in life.

As the nutritional benefits of omega-3s have become better known, it's no wonder that consumption of fish and shellfish has soared 30% in the United States over the past generation. However, many people still don't consume adequate levels of omega-3s. People often ask me if it's true that fish is "brain food," like their grandmothers told them. As you can see,

"People who eat fish three times a week and have the highest levels of DHA in their blood slash their risk of Alzheimer's disease by 39% and other forms of dementia by 47%."

> " People with the highest blood levels of omega-3 fatty acids were significantly less likely than people with low levels to say they felt mildly or moderately depressed."

the research offers powerful evidence that your grandma was right: eating fish really does seem to be good for the brain. The Brainpower Game Plan gives you plenty of ideas for including this nutritional power-house in your weekly meal plan.

Seafood and Your Mood

Eating fish may be good for your emotional health, too. Several studies have shown that depression rates tend to be low in countries where seafood is a popular menu item. For instance, depression is relatively rare in Iceland, where consumption of seafood is five times higher than in the United States or Canada. Mounting research suggests that fish oil may play a role in combating the blues. For example, University of Pittsburgh researchers showed in a 2007 study that people with the highest blood levels of omega-3 fatty acids were significantly less likely than people with low levels to say they felt mildly or moderately depressed.

Fish Benefits for Fish Haters

Some people who don't like fish but want to enjoy the brain boost and other health benefits of fish oil turn to other food sources of omega-3 fatty acids, which include flax-seed, walnuts, canola oil, and soybeans.

Or they shop for "functional" foods, such as eggs, mayonnaise, breakfast cereal, and others that contain added omega-3 fatty acids. Sounds like a great alternative, but unfortunately, most of those foods do not contain the same omega-3s you get from fish oil, which are known as DHA and EPA.

Some of the eggs, mayo, and other food products at your local grocer that are enriched with omega-3s contain a form called alpha-linolenic acid (ALA). That's the same form found in flaxseed and other non-marine sources. While nutrition scientists sing the praises of DHA and EPA, far less is known about the health benefits of ALA. Your body does convert ALA to DHA and EPA, but the process is not efficient. Lab studies show that only a small fraction of the ALA you consume ends up as DHA and EPA. (Note to vegetarians: DHA is also found in algae supplements.)

Some food products promoted as good sources of omega-3s do contain added DHA and EPA, but usually very little. For instance, according to the Center for Science in the Public Interest (a consumer health watch-dog group), a 6-ounce serving of Atlantic salmon has about 100 times more DHA and EPA than a serving of DHA-fortified yogurt or milk. Likewise, one popular brand of yogurt boasts of offering 32 milligrams of DHA per serving. Yet that's the amount you would get from a small bite of salmon.

Including flaxseed, walnuts, canola oil, soybeans, and other sources of ALA in your diet remains a great idea, since they offer other important health benefits. Just keep in mind that eating those foods probably won't significantly increase your blood levels of DHA and EPA. Eating fish (or taking fish oil supplements) remains the best way to get your dose of omega-3s.

Buy the Right Fish

When it comes to seafood, you can toss overboard the usual rules about picking your protein source. While lean cuts of beef and poultry are healthiest, you should choose fish with a high fat content whenever possible. Why? Fish oil is nature's top source of heart- and brain-healthy omega-3 fatty acids. The American Heart Association recommends eating fish twice a week. Beware of varieties of fish that are high in mercury: this element is known to blunt normal brain development in fetuses and children and some studies suggest that consuming too much mercury may also cause cognitive problems in adults, such as poor attention span and learning difficulties. King mackerel, swordfish, and shark are a few varieties that are high in mercury. Women who are or could become pregnant, and all children, should avoid those varieties entirely and limit their consumption of all fish to 12 ounces per week. Studies show that farmed fish such as salmon tend to have higher levels of contaminants than wild varieties do, so if you can find wild salmon or wild rainbow trout at your grocery store, choose that. Here are the 10 fish and shellfish with the highest levels of omega-3 acids per serving and the least amount of contaminants.

| Salmon (wild) |
| Sardines |
| Atlantic mackerel |
| Herring |
| Tuna |
| Halibut |
| Oysters |
| Rainbow trout (wild) |
| Lobster |
| Flounder or sole |

Source: Adapted from *Circulation*, 2002;106:2747–2757

AMP UP YOUR BRAINPOWER WITH ANTIOXIDANTS

You can't feel, hear, or see it happening, but right now cells all over your body—including in your brain—are fending off attack. The villains? Marauding molecules called free radicals, which are waste products your body makes when cells burn fuel to create energy. Stress, smoking, pollution, and other factors can raise your levels of free radicals. Free radicals cause disease by damaging cells through a phenomenon known as oxidative stress. Fortunately, your best defenses against free radicals are close at hand—in your refrigerator, cupboard, and spice rack.

Your brain is unusually vulnerable to attack by free radicals for several reasons. The membranes in your neurons contain large amounts of material that is very sensitive to oxidation—namely, omega-3 fatty acids. Furthermore, your brain burns a lot of fuel. Even though it represents just 3% of your body weight, the brain uses 17% of your energy. That means it makes large amounts of these toxic by-products.

To fight the effects of free radicals, the food in the Brainpower Game Plan is packed with guardian nutrients called antioxidants. These cell defenders disarm and defuse free radicals. Your body produces its own squad of antioxidants, but they need lots of backup—which you can get by eating a variety of delicious foods.

Vegetables

"Eat your vegetables" may be the oldest piece of health advice there is, but it's more valid today than ever. Veggies are among nature's richest sources of antioxidants. Many studies over the years have shown that consuming plenty of vegetables helps prevent various cancers and heart disease. Now scientists say that vegetables protect the brain, too.

For instance, one large study showed that vegetable lovers are more likely than vegetable loathers to maintain brainpower as they age. Researchers at the Rush Institute for Healthy Aging in Chicago tested the basic cognitive skills—that is, the essential brain capacities you need to get through the day—of 3,718 men and women. They retested the group 6 years later and found that people who ate three servings of vegetables a day slowed their overall rate of cognitive decline by 40% compared with those who avoided vegetables.

Some scientists believe that the best bets for your brain are leafy greens and cruciferous vegetables, such as broccoli, cauliflower, cabbage, kale, bok choy, and Brussels sprouts. The reason: these plants with emerald-green foliage are chockfull of antioxidants such as vitamin C and pigments called carotenoids. Some research suggests that eating steamed broccoli, a spinach salad, or other cruciferous vegetables or greens may actually help turn back the clock on your "brain age."

In a 25-year study, Harvard researchers asked more than 13,000 women about their diets, and then gave them a battery of cognitive tests. The top scorers ate plenty of leafy greens and cruciferous vegetables. In fact, the test results showed that women who ate the most greens and cruciferous vegetables lowered their brain age by 1 to 2 years.

Over the years, I've seen clients become much more savvy about including spinach, broccoli, and other leafy vegetables in their diets. If these foods are missing from your diet, it's time for you to go green, too.

Avocados, Oils, Nuts, and Seeds

There are thousands of chemicals in food that act as antioxidants, many with exotic-sounding (and unpronounceable) names. But a few studies suggest that a familiar nutrient—vitamin E—may protect against Alzheimer's disease. In one, Rush Institute researchers followed 815 men and women over age 65 for about 4 years and found that people who consumed the most vitamin E lowered their risk of Alzheimer's disease by 64%.

Keep this in mind, however: only vitamin E from food was linked to a low risk of Alzheimer's; vitamin E supplements didn't seem to make any difference. In fact, studies in which volunteers took vitamin E pills suggest that they have no effect on Alzheimer's disease, even at high doses. So skip the pricey supplements and get your vitamin E from foods such as avocados, olive oil, sunflower seeds, and nuts (which offer a brain bonus, since they're also good sources of monounsaturated fats, another critical part of the Brainpower Game Plan). Need more reasons to eat your spinach? Leafy greens are a good source of vitamin E too.

Chocolate

Flavonoids are another powerful class of antioxidants that may give your brain a boost. These plant pigments give the blue, blue-red, and violet hues to foods such as apples, red grapes, and red onions. However,

yellow onions, broccoli, grains, wine, tea, and beer are also good sources. So is a type of candy that I often recommend as an occasional snack (in small servings, naturally): dark chocolate.

A 2007 study shows how important flavonoids may be to your brain's well-being. Back in 1990, a team of French scientists asked 1,640 men and women over age 65 about their diets, and then gave them a brief quiz that included some basic arithmetic, memory tests, language comprehension tests, and other measures of overall brain functioning. A decade later, the volunteers were tested again. The men and women who ate the most flavonoid-rich foods scored 75% better than the ones who consumed few foods containing the brain-friendly antioxidants.

Curry

Here's a way to turn up the heat in your menu and give your brainpower a boost: pick up an Indian or Thai cookbook. These cuisines feature spicy dishes called curries. Turmeric, an essential spice in curry, contains a chemical called curcumin, which is an antioxidant and fights inflammation. New research in lab mice with Alzheimer's disease shows that curcumin actually clears away proteins called amyloid plaques that may play a role in the brain disorder. Whether the same is true in humans isn't clear yet, but rates of Alzheimer's disease are unusually low among the curry-loving citizens of India. Some studies do suggest that diets rich in curcumin may help preserve brainpower. A 2006 study of 1,010 men and women in Singapore found that people

READ A BRAINPOWER SUCCESS STORY

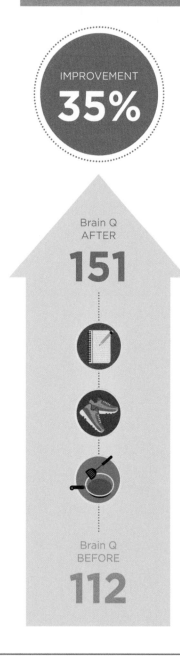

IMPROVEMENT

35%

Brain Q
AFTER

151

Brain Q
BEFORE

112

PANELIST: **Marianne Seminoff**

AGE: **51**

Like most people, I had an occasional memory glitch. But what really got me motivated to try the Brainpower Game Plan was seeing the devastating effects of severe memory loss in my mother, who suffers from dementia. Watching her go through such a huge decline made me want to avoid going through the same thing when I reach her age.

I feel like I've made a giant step toward better brain health for today and years to come. When I took the quiz at the end of the book, it was stunning to me how much better I remembered! The Brainpower Game Plan taught me to use memory strategies to recall the names of new acquaintances. And how's this for a bonus: I lost 4 pounds while eating foods I loved. I'm ecstatic to learn that I can eat well, not be hungry, and still lose weight. And have some fun in the process!

who ate curry at least once a month scored 50% better on a test of basic thinking skills than those who never or rarely enjoyed the hot dish.

Of course, you can add turmeric to many dishes, even if you're not a fan of spicy foods. When I cook for my family, I often add turmeric to pasta sauce and salad dressing, or sprinkle it on roasted chicken. The Brainpower Game Plan offers a variety of ways to incorporate this spice into your meals.

Brain-Boosting Berries

Berries are proof that very good things come in small packages. These bite-size fruits are one of the best sources of antioxidants you'll find at your local grocer. There is no question that berries deserve a prominent place on your menu. But just how much they protect the brain remains unclear.

Berries contain astringent substances called tannins that seem to protect brain cells. Studies have shown that animals fed extracts of certain tannins learned more quickly and improved their memory power. Some scientists think that eating berries protects cell membranes from oxidative stress and helps to build and maintain healthy synapses, the gaps where information flows from one neuron to another.

Unfortunately, there have been no studies designed to measure whether people who eat frequent servings of berries think faster, remember more, or gain any protection against dementia. On the other hand, swapping a sugary dessert for a bowl of blueberries or strawberries certainly won't harm your brain and has plenty of other upsides.

The Top Ten High-Antioxidant Foods

Like cells throughout your body, brain cells can suffer damage from rogue molecules called free radicals. Antioxidants come to your defense by disarming free radicals. A major analysis published in the *American Journal of Clinical Nutrition* in 2006 found that these 10 foods have the greatest concentration of antioxidants by weight (in descending order).

Blackberries
Walnuts
Strawberries
Artichokes
Cranberries
Coffee
Raspberries
Pecans
Blueberries
Ground cloves

Source: *American Journal of Clinical Nutrition*, 2006; 84:95-135

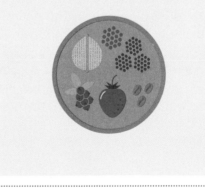

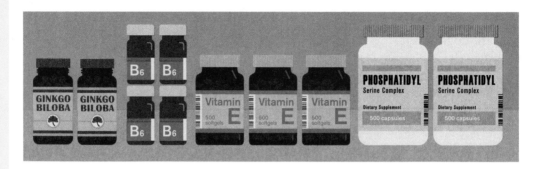

Can Herbs and Supplements Help?

Despite what you might hear from a salesclerk in a vitamin shop or read on the Internet, there is little scientific proof that over-the-counter pills and potions touted as memory aids and brain boosters are effective. You may already know about, or have tried, some of these products. One popular dietary supplement is ginkgo biloba, an herb derived from the oldest species of tree in the world. Others may be less familiar, such as gotu kola and bacopin.

For years, most doctors dismissed the idea of taking dietary supplements to improve memory and mental clarity because of lack of evidence: there had been little rigorous research into whether these various medicinal herbs and other natural products lived up to their billing. However, the growing popularity of dietary supplements has inspired some scientists to look into the brain benefits of the products more closely. Unfortunately, the research hasn't done much to un-muddy the waters.

Ginkgo biloba may be the most widely studied of the so-called memory herbs. Practitioners of traditional Chinese medicine have long recommended herbal preparations containing ginkgo as a treatment for circulation problems and, yes, memory loss. Whether the ginkgo supplements you can purchase over the counter have any medical or cognitive benefits is another matter, however.

In one study, published in *JAMA* in 2002, researchers assembled 203 men and women over age 60. They tested the volunteers' general thinking ability, and then gave half of them ginkgo supplements; the rest received placebo pills. Six weeks later, a second round of cognitive tests revealed that taking ginkgo made no difference.

Yet other studies suggest ginkgo may have important benefits. A 2008 study in *Neurology* found that ginkgo may have helped to prevent dementia symptoms in participants who closely followed the prescribed regimen.

Likewise, many natural medicine proponents recommend supplements containing folic acid and other B vitamins to perk up your brain cells. The bulk of existing scientific evidence suggests they won't help much, but in a few studies B vitamins appeared to provide a brain boost. Other research indicates that various natural products may work best in combination. For instance, a 2008 study found that a supplement containing ginkgo biloba, vitamin B6, vitamin E, and phosphatidylserine (a lipid that's usually derived from soy) improved short-term memory—in a group of aging beagles.

If you decide to try a dietary supplement to enhance your memory or all-around brainpower, keep a few cautions in mind:

● **"Natural" doesn't always mean "safe."** Plant compounds can alter your biochemistry; they would have no benefits otherwise. That means they can also produce unwanted effects. Ginkgo, for instance, is relatively safe, but it may increase the risk of internal bleeding. The same is true of vitamin E in high doses. Talk to your doctor before taking a dietary supplement for any purpose.

● **Quality is a question mark.** The dietary supplement industry is not closely monitored by the government. However, various media outlets and Web sites have conducted laboratory analyses of supplements purchased in retail outlets and online and found alarming quality problems. Products may contain too little, too much, or even none of the herb or other natural compound listed on the label. For example, when the watchdog group Consumerlab.com tested the quality of 13 ginkgo products in 2005, only 6 passed. Even more worrisome: several products were contaminated with lead.

● **Do you really need it?** Following the Brainpower Game Plan will help clear away brain fuzz and keep your mind in mint condition. So why spend a lot of money on expensive memory tonics? As I always remind my clients, you don't need a "cure" for your memory, since it's not sick or broken—it's just out of shape.

While I don't think it's fair to dismiss these products outright, I would like to pass along an observation or two. In my more than 15 years of practice, not one of my clients has told me that a dietary supplement truly helped his or her memory performance. When I began giving lectures on brain health I would ask, "Who takes ginkgo biloba or other memory supplements?" Half of the audience members would raise their hands. When I ask the same question today I rarely see more than five upraised hands. It seems to me that many people have decided there are more effective ways to maintain their memories.

MINDING YOUR FATS

Your mind is a powerful machine. Think of certain dietary fats as the lubricants you need to keep it running smoothly. Earlier, you learned about one type of fat that is essential for a healthy brain, the omega-3 fatty acids in fish oil. However, the fats in other common foods—many of them quite delicious—seem to help keep your mind in motion too.

Meanwhile, other forms of dietary fat appear to have the opposite effect. They shift your cognitive engine into low gear and increase the threat of age-related disorders that cause memory problems and loss of mental clarity. Making sure you're eating the right kinds of fats could prove to be a critical step for better brain health and much more.

Eat More "Good" Fats

Not so long ago, doctors cautioned patients to cut back on all types of fat in their diets in order to reduce their risk of heart attacks. However, over the past generation scientists have shown that consuming certain types of fat actually protects the heart—and possibly the brain too.

Eating more fatty fish such as salmon is a great start, but be sure to include plenty of foods rich in plant oils too. The best choices include cooking oils (preferably olive and canola), nuts, seeds, olives, avocados, and—how sweet is this?—dark chocolate. These foods share an important element: they are all good sources of monounsaturated fats, or MUFAs. Unlike some other fats, MUFAs don't clog arteries. Better still, growing research shows that people who consume plenty of MUFAs gain a valuable defense against dementia.

For example, several studies have found that people who eat a traditional Mediterranean diet seem to lower their risk of Alzheimer's disease. Mediterranean cuisine is diverse—a dinner menu in Marseille, France, won't look much like one you might find in Naples, Italy. However, chefs throughout the region rely heavily on olive oil, one of the richest sources of MUFAs. (People in some parts of the Mediterranean, such as Crete, Greece, consume more than 8 gallons of olive oil per year, on average.) People in the Mediterranean also eat plenty of nuts, another source of MUFAs.

In a 2006 study, neurologists at Columbia University compared the diets of 194 patients with Alzheimer's disease with those of 1,790 healthy people of a similar age. They found that people who adhered closely to a Mediterranean-style diet cut

> " People who adhered closely to a Mediterranean-style diet cut their risk of developing Alzheimer's by 68%."

their risk of developing Alzheimer's by 68%. It's important to point out that this healthful cuisine also includes plenty of fish, fruit, vegetables, and moderate servings of wine, with relatively small portions of red meat and dairy. Yet some studies suggest that olive oil and other sources of MUFAs hold an important key. In one, Italian researchers found that people who consumed large amounts of MUFAs scored significantly better on cognitive tests given 8½ years apart than people who consumed relatively small amounts of this brain-friendly fat.

Avoid "Bad" Fats

What a deal: many of the diet changes you should make for your heart's sake will boost your brain health too. If you're like most people you probably have already taken steps to curb your cardiovascular risk by cutting back on saturated fat. You know the culprits: whole milk, cream, butter, juicy steaks. Eating foods rich in saturated fat raises levels of LDL cholesterol—the "bad" kind—that sticks to artery walls. This buildup can become so thick that it blocks arteries and can cause heart attacks.

However, many scientists now believe that another form of fat, found in packaged snacks such as cookies and chips, is even more dangerous than the saturated variety. Trans fat is the type in partially hydrogenated vegetable oil, which is widely used by food processors and fast-food restaurants, though many companies have switched to other oils, and some cities have banned the use of hydrogenated oil. (Very small amounts of trans fats occur naturally in some foods, such as meat and certain fruits

and vegetables.) In addition to packaged snacks, other foods that may contain trans fat include French fries, doughnuts, stick margarine, pancake mix, and frozen fish sticks, among many others.

Trans fats are a double whammy for your blood vessels. Not only do they raise LDL cholesterol but they lower levels of HDL (high-density lipoprotein) cholesterol—the healthy kind that mops up and whisks away the artery-clogging kind. There is no question that eating too much saturated and trans fat causes heart attacks and strokes. But in case you need another reason to swap your cheeseburger and fries for soup and salad, here it is: both saturated and trans fats have been linked to a higher risk of Alzheimer's disease and other forms of dementia.

In a 2003 study published in the *Archives of Neurology*, researchers examined the diets of 815 people and found that the men and women who ate the most saturated fat more than doubled their chances of developing Alzheimer's disease. However, avoiding cookies, crackers, and other packaged snacks may have had an even bigger benefit. The people who ate the smallest amounts of trans fat were about 2½ times less likely to develop Alzheimer's disease.

It's not entirely clear why limiting saturated and trans fats helps prevent these devastating conditions. However, your neurons rely on steady blood flow for oxygen and nutrients, so clogged arteries in your head can be bad news for your brain. Interestingly, several studies have found that people who take statin drugs such as

Lipitor and Zocor, which lower cholesterol levels, have a reduced risk of Alzheimer's disease. One 2008 study of 1,674 men and women showed that statin users cut their chances of developing dementia in half. Other studies suggest that eating a diet high in saturated fat increases brain deposits of proteins that have been linked to Alzheimer's disease. Meanwhile, taking cholesterol-lowering drugs may prevent these brain abnormalities.

A team of researchers in the United Kingdom and France measured HDL levels in 3,673 men and women, then tested their ability to remember 20 words read aloud in quick succession. The people with the highest HDL levels scored 61% better than those with the lowest. The best way to raise HDL? The monounsaturated fats in olive oil, nuts, and other foods provide a modest increase; consuming small amounts of alcohol helps, too. The top HDL booster? Getting plenty of exercise.

Some scientists think it may be possible one day to use statins to prevent dementia, as well as other neurological disorders such as Parkinson's disease and multiple sclerosis. However, more research is needed before doctors will start prescribing statins for healthier brains. Best bet: help keep your arteries clear the drug-free way by cutting back on saturated and trans fats.

KEEP YOUR BLOOD SUGAR STABLE

Does this ever happen to you? Even though you got plenty of sleep the night before and your day is going just fine, suddenly you feel tired and crabby. You can't concentrate on work. In fact, all you can think about is feeding your groaning belly with a candy bar or one of those oversize chocolate chip cookies.

If these symptoms ring a bell, you might have experienced a blood sugar crash, which can make it a challenge to think clearly and get things done. Taking a few simple steps can help you avoid this between-meal menace.

Your body's main source of energy is glucose, a type of sugar. Levels of blood glucose rise and fall during the day, though most of the time you're unaware of these gentle fluctuations. However, under certain circumstances, your blood glucose may drop too low—and you'll know right away that something is amiss. You might just feel

" The top HDL booster? Getting plenty of exercise."

CHAPTER 1: Nourish Your Brain

hungry and crave sweets. But since glucose is the brain's sole source of fuel, your mental powers may suffer too.

If you're healthy and eating a balanced diet, steep drops in blood glucose should rarely be a problem. Normally, your body converts the carbohydrates in food to glucose during digestion. As your blood-glucose levels steadily rise, the pancreas produces insulin. This hormone "unlocks" cells throughout the body, allowing them to take in glucose and create energy or store it for later use. A few hours after a meal, elevated blood-glucose levels drop back to normal.

This carefully orchestrated process gets thrown off course if you eat too many of the kinds of carbohydrates that produce a rapid rise in blood glucose. When glucose levels in the blood soar too high too fast, they usually plummet just as abruptly to below-normal levels. Low-quality carbohydrates that cause spikes in blood glucose include candy, soda pop, and other sugary foods, as well as refined carbs, such as white bread and white rice.

Avoid mood swings and keep your brain humming along by steering clear of blood sugar crashes with these strategies that the Brainpower Game Plan employs:

- **Favor high-quality carbohydrates.** Limit sweets and soda, of course. (In my house, we get our fix of fizzy drinks by flavoring sparkling water with a splash of fruit juice.) Avoid highly processed carbohydrates such as white bread and white rice. Instead, eat more carbs that raise blood glucose levels slowly. That means plenty of whole grains, vegetables, beans, and fruit.

- **Eat three meals a day with snacks in between.** Staving off between-meal hunger keeps your blood glucose stable.

- **Eat some protein with each meal.** It leaves your belly feeling full and satisfied, which will help to thwart those raids on the candy cupboard between meals—which throw off your blood-glucose levels and cause weight gain. Lean meats, skinless poultry, fish, and soy products (such as tofu, tempeh, and edamame) are the best sources. The Brainpower Game Plan offers plenty of protein to keep you happy and full.

- **Get plenty of fiber.** Adults should aim for 25 grams per day (the typical American eats about 11 grams per day). How can you fiber up? Start reading nutrition labels and ingredient lists. When possible, choose products that contain at least 4 grams of fiber per 100 calories. When buying bread, breakfast cereal, and other grains, be sure the first thing on the ingredient list is whole wheat, whole oat, or some other form of whole grain. Try to include some oatmeal or oat bran, apples, beans, and other sources of soluble fiber, which slows the body's absorption of glucose. (If you have been eating a low-fiber diet, add roughage gradually to avoid gastrointestinal problems. And be sure to drink plenty of water.) The Brainpower Game Plan offers plenty of fiber, too.

THE PLEASURE PRINCIPLE: MODERATION IS KEY

What do a glass of wine, a cup of coffee, and a sprinkle or two of salt have in common? You may include these simple pleasures as part of your diet and never think much about them. But each can influence how well you think. That is, how much, and how often, you enjoy alcohol, caffeine, and salty foods may have an effect on your brain's day-to-day performance and longevity. The secret to savoring these treats? Follow standard guidelines and keep your consumption in balance.

Alcohol

You may raise a glass of champagne and sing "Thanks for the memories" on New Year's Eve, but drinking too much alcohol can blur your ability to recall events, lead to lapses in judgment, and cause a doozy of a headache. However, social embarrassment and hangovers are just the beginning: chronic, heavy drinking can lead to a devastating form of dementia.

Yet the news is hardly all bad when it comes to alcohol. In fact, small amounts of it may even protect the brain.

One study of nearly 12,500 women whose health and habits were tracked for a quarter century found that those who had one drink a day on average scored better than nondrinkers on tests of mental clarity. What's more, moderate drinkers were 23% less likely than nondrinkers to show signs of diminished brainpower.

A number of other studies have reached a similar conclusion: enjoying an occasional grown-up beverage may protect the brain. In one, published in *JAMA*, scientists at several major U.S. medical centers determined that people who had one to six drinks per week were less likely to develop dementia than abstainers, slashing their risk by more than 50%. No one is certain why moderate drinking seems to guard against cognitive diseases. However, some doctors point out that moderate drinkers have reduced rates of heart disease too. It's possible that small doses of alcohol preserve brain health the same way they protect the heart: by preventing blockages in blood vessels.

This much is not in doubt: alcohol abuse is a nightmare for the brain. The same *JAMA* study found that people who had two

STAY ON TRACK!

In the quest for a slimmer waistline, you've probably spent countless hours building up a sweat and dealt with diet after diet. If you have yet to see results, My Health Trackers can help. This easy-to-use tool tracks your progress digitally—no pen or notebook required. Research shows that recording your workouts, foods eaten, and weight can help you recognize and correct bad habits so that you can reach your goals faster. Whether you want to lose weight, eat better, or take control of your health, My Health Trackers will help you succeed! Log on to My Health Trackers today at *prevention.com/healthtracker*.

READ A BRAINPOWER SUCCESS STORY

IMPROVEMENT
18%

Brain Q
AFTER
122

Brain Q
BEFORE
103

PANELIST: **Pilar De Silva**

AGE: **45**

I had one thought when I heard about the Brainpower Game Plan: this seems to be an answer to my prayers. I had been having trouble concentrating, which made me irritable. I was forgetting names, and I was even ready to give up on novels and magazine articles because I found it hard to keep track of what I read. My excess weight was also stressing me out because I knew it was not only bad for my body, but it was also gumming up my brain function.

At the time I started the plan, I was busy caring for my sick father, and then shortly thereafter, I came down with a sinus infection. But, I stuck to the plan and I feel like my dedication paid off. **I definitely feel healthier, and I am more conscious about listening to my body.** In addition to losing 4 pounds, my mood improved. I think the mental exercises help me feel better, and I'm trying to challenge my brain in ways I never thought to before, such as learning to knit. I feel more active, and I realized that I don't have to feel older than my age!

Make It Red Wine

Wine experts love to discuss the complexities of Cabernet Sauvignon, Merlot, and Pinot Noir, but one reason to have a glass of red with dinner is simple: the deeper-hued varieties of wine are unusually rich in resveratrol, an antioxidant and anti-inflammatory that some scientists believe actually slows the aging process. That includes age-related changes in the brain that can cause memory loss and other cognitive problems. So far, scientists have demonstrated resveratrol's fountain-of-youth qualities only in laboratory mice. However, some research suggests that resveratrol may block destructive changes in the brain that cause Alzheimer's disease. Scientists aren't sure what dose of resveratrol might be necessary to slow aging or protect against dementia, but there's probably no harm—and possibly a brain benefit—to sipping a little red now and then. Not a drinker? Although red wine is the top source of resveratrol, grapes and red or purple grape juice pack a respectable dose too. Peanuts are another good source of resveratrol.

or more drinks per day increased their risk of being diagnosed with dementia by 22%. In fact, a distinct form of dementia, known as alcohol-related dementia (ARD), is one of the leading causes of memory impairment in the United States.

Women are more susceptible than men to alcohol's effects. (Consuming too much alcohol increases the risk of a number of other diseases, including breast cancer, colon cancer, and liver disease.) Furthermore, people over age 40 are more likely to forget things after a few drinks. Our bodies become more sensitive to alcohol as we get older. (By the way, the same is true of caffeine.) Simply put, we become less efficient at clearing alcohol from our systems, which allows it to do greater damage to the kidneys, liver, and, yes, the brain.

How does excess booze tax the brain? Doctors have long known that chronic alcohol abuse depletes the body of vitamin B_1, or thiamin, which can lead to memory loss (especially for the recent past) and other disruptions in brain performance. People with ARD have many of the same problems with memory and other basic mental functions that occur with Alzheimer's disease and vascular dementia, though some evidence suggests that the condition may improve if a sufferer abstains from booze. More recent research shows that large doses of alcohol are directly toxic to brain cells. For these reasons, most authorities agree that women should have no more than one alcoholic beverage per day, while men should limit their intake to two drinks. (One drink equals 5 ounces of wine, 12 ounces of beer, or 1½ ounces of liquor.)

Caffeine

Whether we perk our own coffee, pick up a double tall latte on the way to work, or brew a civilized cup of Earl Grey, many of us rely on a dose of caffeine to get rolling in the morning. For most people, consuming small amounts of caffeine isn't a problem (though caffeine is a drug, which means it can interact with certain medications). In excess, however, coffee, tea, certain soft drinks, and other caffeinated products can contribute to cognitive cloudiness.

Caffeine is a stimulant, so it fights off fatigue and increases alertness. In the lab, tests show that caffeine improves attention span, reaction time, and other brain skills. Other research suggests that coffee and tea lovers give themselves a mental edge. A 2007 French study found that women over age 65 who drank three or more cups of coffee a day were better able to recall words and retained greater brainpower than women who consumed little or no caffeine.

Some evidence even hints that coffee may protect against Alzheimer's disease. One scientific review found that coffee drinkers may cut their risk by up to 30%. Another study found that caffeine prevents age-related memory loss—at least in lab rats.

Yet as anyone knows who has ever snapped at a colleague or had to steady a shaky hand after one cup of joe too many, consuming too much caffeine can leave you feeling jittery, impatient, and anxious—just what you don't need on days when you need to focus and concentrate. It may not help your night much, either, since consuming too much caffeine can cause insomnia—an even greater drain on your brainpower.

Counting Caffeine

Experts recommend limiting yourself to 300 to 400 milligrams of caffeine per day, tops. This chart can help you figure out whether you are in the safe zone, but keep in mind that tolerance of caffeine varies greatly. Your best friend may be able to guzzle espresso after dinner and still sleep like a newborn, while you may be wide-eyed in the wee hours if you sip half a cup. How much caffeine can you handle? I usually advise people to be their own guinea pigs: pay attention to how your body reacts to caffeine and judge what works best for you.

	CAFFEINE (in milligrams)
Dark chocolate 1 oz	5 to 35
Iced tea 8 oz	9 to 50
Brewed tea 8 oz	20 to 90
Cola 12 oz	30
Espresso 1 shot	58 to 76
Brewed coffee 8 oz	72 to 130
Red Bull® energy drink 8 oz	80

Sources: *Journal of Analytical Toxicology*, American Beverage Association, Starbucks.com

Salt

Eating chips and pretzels, canned soups, deli meats, and other salty foods may be a stealth villain when it comes to brain health. About 40% of every crystal of table salt (by weight) consists of the mineral sodium. You can't live without sodium; your body needs it to carry out many different functions, such as maintaining normal fluid levels in the blood. However, you probably consume far more sodium than you need. You can get by on 500 milligrams or less of sodium per day, or roughly the amount in a single hot dog. Yet the average American consumes upwards of 3,000 milligrams of sodium daily.

Stealth Sodium in Food

Did you know that a bran muffin can have as much sodium as a slice of pizza? Most experts recommend eating no more than 2,300 mg of sodium per day, which is about the amount in one teaspoon of salt. About 75% of the sodium you consume comes from processed and prepared foods.

FOOD	SODIUM (in milligrams)
Canned vegetable soup 1 c	940
Bloody Mary mix 8 oz	840
Store-bought pasta sauce 1/2 c	756
Reduced-calorie Caesar dressing 2 Tbsp	620
Panera™ cranberry-walnut bagel 1	590
Canned vegetarian baked beans 1/2 c	550
Pancakes, from mix 2 pancakes	477
Large Pizza Hut® Pan Pizza, cheese 1 slice	470
Starbucks® bran muffin 1	470
Cottage cheese 1/2 c	456
Canned green beans 1/2 c	390
Instant chocolate pudding 1/2 c	380
Chocolate fudge cake mix 1/12 cake	350
American cheese 1 slice	250
White bread 1 slice	250
Low-sodium vegetable juice 8 oz	140

Source: *Waiter, There's Too Much Salt in My Cake, prevention.com*

The problem: eating too much sodium may raise your blood pressure, which increases the risk of debilitating strokes and silent strokes, which don't cause obvious symptoms but may lead to memory problems and other cognitive trouble. Not everyone is salt sensitive—that is, some people can eat bag after bag of pretzels and their blood pressure won't budge. Unfortunately, there is no practical test for salt sensitivity. To be on the safe side, it's best to keep your sodium consumption to no more than 2,300 milligrams per day. If you consume a typical American diet, in other words, you may need to cut back.

That's not as hard as it sounds. Simply avoiding processed foods whenever possible is a great start. The payoff is worthwhile: a major review found that people with high blood pressure who reduce their intake of salty foods can produce a modest but meaningful drop in blood pressure.

WATER: THE ULTIMATE BRAIN BEVERAGE

The cooler at your local convenience store is probably stocked with a few so-called smart drinks. These canned and bottled cocktails are infused with vitamins and exotic-sounding herbs that supposedly unleash your brainpower, though any cognitive kick you might get from these drinks likely comes from more familiar ingredients—caffeine and sugar. Save your money. You can get an effective brain boosting beverage from your kitchen tap.

Every cell in your body needs water to thrive, and your brain cells are no exception. In fact, about three-quarters of your brain is water, so it's no surprise that getting too little H_2O can result in misery for your mental muscle. Doctors have long known that severe dehydration can cause a person to become confused or disoriented, and—in extreme cases—to slip into a coma. However, even mild dehydration may be enough to cause a breakdown in brain functioning, some research suggests.

For instance, psychologists at Ohio University used special lab tests to measure the hydration levels of 31 healthy men and women, most in their early 60s. Then they measured the volunteers' memory, attention span, eye-hand coordination, and other cognitive abilities. This small study revealed a clear trend: people whose bodies were well hydrated scored significantly better on tests of brainpower.

Your body's thirst detectors become less sensitive with the passing of time, so your brain cells may be dry even though your throat doesn't feel particularly parched. That's why it's wise to make a habit of sipping fluids throughout the day.

> " Every cell in your body needs water to thrive, and your brain cells are no exception."

Exercise

Exercise burns body fat and builds bigger, stronger muscles by challenging them to work harder. But how could exercise possibly benefit your brain? The answer: in more ways than you might ever imagine.

Think about the last time you worked up a good sweat. Maybe you took a long bike ride, played racquetball, or spent a day pulling weeds and planting perennials in the garden. As you relaxed and caught your breath afterward, you could do so feeling satisfied that you'd just done your body a lot of good. But here's something you may not have realized: that hearty workout was good for your brain too.

It's a fact: vigorous physical activity helps you stay slim and fit. Scientists have discovered over the last generation that your thinking muscle responds to physical exercise in much the same way as your biceps, quadriceps, and other muscles: it produces new cells, nerve connections, blood vessels, and other changes that make it stronger and more efficient. The movement of your body, it turns out, sets off an array of biochemical

"Walking 2 hours or more per week may slash the risk of heart disease in women in half."

changes in the brain that have a profound influence on how you think and feel.

Don't worry—you don't need to train for the Olympics in order to ramp up your brainpower and protect your neurons. Taking a walk after dinner might be all that's required. Harvard researchers surveyed 18,766 women about their exercise habits, then asked each to take a standard test of their basic mental skills. Two years later they retested each woman and found that study participants who got regular, moderate exercise—such as walking at an easy pace for about 90 minutes per week—had a 20% lower risk of developing problems such as poor memory and short attention span than those who did not.

Being active does more than make you feel sharp and alert, however. A good workout boosts your spirits and helps rein in anxiety. It's so effective, in fact, that many doctors routinely prescribe exercise therapy for depression and other mood disorders.

Just imagine: here's a way to promote a healthy, hard-working brain, the side effects of which are a stronger heart, firmer muscles, and a slimmer silhouette, among countless other health benefits. When people ask me to recommend the single best step to take toward better all-around brain health, I don't think twice. Not only does the science supporting exercise grow more compelling every day, but I also know that it works for me. When I have an important meeting or business call coming up, I like to slip on my headphones and take a brisk, 20-minute walk. I do the same thing if I feel burned out after a long day. Moving my limbs never fails to energize my mind— I feel more focused, alert, and productive. You will too.

MOVE MORE TO PREVENT DEMENTIA

You don't slip on your running shoes or hit the weight room just to get buff, of course. Studies involving thousands of participants show that exercise is a major force in the battle against disease. For instance, one study involving more than 39,000 women found that walking 2 hours or more per week may slash the risk of heart disease by half.

Now a fast-growing body of research gives you another reason to start exercising: sweating seems to ward off dementia too. I know that dementia is on the minds of many baby boomers, particularly those who have seen a parent struggle with the condition—or both parents, as in the case of Teresa McCoart, 52, of Van Lear, Kentucky (see page 29 for her Brainpower Success Story). "I want to maintain both my physical and mental health, for my sake as well as for my two daughters," said Teresa, who was one of our panelists.

Getting regular exercise offers just the twofer Teresa—and you—will need to help fend off dementia. Consider what scientists have discovered about the brain health of people who work out regularly.

Researchers at Group Health Cooperative (an HMO) in Seattle looked at the exercise habits of 1,740 people and found that those who performed some form of physical activity at least three times per week—

" People who get the most physical activity cut their risk of dementia by as much as 50%."

whether it was walking, jogging, swimming, or any other workout—were 38% less likely to develop dementia than those who sat on the sidelines.

In Bologna, Italy, researchers followed 749 men and women age 65 and older who were healthy at the start of the study. Four years later, 27 of the participants had developed vascular dementia, the form caused by clogged blood vessels in the brain. When the Italian team measured how much physical activity each participant had been engaging in, they discovered that the people who got the most exercise reduced their risk of vascular dementia by 71% compared with those who were less active.

An ongoing study of Japanese-American men living in Honolulu offers further evidence that it's never too late to start exercising for a healthier brain. After following a group of 2,263 men over age 71 for 6 years, researchers have concluded that participants who get the most physical activity cut in half their risk of dementia.

To be fair, these studies show only that fitness lovers have low rates of dementia. In other words, they don't prove that exercise is the key—the same people who work out frequently may also eat foods that boost brain health, for example. However, a new

wave of studies has begun formally testing whether exercise actually prevents disorders of the brain—with convincing results.

For instance, Australian researchers tested the memory, language skills, and other mental abilities of 138 people, and then divided them into two groups. All of the participants were people who complained of memory problems and had been identified as at risk for dementia. The first group received educational materials about eating a healthy diet and taking other steps that may improve memory, though the literature didn't mention exercise. Members of the second group received the same educational materials but were also encouraged to exercise three times a week for 50 minutes per session. (Most participants chose walking as their workout.)

Six months later, a second round of tests showed that the exercisers' memories had improved while the other study participants' scores had actually fallen. This study offers some of the first solid proof that you can battle brain disease by picking up a good pair of walking shoes—and using them.

How does staying active safeguard neurons? To begin with, we know that regular exercise helps prevent heart disease,

READ A BRAINPOWER SUCCESS STORY

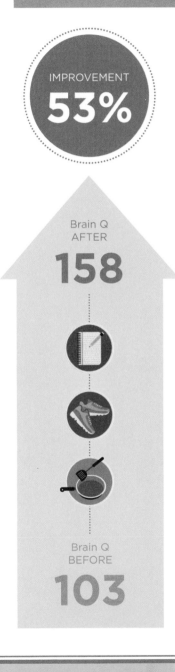

IMPROVEMENT
53%

Brain Q
AFTER

158

Brain Q
BEFORE

103

PANELIST: **Jane Hess**

AGE: **61**

As soon as I finished the Game Plan, I was ready to start over! Even though I was in the midst of a hectic period in my life, I jumped at the chance to be part of the Brainpower Game Plan panel. One reason: I run a small embroidery business with many repeat customers, but struggle to remember their names and order information. It can be embarrassing, and it can also be bad business.

That's changing fast now, as I've learned memory strategies that I can use on the job. **I can sense a difference, and I've surprised myself—and my customers—with my new, improved memory for faces.**

On the Brainpower Game Plan, I enjoyed the daily puzzles and other Brain Train activities—and I didn't mind losing 5 pounds eating foods that I found surprisingly tasty, either. I really liked the shrimp tortillas, which I never would have thought to put together. Regular workouts have been good for my body and my brain. After exercising the night before, I wake up the next morning feeling ready to go.

which seems to raise the risk of dementia. Exercise fights cardiovascular problems by improving the circulation of oxygen-rich blood to the heart. It improves blood flow to the brain too, which keeps your neurons nourished. Also, during physical activity, hard-working muscle cells soak up glucose, keeping blood-glucose levels under control and helping to prevent type 2 diabetes. Chronically elevated blood glucose, which occurs in people who have poorly controlled diabetes, can damage tiny blood vessels in the brain, potentially leading to memory loss and other cognitive problems.

By the way, you'll see the word *cognitive* now and then in this book. It's a form of *cognition*, which refers to the whole range of mental processes, including awareness, perception, reasoning, and judgment.

But there's reason to think that exercise protects the brain in other ways. For instance, scientists have studied the brains of animals and found that regular physical activity decreases deposits of amyloid, the protein that forms plaques in the brain, which may cause Alzheimer's disease. Studies of humans using MRI scans show that people who get plenty of aerobic exercise retain more brain cells than people who avoid exercise, which may help keep their minds clear and sharp. Scientists believe that many of the changes in brain chemistry that promote long-lived neurons may also improve daily brain performance, as you will discover next.

THE SMART WORKOUT

Spending 30 minutes on a treadmill won't raise your IQ; if it did, your local fitness club would probably hold Mensa meetings. However, getting more exercise will make you feel more attentive, focused, and in control of your daily doings. Groundbreaking research shows that you can sharpen the very brain skills that tend to dull with age by hitting the road or the gym.

The types of brain skills that seem to respond best to exercise are known as executive functions. That includes your short-term memory—start working out more and you may find it easier to remember names and phone numbers—as well as your ability to make plans, set and stick to a schedule, prioritize, and multitask.

Aerobic Exercise

What's the best exercise for your brain? Any form of aerobic exercise, such as jogging, swimming, or other sustained physical activity that gets your heart beating faster and lungs working harder. What matters most is making sure you are not part of the large and lazy majority in the United States: three out of four Americans do not exercise regularly.

Pumping Iron

No doubt about it: walking, jogging, swimming, and other types of aerobic exercise are dependable brain boosters. But be sure your regimen includes strength and flexibility training all the same: working out your muscles, tendons, and ligaments does more than build strength and flexibility. Well-trained limbs improve balance, which becomes increasingly important with age, since falls pose the threat of bone fractures. Strength training also builds endurance, which helps fight fatigue. What's more, bigger muscles burn more calories by raising your metabolism. Strength training, which you'll be doing in the Brainpower Game Plan, also helps the body control blood glucose, while lowering levels of cholesterol and other blood fats.

Two Keys: Challenge and Complexity

We created the Brainpower Game Plan with two key rules in mind. First, keep challenging yourself—a little perspiration on the brow is a good thing. That doesn't mean you should pound away on the treadmill until your legs turn to jelly and you collapse, which could lead to injury. On the other hand, a workout should never feel too easy—the minute that happens, the benefits begin to plateau. And that's true whether you're working out at the gym or working on a crossword puzzle.

The reason? "Both your muscles and your brain respond to challenge and stress," explains John Ratey, MD, author of *Spark: The Revolutionary New Science of Exercise and the Brain.* Strenuous physical exercise is a form of stress, which breaks down

muscle fibers, Ratey notes. Muscle grows during the recovery phase following a workout, as it repairs broken fibers. Not only do hard-working limbs develop more and bigger muscle fibers, but they sprout more blood vessels, too.

Likewise, challenging yourself to think hard by solving difficult crosswords or Sudoku puzzles exposes your brain to a beneficial form of mental stress, according to Ratey. Just like your muscles, your brain undergoes a recovery period after you put down your pencil. During that time, your brain builds new branches between brain cells and strengthens existing connections. Stress also causes brain cells to produce an internal "janitorial staff" of antioxidant enzymes that clean up waste products, says Ratey.

A second key rule: keep it complex. Walking and jogging are terrific forms of aerobic exercise, but the Brainpower Game Plan is all about mixing it up. That is, don't think of your workout as a routine but as an opportunity to expose your mind to new experiences. Participating in a variety of workouts—especially group activities—will dramatically increase the brain boost you get from exercise. Not only will learning new disciplines keep your neurons on their toes, but you will gain cognitive and psycho-

> " A workout should never feel too easy— the minute that happens, the benefits begin to plateau."

logical benefits by socializing with others in group workouts. Plus, I tell my clients, mixing up your fitness regimen is fun, which can help keep you motivated to sweat some more tomorrow. (Our panelists agreed that mixing it up was a plus. "One thing I really liked about the Brainpower Game Plan was its diversity," says Teresa McCoart. "The variety kept it from becoming routine and boring.")

To give your brain an extra-large boost, plan on adding group activities that require complex movements, such as dance or yoga. Complex exercises challenge your brain's ideomotor function—that is, the capacity to think and do. In theory, learning a new dance step or yoga position should require your brain to work in new ways. That stimulates your neurons and encourages them to grow and create new connections between one another, which should result in more brainpower.

Want proof? A preliminary study by researchers at Deakin University in Australia offers intriguing clues that learning a new dance may improve your memory. The team asked people to play a popular video game called *Dance Dance Revolution*, in which competitors must perform dance steps on an electronic mat while watching arrows flash across a video screen that instruct them where to move their feet. Players who are able to learn and remember the sequence of steps achieve the highest scores. If you have ever seen kids play this game in an arcade—or if you have tried it yourself—you know that it not only requires some pretty fancy footwork, but it calls for deep concentration and focus too.

The study found that people who excel at *DDR* also tend to score exceptionally well on tests of short-term memory. Of course, it could be that people with good memories are simply better at learning new dance steps in the first place. However, the study does suggest that learning and recalling a complex sequence of dance steps may not only stretch your leg muscles but also expand your attention span.

Dancing has the added benefit of keeping you socially engaged, which we know also promotes a healthy brain. So if you love to trip the light fantastic, think of a night out dancing as a bonus for your body and your brain. But no matter how much you might like to cut loose and rock it on the dance floor, keep in mind that dance styles requiring specific patterns of steps, such as ballroom or square dancing, offer your brain the most benefit.

> " Participating in a variety of workouts— especially group activities—will dramatically increase the brain boost you get from exercise."

A Bigger, Better Brain?

Don't panic, but your brain may be shrinking. Fortunately, you can take steps—literally—to slow and perhaps even reverse this trend.

Studies show that people who exercise regularly have bigger brains than those who slack off. Of course, brain size alone tells us nothing about a person's thinking capacity. Women have smaller brains than men, after all, yet there is no difference in intelligence between the sexes. However, studies suggest that losing large amounts of brain volume as you age increases the risk of dementia and other cognitive problems. Physical activity, especially aerobic exercise, seems to help you retain brain cells and may even help restore lost neurons.

By the time you reach 40, you begin to lose microscopic amounts of brain tissue every day as a natural consequence of aging. It's a slow process, of course, but over time the gradual loss of brain volume may contribute to cognitive frustration—memory lapses and attention problems, for instance. Severe brain shrinkage, known as cerebral atrophy, occurs with dementia and other neurological disorders. In one 2006 study, Dutch researchers showed that people with reduced volume in certain parts of the brain were more likely to develop dementia later in life.

However, how much your brain shrinks as you age may depend in part on how much aerobic exercise you get. Psychologist Arthur Kramer, PhD, and his colleagues at the University of Illinois performed MRI exams on 59 older adults, then asked half of them to start an aerobic exercise program (such as walking or jogging). The rest participated in a stretching and toning program. After 6 months, Kramer and his team performed a second round of MRIs, which they compared to the original ones. The scans showed that the aerobic exercisers had significantly increased the volume in certain parts of their brains; there was no change in the brains of the other study participants. Kramer's study suggests that exercise can help rebuild and bulk up your brain.

LEGWORK AND LEARNING

Scientists have been studying the link between physical activity and cognition for only a short time, but some intriguing evidence has emerged. For example, a 2004 study by Dr. Arthur Kramer, PhD, of the University of Illinois, and his colleagues found that men and women who got plenty of aerobic exercise and were physically fit made snappier decisions and fewer errors on computer tests than others who were out of shape. But that study didn't necessarily prove that exercise improves cognitive ability; it left open the possibility that quick-witted, keen-eyed people are simply more likely than others to be in good condition.

To find out whether exercising directly improves brain performance, Kramer and his colleagues gave a group of 15 sedentary people a computer test that measured their ability to pay attention and focus. Next, they asked the study participants to start an aerobic exercise program. Before long, most of the participants were walking for 45 minutes 3 times a week. After 6 months, the newly active volunteers took the attention-and-focus test a second time and their scores improved by 11% on average. By contrast, a control group of study participants who didn't perform regular aerobic exercise showed no improvement on the computer test.

While exercise doesn't make you smarter per se, it does seem to improve learning ability. Several of Kramer's colleagues evaluated the overall health of 239 children in the third and fifth grades at four elementary schools. Then they obtained the students' scores on standard reading and mathematics tests. This 2007 study, published in the *Journal of Sport & Exercise Psychology*, found that kids who were physically fit and trim tended to have the best academic scores. That trend held true for boys and girls, regardless of their race or economic background.

Another 2007 study, involving 94 overweight children (average age 9) in Augusta, Georgia, reached a similar conclusion. Catherine L. Davis, PhD, of the Medical College of Georgia, and her colleagues split the children into two groups: one group played tag and other energetic games for 40 minutes a day 5 times a week, while the second group got little or no exercise. After 4 months the children who exercised daily scored significantly better on standardized

> " Men and women who get plenty of aerobic exercise and are physically fit make snappier decisions and fewer errors."

> " A good, hard workout may even produce new brain cells, in a process called neurogenesis."

academic tests and special cognitive exams that measure a child's capacity to plan, organize, and solve abstract problems.

Israeli researchers gave a group of men and women over age 50 a test of their cognitive flexibility, or the capacity to "think outside the box." (In such a test, you might be asked to list as many alternate uses for a newspaper as you can think of, such as swatting flies, packing fragile items, or making papier-mâché crafts.) Then they asked half the volunteers to spend 35 minutes walking at a moderate pace on treadmills. Later, all the study participants took the cognitive tests a second time. Only the walkers showed significant improvements in their scores.

How Exercise Grows Neurons

Getting in shape boosts brainpower in several important ways. Dr. Kramer and his team performed MRI scans and found that—compared with sedentary adults—physically fit men and women have better blood flow and more activity in the regions of the brain that control attention. Studies of animals show that exercise stimulates the production of chemicals called vascular endothelial growth factor (VEGF) and insulin-like growth factor 1 (IGF-1). One role for these molecules is helping to produce new blood vessels in the brain. New blood vessels mean better circulation, which should, at least in theory, mean a more efficient and harder-working brain.

A good, hard workout may even produce new brain cells, in a process called neurogenesis, according to some animal studies. That's probably because exercise triggers the rise of another key chemical, known as brain-derived neurotrophic factor (BDNF).

Your neurons need BDNF to grow and thrive, which is why John Ratey calls the substance "Miracle-Gro for the brain." To be sure, BDNF is a kind of neuronal fertilizer, since it increases the volume and longevity of cells in the hippocampus, the brain region that neuroscientists believe plays a vital role in learning and memory.

BDNF seems to promote healthy neurons, helping them to perform their daily tasks. But this intriguing protein may also help prevent dementia. People who develop cognitive problems such as Alzheimer's disease experience a dramatic drop in the number of neurons in the hippocampus. Although the theory remains controversial, some scientists believe that increased BDNF may be why exercising regularly appears to improve brainpower and reduce the risk of dementia.

Want to boost your BDNF? Researchers at Texas Tech University found that men and women who took intense 30-minute spins on stationary cycles experienced significant spikes in their BDNF levels. While studies have not been done to show that the nifty bump in beneficial brain chemicals you get from a single workout lasts, research is clear that regular aerobic exercise is a dependable BDNF booster.

HOW EXERCISE MODERATES YOUR MOOD

Stand outside a gym and you'll notice something about the people walking out the door: most are smiling and have a little spring in their step.

If you don't already exercise regularly, here's a bonus you'll earn by starting on the Brainpower Game Plan: exercise is good for the psyche and can leave you feeling a unique sense of satisfaction, accomplishment, and pleasure—even joy and exhilaration.

It's a fact: working out is a cheap and effective antidepressant, stress buster, and all-around attitude adjuster. Large-population studies indicate that people who follow an exercise regimen are more content with their lives, less likely to be depressed, and less stressed out than sedentary types.

What's their secret? Growing research tells us why exercise is such powerful mood medicine.

For starters, exercise helps to offset mood wreckers such as stress, depression, and anxiety. Stress isn't all bad. Feeling a little nervous tension before going to a job interview or giving a speech can help you stay focused and alert. However, stress-filled days sap your memory and concentration. Worse, unremitting stress is toxic for the brain—literally. During stressful times, the body releases hormones called glucocorticoids. Lab studies have shown that chronic exposure to these stress hormones can damage cells in the hippocampus, the brain region that governs learning and memory.

Depression and anxiety appear to be bad for the brain, too. A number of studies show that when a person experiences these negative states of mind, his or her hippocampus stops sprouting new brain cells, making it harder for the person to learn and retain new information.

Good news: compelling research suggests that exercise is a terrific antidote to mood disruptions that can drain your brain. For years, many scientists credited hormones called endorphins for the emotional boost that comes with physical activity, especially extended, vigorous workouts.

> " Good news: compelling research suggests that exercise is a terrific antidote to mood disruptions that can drain your brain."

> " Getting in shape makes you feel confident and positive about yourself, which can help overcome feelings of stress and depression."

(Long-distance runners in particular have reported experiencing a "runner's high.") Blood levels of endorphins—which are chemically similar to the painkiller morphine—soar to five times their normal level or higher in response to a hard workout, apparently to help you cope with the discomfort and stress of intense physical activity.

However, many scientists are skeptical about the idea that endorphins alone explain why exercise lifts the spirits. Research has shown, after all, that exercise increases levels of other brain chemicals that influence your emotions. For instance, physical activity boosts serotonin, a mood-regulating brain chemical that is targeted by fluoxetine (Prozac) and similar antidepressants. Exercise also increases dopamine and norepinephrine, two other neurotransmitters that appear to play roles in depression.

One 2007 study found that exercise may be just as effective as medication for overcoming depression. Duke University psychologist James A. Blumenthal, PhD, led a team that randomly assigned 202 men and women with serious depression to different treatment groups. Some received the antidepressant sertraline (Zoloft), while others got a different type of prescription: exercise, either in a supervised group or on their own at home. After four months, the depression of 40 to 45% of the patients who exercised had gone into remission—roughly the same number as those receiving drug therapy.

Some experts say that the real psychological benefit of exercise is simple: getting in shape makes you feel more confident and positive about yourself, which can help overcome feelings of stress and depression. Think about it: the first time you jump on a stair-climber at the fitness club you may poop out after 5 minutes of pumping your legs up and down. But keep at it and after a few weeks you will probably find that you can grind through 30 minutes or more. That produces a feeling of what psychologists call "self-efficacy," the confidence that you can achieve your goals. Studies show that self-efficacy can act as an antidepressant.

If you're plagued by the blues or feel stressed out much of the time, exercising may seem like it will take more energy than you can spare. Trust me, making the effort will pay off. Countless clients I have worked with who complained about having a poor memory and other cognitive fogginess reported that once they got moving their memories and mood improved dramatically.

The 9 Secrets to Success on the Brainpower Game Plan

Between all of our various obligations, such as work and family, sticking to an exercise program can sometimes be more challenging than the workout itself. Author and trainer Sue Fleming offers these nine strategies to boost your commitment and chances for success.

1 **Find a workout buddy.** Having a partner can help on those days when you don't feel like exercising. "It's very easy to cancel on yourself," says Fleming. "But you think twice about canceling on someone who's relying on you." Several studies show that getting social support helps people stay the course. For instance, a 2008 study in the *Journal of Exercise Physiology* found that women who were trying to lose weight were more likely to succeed if they joined a support group than if they worked out alone in a gym.

There are several other good reasons to shop for a workout buddy. Exercising with a friend is more fun than going it alone. It also provides you with an hour or so of socializing, which also boosts your brainpower. Caution: your best friend will not necessarily make a great workout partner. Ask someone who is serious about getting in shape, advises Fleming, but avoid "Debbie Downer" types. "You want someone with good energy," she says.

2 **Set a date.** Want to look fabulous at your niece's wedding? Fill your exes with regret at your high school reunion? Quit sucking in your belly at the beach? Choose an occasion sometime in the future for which you know you'll want to look and feel great—and make that your goal. "That seems to help a lot of people stay motivated," says Fleming. You don't need to choose a specific event. "Maybe summer is coming and you have always wanted to wear a sleeveless blouse," says Fleming.

One of Fleming's clients who wanted to slim down for her wedding day combined these first two strategies: she asked her maid of honor to work out with her 4 months before her trip down the aisle. "It was so much more fun for both of them," says Fleming. Effective, too: the bride-to-be lost 42 pounds.

3 **Start slow.** Don't try to make up for years of sofa-surfing on the first day. If you don't currently exercise, starting out with a 10-minute walk is a perfectly reasonable goal, says Fleming. Try that for a few days, then add 5 minutes at a time until you reach your daily goal (which you will learn about later). One major advantage of starting out slow: you greatly reduce the risk of sore muscles that inevitably follow over the next day or two.

4 **Keep an exercise log.** Every time you work out, write down in a notebook or journal what you did and how long you did it. Seeing your progress on paper will give your psyche a lift.

5 **Make time.** Block out time in your schedule for a workout. If you write down "20-minute walk" in the space for noon in your day planner, treat the walk like an appointment that you can't miss or reschedule. If you decide to work out first thing in the morning, put your alarm clock on top of your sneakers and lay out your exercise togs the night before.

6 **Become a motivational speaker.** And start talking to yourself. Repeating positive messages in your head while exercising, such as "This is good for my body and for my brain," can help persuade you to finish a hard workout.

7 **Find your rhythm.** Listening to music while you exercise makes a workout more fun and can add some bounce to your stride, so get some earphones and an MP3 player. If you're computer savvy, create playlists of up-tempo tunes to download onto your device.

8 **Reward yourself.** Use positive reinforcement—it really works. When you complete your exercise plan for the week, give yourself a new song download to add to your workout playlist. Or maybe buy a new workout top after your first month. You'll be surprised how much an occasional pat on the back helps you to stay excited about exercise.

9 **Don't beat yourself up.** So you missed a workout—or two or three. Don't freak out. Instead, think about what got you off track. Did you start your new regimen during a chaotic week? Did you push too hard? Choose an exercise that you find boring? Once you have detected the problem, make the necessary changes and get rolling again.

Play Brain Games

Mounting scientific evidence suggests that people who constantly challenge their minds to solve problems and absorb new information have the sharpest, clearest, and hardest-working minds.

Brain training—the act of purposely challenging your memory, focus, and concentration—is like giving your brain a workout. And like the benefits of any good workout, brain training will make you feel more alert and on the ball, plug up holes in your memory bank, and shore up your defenses against Alzheimer's disease and other forms of dementia. While choosing the right foods and getting plenty of physical activity are absolutely critical for a healthy brain, making sure you get lots of mental activity is essential for boosting your brainpower.

But don't your brain's gears churn away all day? Yes, but I advise all of my clients to make sure that brain training is part of their overall plan for good health.

Brain training seems to protect and perk up the brain in several ways:

● **Practice helps keep brain skills intact.** You rely on a wide range of basic brain skills to get through the day. However, these skills are subject to the "use it or lose it" concept—if you don't put your memory, focus, concentration, and other fundamental brain skills to work, they're bound to fade. Several recent studies suggest that it's possible to fight the effects of aging and retrain your brain to hold on to more of these vital functions. (Don't worry—practicing your brain

CHAPTER 1: Nourish Your Brain

skills is nothing like those endless hours spent at the piano or memorizing multiplication tables. Brain training is actually fun and will become a welcome break you look forward to every day.)

● **Novelty builds and rewires the brain.** Studies in humans and animals offer exciting evidence that the brain changes in response to new experiences and mental challenges. Novelty—as in anything new that you try, from joining a soccer league to learning a language—triggers the release of chemicals that spawn new brain cells and connections between neurons.

● **Mental activity fills your cognitive reserve.** Some scientists believe that continuously challenging the mind creates backup brainpower known as cognitive reserve. If dementia or any other disease harms one network of neurons, the theory goes, the brain of someone with deep cognitive reserve can recruit and train a new network of healthy neurons to take over for the damaged brain cells.

● **Socializing stimulates your brain.** Staying connected with friends, family, and colleagues keeps your brain active by exposing you to new ideas and opinions, which keeps your neurons and synapses in fighting shape.

Here's the beauty of building up your brain with mental activity: it's easy to weave exercise for your mind into the fabric of your daily life. You give your brain a workout when you read a book or take a class, of course. But you can increase your intake of this critical brain medicine in hundreds of other ways. (And you will when you start the Brainpower Game Plan!) If you're stuck in a doctor's waiting room, don't just leaf through a 3-year-old magazine—take out your cell phone and play a game (most cell phones are preloaded with several games and you can download more from your provider's Web site). Have you fallen into the rut of staying home at night and watching tepid sitcoms? Attend a lecture on global warming. Even getting together with an old friend for dinner can stimulate your neurons in a new and beneficial way.

Giving your mind plenty of exercise will do more than keep your brain cells healthy. Making brain training part of your daily regimen will likely leave you feeling more in control and on your toes. Life may even feel richer and more exciting. You will probably discover, in fact, that a more active mind is a happier one.

> " Some scientists believe that continuously challenging the mind creates backup brainpower known as cognitive reserve."

POWER UP YOUR BRAIN WITH DAILY PRACTICE

Sticking to a regular workout schedule has a major payoff: you maintain those toned muscles you worked so hard to build up. You can do the same thing for your brain. Fascinating studies show that regular exercise for the mind helps keep your basic brain skills in shape, which allows you to think faster, learn more, and forget less.

What are brain skills? They are the fundamental functions your thinking software must perform to get you through the day. They include:

- **Attention**—how well you acquire information through your senses
- **Processing speed**—how quickly your brain interprets information
- **Mental flexibility**—how well your thoughts adapt to new circumstances
- **Encoding**—how well you learn new information, such as names and addresses
- **Retrieval**—how efficiently your brain fetches information from long-term storage
- **Reasoning**—how well you solve problems

Reality check: those skills can ebb as you age. That's why you have those maddening moments that can really mess up your day—like when you forget what you were saying in the middle of a sentence or why you walked into a room.

Everybody finds these brain cramps frustrating, but good news: they are not inevitable. Too many people fall into the trap of saying, "Well, I'm just getting older" when they miss the exit on the highway or neglect to add a key ingredient to a recipe. But practicing brain skills regularly can help keep them largely intact—the research says so.

Take, for example, one national study published in *JAMA*, which showed how it's possible to improve your focus. In the study, 2,832 men and women over age 64 underwent 10 training sessions with a special computer program that required them to search for information on a computer screen while ignoring distracting sounds and images. This program was designed to test how quickly the participants' brains processed information. Researchers made each successive test more difficult. At the end of the experiment, 87% of participants had revved up the processing speed of their brains.

That's right: nearly 9 out of 10 people were able to train themselves to think faster and concentrate better with only 10 days of practice. Just imagine what you could do for your brain by giving it a daily mental workout from now on.

Of course, speed isn't everything. Every day you probably find yourself faced with issues you need to sit down and think about long and hard—knotty problems you need to resolve. Problem solving exercises your brain's reasoning skills—that is, your ability to think logically and reach conclusions. The authors of the *JAMA* paper you just read about conducted another study that shows you can whip your problem solving ability into shape, too.

Researchers had study participants work on their reasoning skills by looking at strings of letters or numbers, such as "1, 5, 9, 13," and figuring out what the next number should be. (In this case, the answer is 17, since each number increases by four.) Not only did the volunteers improve their reasoning skills, tests showed, but 5 years later they had significantly fewer problems with daily living—for example, preparing meals, managing money, and shopping for groceries and personal needs. Once again, these potentially life-altering brain changes took hold after just 10 practice sessions. Think of it: a few minutes of brain training every day could be potent medicine for your mind.

Mental workouts are a great way to keep your head in the game, making your mind ready for whatever the day throws your way. But some scientists say that brain training may go a step further. In fact, they claim, challenging your thinking muscles in certain ways may even increase your intelligence.

Sound too good to be true? Experts have long believed that it's not possible to boost your IQ, but a 2008 study hints that the right kind of brain training may do just that. Specifically, it may be possible to improve upon a mental ability called "fluid intelligence," which your brain uses to solve problems and make sense of new concepts. Most scientists argue that your level of fluid intelligence is like freckles or dimples— that is, it's something you're born with that never changes. But that may not be true. Neuroscientists have learned that certain circuits in the brain light up when a person uses fluid intelligence. The very same brain circuits also seem to control working memory, or the ability to store information you need to recall for only a short time—such as a phone number you just looked up.

A team at the University of Michigan wondered this: is it possible to boost your fluid intelligence by improving your working memory? The team asked 35 healthy young people (average age 26) to perform a specially designed computer task that challenged their working memory: think of a devilishly difficult version of the children's game *Concentration* (in which a deck of cards is spread out facedown and players try to make pairs by turning over one card at a time and remembering where matching cards lie). The "game" was designed to become more difficult as the user's working memory improved. The study participants trained with the program anywhere from 8 to 19 times.

Got a thorny problem to solve? You might want to deal out a hand of *Concentration* to get your brain bubbling. Tests given before and after the experiment showed that the participants who worked out their brains with the memory training game improved their fluid intelligence more than twice as much as people in a control group who didn't undergo training. In fact, 100% of the trainees showed at least some improvement in performance. The more days they spent using the computer program, the higher their fluid intelligence rose.

You don't need to sign up for a study to get the same sorts of brain benefits.

In fact, volunteers often quickly lose the gains they earn in these studies, for an obvious reason: they quit practicing once the experiment ends.

No surprise there. Remember, your brain is like any other body part. A few workouts might have your biceps or quads feeling firmer and tighter, but you have to form an exercise habit to keep them that way. The Brainpower Game Plan will help you discover ways to form an exercise regimen for your brain that you'll stick with. Why? Because the games, puzzles, and other mental challenges that you'll be doing each day as part of the plan are fun. "I love that kind of stuff," says one of our panelists, Jane Hess, 61, of Danville, Pennsylvania. Her dedication showed: Jane's score on the everyday brain skills portion of the Brain Q Quiz increased 58% after completing the Brainpower Game Plan.

If you're ready to start training your brain on your own, playing games and solving puzzles are great workouts. Just bear one thing in mind: the best way to boost brain skills is to play against a clock. The pressure of time ticking away shifts your attention, processing speed, and other brain skills into overdrive. The faster they need to work, the more your brain skills will improve.

Most video games require you to think and maneuver quickly as seconds slip away, or as aliens pursue you. If most newer video games seem too violent, old arcade favorites such as Pac Man and Tetris are still around. If your favorite games or puzzles don't involve a time element, add one. For instance, if you do the daily crossword in your local newspaper, give yourself the goal of completing it in less than 30 minutes. If that becomes too easy, cut your time limit to 25 minutes. (Need a goal to aim for? Champion puzzle solvers can complete the daily *New York Times* crossword in as little as 2 minutes.)

Strategize

In the Brainpower Game Plan you will discover simple and practical mental techniques (some that date back to the ancient Greeks) you can learn in a few minutes that literally make information you need to remember—like the name of the person you just met at a cocktail party— more memorable. (By the way, the strategies I'll introduce later on are much easier to

> " Researchers at the Albert Einstein College of Medicine found that men and women who frequently spent time reading, playing board games, or playing musical instruments had a significantly reduced risk of dementia."

CHAPTER 1: Nourish Your Brain

use than other methods you may have read about in "memory improvement" books. And if one doesn't suit your style, I promise you'll find another that will.)

Memory strategies have been around so long and work so well that there has been little recent research on their effectiveness. Scientists simply haven't seen the need. However, in a 2002 study led by researchers at the University of Alabama, 711 people learned how to use memory strategies to recall information such as grocery lists. Two years after taking the 10-session program, 26% of the participants still showed significant memory improvement.

Changing your diet, exercising, and ramping up your mental activity are essential for a healthy brain. However, using memory strategies will help you cut back on everyday forgetfulness and boost your brainpower to its highest level.

Play

Boosting brainpower with mental activity isn't all work and no play. Far from it: the leisure-time activities you choose—you know, the stuff you do for entertainment, pleasure, or just for kicks—may have a major impact on your brain's long-term health. Several studies have shown that people who regularly take part in activities that keep their minds challenged—what I like to think of as giving your brain a good stretch—appear to gain impressive protection against dementia.

It's true. Spending your free time working on puzzles, learning to play the piano, or plowing through novels with complex plots builds stronger connections between your neurons. Scientists say that building up new networks of neurons could deepen your cognitive reserve—that is, your brain's backup power—which may help you overcome any damage to brain cells caused by dementia.

Neuropsychologist Robert Wilson, PhD, of Chicago's Rush Alzheimer's Disease Center, led a 2007 study in which he and his colleagues asked more than 700 elderly men and women to describe the leisure activities they engaged in that required their brains to seek or process information. Did they read newspapers, books, or magazines? Attend the theater or go to concerts? Play chess? Five years later, the study showed that participants who kept their brains busy were more than 2½ times less likely to develop Alzheimer's disease and other forms of dementia than those who spent less time using their heads.

In another study, published in the *New England Journal of Medicine*, researchers at the Albert Einstein College of Medicine found that men and women who frequently spent time reading, playing board games, or playing musical instruments had a significantly reduced risk of dementia. In fact, compared with people who rarely participated in mentally challenging activities, those who kept their minds in motion cut their dementia risk by an impressive 63%. Neurologist Joe Verghese, PhD, who led the study, later oversaw another investigation, which showed that people who spent the most time engaged in stimulating leisure activities were 54%

READ A BRAINPOWER SUCCESS STORY

IMPROVEMENT
78%

Brain Q
AFTER

157

Brain Q
BEFORE

88

PANELIST: **Barbara Capalbo**

AGE: **52**

This plan saved my life! I was coping with serious personal problems at the time I started the Brainpower Game Plan. Plagued by stress and depression, I was chronically feeling spacey, in a fog. I lost track of what I was talking about in mid-sentence or would zone out in the middle of the day for no reason.

After just one week on the plan, I began to regain a sense of control. I feel so much better. More with it, more in the moment, less spacey. **I'm much more energetic and organized now. In better shape, too: I lost 10 pounds on the plan.** I'm proud to say that my doctor said I look great.

I really enjoyed doing the Brain Train exercises with my 11-year-old daughter, especially the puzzles. And I'm telling you: the hard work pays off. After 4 weeks, my memory improved. More important, I feel like my old self has returned. I'm back to normal again and I'm psyched to keep going.

less likely to develop a condition called amnestic mild cognitive impairment, which often precedes Alzheimer's disease.

You don't need to give up frivolous fun, of course. Just bear in mind that no matter how intensely you focus on the plot of *Grey's Anatomy* or *The Office*, watching typical TV fare does not qualify as a challenging leisure activity. So put down the remote and try something new. Learn to throw pottery. Take up knitting. Sign up for guitar lessons. The Brainpower Game Plan will jog your mind and help you come up with a month's worth of other cool ways to stretch your brain and keep your cognitive wheels turning.

Learn

Have you ever dreamed of enrolling in a literature course at your local college and finally figuring out what Faulkner or Fitzgerald was really talking about? If fiction's not your thing, maybe you're a history buff or a budding botanist. Or perhaps you're intrigued by opera, ornithology, or origami.

Whatever your passion, if you have ever thought of taking a class or two in some subject—or even pursuing a degree—quit stalling and sign up soon. You'll do far more than homework. You just might reduce your risk of Alzheimer's disease and other types of dementia, researchers say.

Take one landmark study conducted in the mid-1990s, in which a group of scientists from the University of Kentucky gave a standard test used to screen patients for dementia to 678 Catholic nuns (the youngest was 75). When they repeated the test about a year and a half later, a pattern was obvious: the sisters who had college degrees were the least likely to show signs of dementia.

The take-home lesson? Over the past generation, scientists who study the brain have discovered that going to school may do more than fill your head with facts. Education appears to be a powerful form of preventive medicine. A number of studies have linked learning and brain health: the more years a person spends immersed in academia, the longer he or she is likely to remain sharp, lucid, and free of cognitive disease.

Getting an education is probably the most obvious way to build up cognitive reserve, or backup brainpower. Postmortem studies have shown that some people die with their

> " The more years a person spends immersed in academia, the longer he or she is likely to remain sharp, lucid, and free of cognitive disease."

brains full of plaques, clogged arteries, and other destructive changes that may cause the various forms of dementia—yet never showed any obvious signs or symptoms of cognitive disease during their lifetime. This phenomenon—developing damage to brain tissue without developing memory loss or other serious cognitive problems—occurs more often in well-educated people than in people with less schooling, according to a 2007 study. Scientists theorize that the mental stimulation that comes with getting an education allows some people to build stronger brains and blunt the symptoms of dementia.

Some scientists suspect that learning itself may not be the secret to brain health. They point out that people with little education are more likely than degree holders to smoke, eat poorly, and have other unhealthy habits that may increase the risk of dementia and other diseases. Yet other studies have ruled out these influences and still show a connection between schooling and long-term brain health.

These studies don't offer the final word on whether education reduces the risk of dementia. Then again, there is probably little harm in and a lot to be gained by staying a student in one form or another throughout your life. Most communities have programs for adults who want to continue their educations. My town has a thriving adult-ed school that offers courses in everything from Jane Austen to identifying birdsongs. Your local library or community center probably hosts lectures and discussions on topics that may interest you.

Get a schedule and check them out: your brain will thank you.

Get a Little Help from Your Friends

Everybody knows that spending time with the people you care about most—a close sibling, perhaps, or a trusted old friend—is good for your psyche. After a lunch of telling stories, venting about problems, or just laughing, you walk away feeling understood, reassured, and spiritually nourished.

So why do we let these close—and important—encounters slip through the cracks? Between work, family, and your many other obligations, sometimes it can seem hard to make friends a priority. As a working mother, I know that sometimes time with friends can be one of the hardest things to fit in your schedule. Those dates, however, should be on the top of your priority list. Hanging out with friends isn't just good for the psyche. Remarkably consistent research shows that it's a powerful way to protect your brain, too.

For starters, a number of studies show that people who spend plenty of quality time with family members, friends, and other social contacts are more likely than recluses to retain keen wits and healthy brains as they age.

For example, in a 2008 study involving 16,638 adults age 50 and older, researchers at the Harvard School of Public Health found that staying connected with others could actually double memory power.

In the study, each man and woman was shown a list of 10 words, then asked to recall as many of the words as possible 5 minutes later. Next, the researchers asked each participant a series of questions about his or her degree of "social integration." Are you married? How much time do you spend with your parents, children, or neighbors? Do you do any volunteer work? Six years later, the men and women in the study took the word-recall test a second time. The results: The memories of the people with the most social connections were twice as strong as those of the ones who spent little time with friends and loved ones.

That's just one of many studies to show that staying connected with others may strengthen your defenses against dementia. In another 2008 study, researchers at a Southern California HMO asked 2,249 older women about the size of their networks of friends and family, as well as how often they were in contact with others and how close they felt to people in their social circle. Most important, they also asked the women if they had confidants they could speak with about personal issues. After 4 years, the study showed that women who reported plenty of close social contacts cut their risk of dementia by 26%. Other studies have shown that a busy social schedule may reduce the risk even more—by up to 60%.

What is it about spending time with others that's so good for the brain? Scientists think that filling your social calendar builds up your brainpower by increasing your mental activity. Hanging out and interacting with other people exposes you to new ideas and forces you to articulate your own thoughts, which gives your neurons and synapses a great workout.

Staying socially engaged is also the best antidote to loneliness, which seems to be bad for the brain. Feeling lonely is stressful, and scientists have known for

Better Brainpower: Is Love the Answer?

Have you ever known a husband and wife who were together so long they began to look and talk like each other? Some research hints that long-term spouses may even start to think alike—and that one partner's braininess rubs off on the other.

Scientists tested the intellectual skills of 169 married couples in the Seattle area every 7 years from 1956 to 1984. Early on, test scores revealed a significant gap in brainpower within many couples. But over the years, something intriguing occurred: those gaps tended to narrow as lower-performing spouses improved their test scores. This study suggests that spending time around brilliant, clever people may promote a healthier brain by keeping your mind stimulated. Your heart, of course, is another matter.

years that stress makes your body produce hormones that appear to damage parts of the brain that govern your ability to learn and recall information. This may help explain why lonesome sorts are more vulnerable to dementia.

In a 2007 study, Robert S. Wilson, PhD, of Chicago's Rush Alzheimer's Disease Center, and his colleagues interviewed 823 residents at senior citizen facilities. They asked the study participants to rate, on a five-point scale, how much they agreed with statements such as "I miss having people around" and "I feel like I don't have enough friends." After 4 years, 76 of the study volunteers had developed Alzheimer's disease. Based on the earlier test results, researchers estimated that the risk of Alzheimer's was doubled among people who said they often felt lonely.

Loneliness can sneak up on you—don't let it. If you check in frequently with your friends about jobs, family, or local goings-on, then you're on the right track. On the other hand, if you can't recall the last time you spoke with your best buddy, start dialing—or typing or texting—and set up a date.

Better yet, take your cue from the social butterfly on your block—the one who always seems to be making new friends and organizing big get-togethers. If you prefer more intimate gatherings, reconnect with an old friend or two from high school and arrange a mini-reunion. Start a book club or walking program with a neighbor.

Bottom line: make spending time with family, friends, and other people in the community a priority. Staying connected with others may be one of the most pleasurable, satisfying, and—let's face it—easy steps you can take toward building a better, healthier brain.

Work

What's a typical day on the job like for you—or is there no such thing? Are you constantly switching hats, making new contacts, and putting out fresh fires? If so, a stack of year-end bonuses can't match the windfall that you may be building up: healthier brain cells.

Past studies have shown that people who work in occupations that require training in a skill or advanced schooling seem to gain added protection against dementia. Scientists speculated that the key was education—after all, other studies have shown that Alzheimer's disease and other cognitive disorders are less common among people who have had lots of learning.

> " Hanging out and interacting with other people exposes you to new ideas and forces you to articulate your own thoughts, which gives your neurons and synapses a great workout."

CHAPTER 1: Nourish Your Brain

> "Giving your brain some daily exercise strengthens the connection networks among brain cells, creating a more powerful defense against cognitive diseases."

However, more recent research suggests that certain types of jobs—not just the education or training you bring to them—can protect your brain, too. A 2008 study published in the *American Journal of Epidemiology* may help you determine whether you're getting a healthy brain boost in the workplace.

Researchers at Laval University in Quebec and several other institutions looked at the work histories of 3,557 men and women over age 65 who'd participated in the Canadian Study of Health and Aging. The team used a grading system to determine whether a person's job involved complex interactions with people, things, or data.

For instance, if you're a teacher or instructor, or you act as a mentor to other employees, then your post requires highly complex interactions with people. The same is true for managers and supervisors. Likewise, the authors of this study judged jobs that involve persuasion (such as being a copywriter) and negotiation (such as being an attorney) to require very complex interactions with people, too. By contrast, they judged bookkeepers—who typically work in relative solitude—to have few complex interactions with others.

The researchers graded people who operate machinery or who do work requiring great precision (jewelers, perhaps) as having highly complex interactions with things. (Farming was the most common job in the study to fit that description, since agriculture requires plenty of interacting with crops and livestock.) Finally, the scientists judged people who spend most of their time working with numbers and facts (such as stock analysts) to have highly complex interactions with data.

Next, the team compiled a list of which study participants developed dementia. When they combined this information with the job complexity rankings, some clear trends emerged. In particular, those who dealt the most with other people reduced their risk of dementia by 34%. Meanwhile, others who had complex interactions with things lowered the threat by 28%.

The authors of the study theorized that one way a mentally stimulating job may help guard against dementia is by building up cognitive reserve. In other words, giving your brain some daily exercise in the workplace helps to strengthen networks of connections between brain cells, giving it a more powerful defense against cognitive diseases. That may allow your brain to

" A mentally stimulating job may help guard against dementia by building up your cognitive reserve."

continue functioning effectively even if you do develop the pathological changes that cause dementia.

Interestingly, the study found clues that crunching numbers and poring over spreadsheets may not be the fast track to better brainpower. In fact, participants in this study who spent 23 years or more working with data actually increased their risk of dementia, possibly due to high stress levels. People who have highly complex relationships with others on the job by necessity build wide social networks, which other studies suggest protect the brain, too. In fact, another large study, of twins in Sweden, found compelling evidence that siblings who had people-oriented jobs were also less likely to develop dementia.

Some people prefer solitary jobs—where else would we get lighthouse keepers? However, if too much solo time at work is a problem, try to team up on projects with colleagues whenever possible. If you feel bored and uninspired on the job, maybe it's time to update your résumé and start shopping for a more stimulating post. If your career seems like it has hit a dead end, consider rerouting your life altogether and trying a new field, even if it means going back to school.

If you don't have a formal job, try volunteering, which rewards the soul and health, it turns out. Researchers at Johns Hopkins University studied 125 men and women over age 60 who volunteered to assist teachers in Baltimore public elementary schools. After just 4 to 8 months, the volunteers had improved their overall health, but the researchers discovered something else: participants in the study were also stretching their minds more and spending less time watching TV and more time involved in mentally stimulating activities.

Get Mindful

Imagine a child tying her shoe. As the little girl struggles to master this simple task, she has to block out all distractions and focus intently on entwining the laces. Achieving that kind of focus can be just about impossible when your mind is frazzled by everyday responsibilities. If you're like me, you sometimes find yourself trying to pack a lunch while getting dressed, with a cell phone pressed to one ear. Not a very Zen state of mind, I must admit. But what if you could regain the ability to concentrate as well as that child?

Meditation is a general term for various forms of contemplation that help to focus the mind. Some studies suggest that this ancient practice can help to hush the internal chatter and noise in our brains that blur mental focus. For example, psychologists at the University of Pennsylvania found that asking people to practice a style of meditation known as "mindfulness" for 30 minutes per day for 8 weeks helped improve their ability to quickly and accurately focus their attention while using a special computer program. Other studies have revealed similar benefits.

In the Brainpower Game Plan you'll learn about a famous exercise created by Jon Kabat-Zinn, MD, to introduce newcomers to mindfulness. Kabat-Zinn, founder of the Stress Reduction Clinic at the University of Massachusetts Medical Center, has used various exercises to help people realize that they often go through life on autopilot, without truly thinking about their actions. Unlike the impression many people have of meditation, mindfulness is not about emptying your brain of thoughts. Instead, practicing mindfulness helps you to focus your thoughts on what's happening in your life right now—and sustain that

focus. In other words, mindfulness helps you to stay "in the moment," as proponents like to say. (Bonus: as the name of the clinic Kabat-Zinn founded suggests, meditation is a great stress buster too.)

I have taught mindfulness exercises to classes for years, and the results are consistent: people say they feel more relaxed afterward and they're happy to learn that chilling out is part of brain training. What I find so great about mindfulness training is that you can use it in daily life—when you're walking down the street, for instance, or eating a meal. I especially recommend mindfulness training to clients when it's clear that stress is making them forgetful. There are many books about mindfulness, but the easiest entrée into the topic may be Kabat-Zinn's audio book, *Mindfulness for Beginners*. And your local hospital or community center may offer mindfulness classes. In the Brainpower Game Plan you will learn how to practice meditation, and even try yoga, which allows you to merge the mind-calming effects of meditation with the brain-boosting benefits of physical activity.

> " Practicing a style of meditation known as 'mindfulness' for 30 minutes per day for 8 weeks may help improve your ability to quickly and accurately focus your attention."

BRAINPOWER GAME PLAN

Getting Started | The Plan

Getting Started

It's amazing. For years, scientists ignored brain fitness, but an abundance of new studies show that it's possible to buff up your brain, improve your memory and other vital thinking skills, and ward off dementia.

Now I'm going to show how to put that research to work for you with the Brainpower Game Plan.

I'm confident that you've never tried a diet or fitness strategy quite like the Brainpower Game Plan. Every day for the next four weeks, you will perform mentally challenging tasks, eat a carefully designed diet, and get your body moving in new ways. The goal: to feed and fortify your brain, with the added benefit of slimming and toning your body.

GIVING YOUR BRAIN WHAT IT WANTS AND NEEDS

There are three components to the Brainpower Game Plan: Eat Well, Exercise, and Play Brain Games.

The pages that follow include brain-training activities, exercises, and meals for weeks 1 through 4. For each week, you'll find a grocery list and an overview of the exercises and brain-training activities you'll be doing. Don't worry—although I'm prescribing strategies that are based on solid science, there's plenty of variety woven into the plan. For instance, we include ideas for quick meals you can whip up as substitutes for other dishes—after all, who doesn't get too busy to cook once in a while? You can also adapt all of the exercises to suit your physical fitness level.

Here's a preview of each component of the plan.

EAT WELL

Eating the right foods is critical for boosting brainpower. That's why we asked nutritionists Willow Jarosh, MS, RD, and Stephanie Clarke, MS, RD, to create a 4-week meal plan that's easy to follow, will help you maintain a healthy weight, and features plenty of brain-friendly foods, such as fish, avocado, oil, nuts, curry, and berries. The Brainpower Game Plan diet supports overall health while making the mind work more efficiently and reducing the risk of Alzheimer's disease and other forms of dementia.

Words of Wisdom

There's plenty of flexibility in the daily meal plans, but try to follow a few basic principles:

- **Eat a variety of meals.** You don't have to choose the exact meal provided for any given day, but eat at least two different breakfasts, lunches, and dinners each week.

- **Mix up your choice of fruits and vegetables by color.** That way you'll consume a broad spectrum of antioxidants, which appear to guard against dementia.

- **Eat at least two servings of fatty fish each week.** It's the best source of brain-friendly omega-3 fatty acids. Good choices include salmon, albacore tuna, mackerel, and sardines. Regarding albacore tuna, eat no more than six ounces per week. Note: shrimp contains omega-3 fatty acids, but not enough to count as a serving of fatty fish.

- **Eat protein with every meal.** All Brainpower Game Plan meals include protein, so following this rule shouldn't be too hard.

- **Want to swap out ingredients in a meal?** You can, so long as your swap falls within the same food group, such as chicken for turkey or an orange for an apple. For a complete substitution guide, go to page 264.

> " Eating the right foods is critical for boosting brainpower."

EXERCISE

Getting up and on the move not only increases the flow of oxygen and nutrients to your mental muscle—it also kick-starts production of chemical compounds that are critical for brain health. I asked fitness trainer and author Sue Fleming to create a workout plan that incorporates all of the following:

● **Aerobic exercise:** Some call it "cardio," since it strengthens the heart, but aerobic exercise—any workout that gets you huffing and puffing—does much more. Not only does aerobic exercise (such as walking or jogging) help you keep the pounds off, but impressive research shows that it slashes the risk for Alzheimer's disease and other forms of dementia.

● **Stretching, yoga, and Pilates:** Physical activity that improves flexibility and range of motion not only helps prevent bone and muscle injuries, but the calming nature of these meditative exercises can also relieve stress and declutter your mind.

● **Dance:** Don't be a wallflower—dancing is fun and fantastic exercise. Even better, some research suggests that learning a style that requires specific steps may improve memory.

● **Strength training:** Although it has less direct benefit for the brain, strength training is critical nonetheless. Weight lifting and other forms of strength training improve muscle tone, balance, and endurance. In other words, they help you stay active—a definite boon for your brain.

Words of Wisdom

Whether you're a gym rat or sofa surfer, it's easy to adapt the exercise component of the Brainpower Game Plan to fit your fitness level. Just look for the words "Make It Easier" and "Make It Harder" below each exercise. Follow these basic guidelines to ensure your success:

● **Always stretch a few minutes before—and a few minutes after—exercising:** Stretch muscles only until you feel light tension to avoid injury.

SHOULD YOU SEE A DOCTOR FIRST?

If you're under age 50 and you don't have any serious medical conditions, it's probably safe to start a new workout plan without checking first with a physician. Women over 50 (and men over 40) should speak with a doctor before embarking on a new regimen. That's especially true if you have any of the following conditions, no matter what your age: heart disease, high blood pressure, diabetes, osteoporosis, asthma, or obesity. You should also talk about exercise safety with your doctor first if you have a family history of heart disease or stroke, or you have been eating a poor diet.

- **Drink up.** It's critical to keep your body well hydrated during a workout. Drink a cup or two of water before starting and ½ to 1 cup for every 15 minutes you exercise.
- **Don't beat yourself up if you miss a day or two along the way.** Just try to get back on track ASAP.
- **If you're new to weight lifting, here are a few things to know:**
  - Aim to perform 12 repetitions (or "reps") of each exercise, which constitutes one "set." There are usually two or three sets required for each exercise. Rest for 30 to 45 seconds between each set.
  - Work with just enough weight so that your muscles feel fatigued when you perform the final rep of your last set. If the final rep feels too easy, increase the weight by 2 pounds. Don't worry if finding the right weight for each exercise takes some trial and error.

HERE'S WHAT YOU NEED:

- ☑ A good pair of sneakers
- ☑ Workout clothes, including a sports bra for women
- ☑ An mp3 player (or any type of music player) full of music that inspires you to move
- ☑ An exercise mat
- ☑ A set of dumbbells (weights ranging from 2 to 10 pounds)
- ☑ A bottle of water
- ☑ Optional: a fitness ball

"Getting up and on the move: kick-start production of chemical compounds that are critical for brain health."

> With practice, these easy-to-learn strategies will make those frustrating brain cramps, like forgetting a name or a number, disappear."

PLAY BRAIN GAMES

Every day, you'll perform activities and practice strategies that will improve your basic memory and thinking skills—you may never forget another name!—and promote your brain's overall health. I've been teaching these activities and strategies for years, and the feedback I get is unanimous: they're incredibly effective—and fun too.

Words of Wisdom

The guidelines for your daily brain-training session are pretty simple. For most activities, you'll need to block off about a half hour a day and find a quiet space where you won't be interrupted. Each brain-training session includes three components:

- **Sharpen your wits with timed exercises.** Each day of the plan includes a game that requires you to race against the clock. These timed exercises will improve your attention span and your cognitive flexibility—that is, your ability to multitask and think quickly.

- **Step out of your routine.** We'll give your brain a "stretch" each day that may ask you to try something new or see something a new way. These daily challenges can help safeguard your brain against Alzheimer's disease and dementia.

- **Learn how to make information more memorable.** The plan offers simple and practical mental techniques designed to make information you need to remember—like the name of the person you just met at a cocktail party—unforgettable. With practice, these easy-to-learn strategies will make those annoying brain cramps, like forgetting a name or a number, disappear.

HERE'S WHAT YOU NEED:

- ☑ A pad of paper with lines, such as a legal pad
- ☑ A pencil
- ☑ A stopwatch (or timer)
- ☑ 3 tennis balls
- ☑ A deck of playing cards
- ☑ 10 jacks and a small rubber ball
- ☑ A box of crayons

■ USE THIS SPACE TO TAKE NOTES

Here is your space for taking notes on your progress throughout the week. You can keep track of your weight, note which meals, exercises, and brain games you enjoyed (or hated!), or simply use it to track how you're feeling.

EAT WELL

MY WEIGHT:

EXERCISE

CHAPTER 2: Brainpower Game Plan

PLAY BRAIN GAMES

■ GROCERY LIST

VEGETABLES

- ☐ Baby carrots, 1 lb bag
- ☐ Baby spinach, 6–7 oz bag
- ☐ Broccoli, 1 medium bunch
- ☐ Celery, 1 small bunch
- ☐ Cucumber, 1 large
- ☐ Fennel, 1 small bunch
- ☐ Garlic, 1 small head
- ☐ Lettuce, 1 small head
- ☐ Mushrooms *(white or baby bella)*, 5–8 oz package
- ☐ Red bell pepper, 1 small
- ☐ Red onions, 1 large or 2 small
- ☐ Red potatoes, ¾ lb
- ☐ Sweet potato, 1 large
- ☐ Zucchini, 1 small

FRUIT

- ☐ Apples, 2 medium
- ☐ Avocado, 1 small
- ☐ Bananas, 2 small
- ☐ Blueberries, 1 pt
- ☐ Orange, 1 small
- ☐ Peach *(if not in season choose 1 pear or apple)*, 1 medium
- ☐ Tomatoes, 3 medium

OTHER

- ☐ Hummus, 10 oz container

DAIRY

- ☐ 1% reduced-sodium cottage cheese, 16 oz container
- ☐ Eggs, ½ dozen
- ☐ Low-fat plain yogurt, 32 oz container
- ☐ Nonfat milk, 1 qt
- ☐ Parmesan cheese, 4 oz container
- ☐ Reduced-fat feta cheese, ¼ lb or 1 small container
- ☐ Reduced-fat shredded Mexican-blend cheese, 8 oz bag
- ☐ Reduced-fat sliced Swiss cheese, ¼ lb

BAKERY

- ☐ 8" diameter, whole-wheat tortillas, 1 package
- ☐ Corn tortillas, 1 small package
- ☐ Whole-wheat English muffins, 1 package

FROZEN FOODS

- ☐ Frozen blueberries, 10 oz bag or box
- ☐ Frozen broccoli, 10 oz bag or box
- ☐ Whole-grain waffles, 1 package

DRY GOODS

- ☐ Beets, 1 small can
- ☐ Chopped walnuts, 1 small bag
- ☐ Dark chocolate chips, 12 oz bag
- ☐ Dried cranberries or cherries, 1 small package
- ☐ LÄRABARs®, 4
- ☐ Low-sodium chicken or vegetable broth, 1 can
- ☐ No-salt-added corn, 15 oz can
- ☐ Reduced-sodium black-bean soup, 1 can
- ☐ Reduced-sodium black beans, 1 can
- ☐ Reduced-sodium white beans, 1 can
- ☐ Slivered almonds, 1 small bag
- ☐ Tomato sauce, 1 small jar
- ☐ WASA® Fiber Crispbread, 1 box
- ☐ Whole-wheat pasta, 16 oz box

MEAT/SEAFOOD

- ☐ Raw ground turkey, 8 oz
- ☐ Raw salmon, 9 oz
- ☐ Raw shrimp, 12 oz
- ☐ Raw skinless, boneless chicken breast, 9 oz
- ☐ Raw top sirloin beef, 6 oz

■ PANTRY

The following foods will be used throughout the plan.

DRY GOODS

- ☐ Balsamic vinegar, 1 small bottle
- ☐ Bite-size shredded wheat, 1 small box
- ☐ Brown sugar, 1 box
- ☐ Coffee, 1 jar
- ☐ Dijon mustard, 1 jar
- ☐ Ground or milled flaxseed, 1 small box
- ☐ High-fiber cereal, 1 small box
- ☐ Honey, 1 jar
- ☐ Kashi® GoLean® cereal, 1 box
- ☐ Ketchup, 1 small bottle
- ☐ Low-fat balsamic vinaigrette, 1 bottle
- ☐ Low-sodium soy sauce, 1 small bottle
- ☐ Natural peanut butter, 1 jar
- ☐ Olive oil, 1 small bottle
- ☐ Pumpkin puree, 15 oz can
- ☐ Reduced-fat mayonnaise, 1 small jar
- ☐ Red-wine vinegar, 1 bottle
- ☐ Rolled oats, 1 container
- ☐ Salsa, 1 jar
- ☐ Wheat Chex®, 1 small box

SPICES

- ☐ Fresh ginger, 1 small piece

Small containers:

- ☐ Chili powder
- ☐ Cumin
- ☐ Dried dill
- ☐ Dried or fresh rosemary
- ☐ Garlic powder
- ☐ Ground cinnamon
- ☐ Pepper
- ☐ Turmeric
- ☐ Vanilla extract

CHAPTER 2: Brainpower Game Plan

■ GRAB AND GO MEALS

These meals can be substituted for any of the designated meals for this week, for example: breakfast for breakfast, lunch for lunch, or dinner for dinner. However, try not to substitute more than one meal per day.

⊕ BREAKFAST

PEANUT BUTTER AND BANANA ON WHOLE-WHEAT BREAD
Top a slice of whole-wheat bread with 2 teaspoons all-natural peanut butter and ½ banana (sliced). Serve with 6-ounce container nonfat fruit yogurt.
calories: 346; protein: 14 g; carbohydrate: 61 g; dietary fiber: 4 g; total fat: 7 g; saturated fat: 1.4 g; cholesterol: 3 mg; sodium: 270 mg

⊕ LUNCH

VEGGIE BURGER AND BROCCOLI
1 veggie burger (such as Gardenburger®) with 1 slice reduced-fat cheese on an English muffin (or 2 slices whole-wheat bread). Serve with 1 ½ cups broccoli, microwaved. Top broccoli with 2 tablespoons grated Parmesan cheese.
calories: 480; protein: 36 g; carbohydrate: 52 g; dietary fiber: 13 g; total fat: 15.9 g; saturated fat: 5.9 g; cholesterol: 25 mg; sodium: 1024 mg

⊕ DINNER

BEAN AND CHEESE BURRITO
Heat ½ cup fat-free refried beans. Spread beans on whole-wheat tortilla and top with ¼ cup reduced-fat shredded Mexican-blend cheese. Heat in microwave until cheese is melted. Add 2 tablespoons salsa and 1 tablespoon of low-fat plain yogurt or reduced-fat sour cream. Serve with 1 cup baby carrots and ⅓ cup hummus.
calories: 559; protein: 26 g; carbohydrate: 81 g; dietary fiber: 16 g; total fat: 16.5 g; saturated fat: 5.5 g; cholesterol: 26 mg; sodium: 1198 mg

■ BREAKFAST

YOGURT PARFAIT

Layer 3/4 cup low-fat plain yogurt with 1/2 cup shredded wheat squares, 1/4 cup high-fiber cereal, 1 tablespoon chopped walnuts, 1/4 banana, sliced, and 1/4 cup berries.

calories: 336
protein: 16 g
carbohydrate: 59 g
dietary fiber: 10 g
total fat: 8.9 g
saturated fat: 2.4 g
cholesterol: 10 mg
sodium: 159 mg

■ LUNCH

GRILLED VEGGIE AND BEAN BURRITO

Roast 3/4 cup combined 1" pieces of carrot, red onion, zucchini, and mushrooms in 1 teaspoon olive oil at 350°F for 15 to 20 minutes or until vegetables are tender. Fill an 8" whole-wheat tortilla with roasted vegetables, 3/4 cup reduced-sodium canned black beans, rinsed and drained, and 1/4 cup shredded reduced-fat Mexican-blend cheese. Serve with 1 medium apple.

calories: 506
protein: 25 g
carbohydrate: 82 g
dietary fiber: 20 g
total fat: 11.5 g
saturated fat: 3.8 g
cholesterol: 20 mg
sodium: 665 mg

■ DINNER

GRILLED CHICKEN SANDWICH WITH VEGETABLE SOUP

Mix 1 cup low-sodium vegetable soup with 2 tablespoons Parmesan cheese. Top 1 slice whole-grain toast with 4 ounces grilled chicken breast, 1 slice reduced-fat Swiss cheese, and 1 sliced purple onion sautéed in 1 teaspoon olive oil. Add lettuce and tomato (if desired), spread with 1 teaspoon mustard or hummus, and cover with another slice whole-grain toast.

calories: 559
protein: 52 g
carbohydrate: 45 g
dietary fiber: 7 g
total fat: 18 g
saturated fat: 6.9 g
cholesterol: 117 mg
sodium: 1141 mg

■ BRAINPOWER SNACKS   Choose 1 snack   Eat both snacks

BERRIES AND CHOCOLATE

Top 1 cup berries with 1 tablespoon dark chocolate chips and 1 tablespoon chopped nuts.

calories: 184; protein: 3 g; carbohydrate: 29 g; dietary fiber: 5 g; total fat: 8.5 g; saturated fat: 2.4 g; cholesterol: 0 mg; sodium: 3 mg

HUMMUS AND VEGGIES

Serve 1/3 cup hummus with 1 1/2 cups combined celery and baby carrots.

calories: 196; protein: 5 g; carbohydrate: 28 g; dietary fiber: 7 g; total fat: 7.4 g; saturated fat: 1 g; cholesterol: 0 mg; sodium: 336 mg

■ NAME YOUR COLORS

This classic test of attention challenges your ability to stay focused in the face of distraction. At right, you'll find the words for five common colors that have been printed in different colors of ink. Your task is to go through the list as quickly as possible and say out loud the color that each word is printed in—not the word itself. Try it several times to see if you can improve your ability to pay attention and concentrate.

BLACK	BLUE	**GREEN**
RED	**YELLOW**	RED
BLUE	**RED**	**YELLOW**
GREEN	**BLUE**	**BLACK**

■ TELL ME SOMETHING NEW

Choose a mentally challenging activity—preferably one that's fun—that you have never done before, like starting a blog, signing up for a new course, joining a book club, or volunteering with kids or senior citizens.

■ KNOW YOUR NUMBERS

Knowing important numbers—such as frequently dialed phone numbers, and PIN numbers—off the top of your head can make life easier, but it's difficult to commit a random series of digits to memory. **REHEARSE** and **RESIZE** are dependable memory techniques. **REHEARSE:** this strategy requires you to repeat the information you are learning. That's right: you simply restate the information you need to learn. Repeat the information as many times as you like, either aloud or to yourself. **RESIZE:** most people find it easier to remember several shorter lists of items—such as numbers—than to recall a long string. For example, we tend to remember a phone number by breaking it up into groups of digits. With the **RESIZE** technique, you break up a longer list of words or numbers into several shorter lists.

NUMBER LIST

529

25186

4295014

317492706

1528469537

Try using the **REHEARSE** and **RESIZE** strategies to remember the lists of numbers at right. To test yourself, write down each number string after you've used the strategy for it. See how you did.

CONTINUE TO NEXT PAGE →

■ CARDIO | 30 MINUTES

THE BRAINPOWER WALK

BASIC AND BRISK PACE: 10 MINUTES
Walk at a lively pace, but not so fast that you couldn't carry on a conversation if you had to. Pump arms slightly, keeping them close to your body with elbows bent.

POWER-IT PACE: 10 MINUTES
Challenge yourself by picking up pace. **A** Create loose fists with hands. **B** Bend elbows to slightly less than 90-degree angle, and swing arms back and forth. Do not swing elbows higher than sternum.

BASIC AND BRISK PACE: 10 MINUTES
Downshift to the Basic and Brisk pace for the last 10 minutes of the Brainpower Walk.

Make It Harder:
Make your Basic and Brisk pace a jog and Power It by sprinting.

■ STRENGTH TRAINING

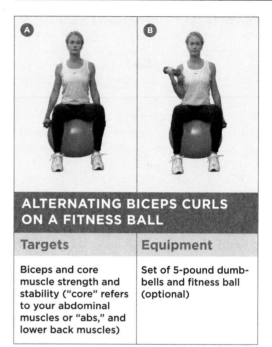

ALTERNATING BICEPS CURLS ON A FITNESS BALL

Targets	Equipment
Biceps and core muscle strength and stability ("core" refers to your abdominal muscles or "abs," and lower back muscles)	Set of 5-pound dumb-bells and fitness ball (optional)

Sit on fitness ball with feet flat on floor, shoulder-width apart. **A** Hold dumbbell in each hand, palms facing inward. **B** Slowly bend elbow upward, rotating forearm so palm faces left shoulder. Pause, then lower arm to starting position. Repeat with other arm. Do 2–3 sets, 12 reps each arm.

Make It Easier:
Use 3-pound dumbbells.
Make It Harder:
Use 8- to 10-pound dumbbells.
If You Don't Have A Ball:
Use a chair and remember to engage your core.

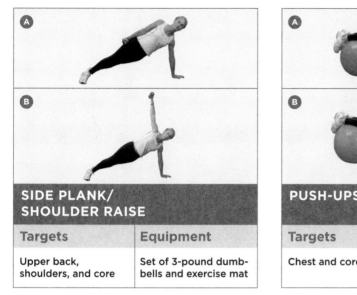

SIDE PLANK/ SHOULDER RAISE

Targets	Equipment
Upper back, shoulders, and core	Set of 3-pound dumb-bells and exercise mat

PUSH-UPS ON A FITNESS BALL

Targets	Equipment
Chest and core	Fitness ball (optional) and exercise mat

Ⓐ Place left hand on floor, so that it is aligned with left shoulder. Then extend both legs to one side, placing left foot behind right. Tighten abs so body forms a straight line from head to feet. Ⓑ Hold dumbbell in right hand, arm extended, palm facing inward and resting on hip. Keep head steady, looking forward. Keeping right arm straight, lift it until arms form a T, then slowly lower right arm to starting position. Do 2–3 sets, 12 reps each arm.

Make It Easier:
Put your inside knee down for extra support.
Make It Harder:
Use 5-pound dumbbells.

Ⓐ Position body so that shins are resting on fitness ball and hands are flat on the mat, shoulder-width apart. Keep legs and back straight. Hold head steady. Ⓑ Slowly lower body to mat, bending arms at elbow. Once nose has almost touched mat, slowly raise up to starting position. Do 2 sets of 12 push-ups.

Make It Really Easy:
Stand and push-up against wall with feet 3 feet from wall. Do 2 sets of wall push-ups.
Make It Easier:
Place ball closer to hips and rest weight on ball.
Make It Harder:
Do 3 sets of 12 push-ups.
If You Don't Have A Ball:
Do 2 sets of push-ups on the floor and on your knees.

END OF DAY 1

■ BREAKFAST

PEANUT BUTTER AND BANANA ROLL-UP
Spread one 8″ whole-wheat tortilla with ½ tablespoon peanut butter. Top with ½ banana, sliced, and roll up. Serve with ½ cup low-fat plain yogurt topped with ¼ cup high-fiber cereal.

calories: 391
protein: 19 g
carbohydrate: 68 g
dietary fiber: 10 g
total fat: 8.4 g
saturated fat: 2.9 g
cholesterol: 11 mg
sodium: 419 mg

■ LUNCH

HEARTY GRILLED CHICKEN SALAD
Over 1 cup mixed greens toss ½ cup each of cucumber, carrots, and mushrooms, ½ cup canned reduced-sodium white beans, rinsed and drained, ¼ cup crumbled reduced-fat feta cheese, ¼ cup dried cranberries, 1 tablespoon chopped walnuts, and 3 ounces grilled chicken. Dress with 1 teaspoon olive oil and 1 tablespoon balsamic vinegar. Serve with ½ whole-wheat English muffin.

calories: 489
protein: 27 g
carbohydrate: 72 g
dietary fiber: 18 g
total fat: 12.5 g
saturated fat: 1.9 g
cholesterol: 36 mg
sodium: 296 mg

■ DINNER

GRILLED SALMON WITH SWEET POTATO
Grill 4 ounces wild salmon with 1 teaspoon olive oil, a splash of freshly squeezed lemon juice, and freshly ground black pepper to taste on medium flame until salmon begins to flake. Serve with 1 ½ cups broccoli, steamed and drizzled with 1 teaspoon olive oil and 2 tablespoons Parmesan cheese, and 1 large baked sweet potato drizzled with 1 teaspoon olive oil.

calories: 536
protein: 36 g
carbohydrate: 47 g
dietary fiber: 10 g
total fat: 24 g
saturated fat: 5 g
cholesterol: 60 mg
sodium: 315 mg

■ BRAINPOWER SNACKS   👩 *Choose 1 snack*   👨 *Eat both snacks*

CEREAL TRAIL MIX
Combine ½ cup whole-grain cereal, ¼ cup raisins or dried chopped apricots, cranberries, or cherries, and 1 ½ tablespoons chopped walnuts or slivered almonds.
calories: 207; protein: 4 g; carbohydrate: 33 g; dietary fiber: 5 g; total fat: 8.5 g; saturated fat: 1 g; cholesterol: 0 mg; sodium: 109 mg

LÄRABAR®
1 LÄRABAR® (cherry pie, cocoa mole, pecan pie, cranberry almond, or Jŏcolat chocolate cherry).
calories: 190; protein: 4 g; carbohydrate: 27 g; dietary fiber: 5 g; total fat: 9 g; saturated fat: 2 g; cholesterol: 0 mg; sodium: 0 mg

LÄRABAR® nutrition facts may vary slightly depending on the flavor.

■ COUNT BACKWARD

Here's a simple yet effective brain workout that will help keep your mind on track. Try these three exercises in simple subtraction.

● Beginning at 200, count backward, subtracting 5 each time (200, 195, 190 . . .)

● Beginning at 150, count backward, subtracting 7 each time (150, 143, 136 . . .)

● Beginning at 100, count backward, subtracting 3 each time (100, 97, 94 . . .)

■ OPPOSITE DAY

Build new neuronal connections by putting your nondominant hand into action. Use the hand that you don't usually use to perform daily tasks such as brushing your teeth, combing your hair, applying makeup (careful with mascara!), eating, and so on. Try writing with your other hand too. Does using the non-dominant hand get any easier over the course of the day?

■ KNOW YOUR NUMBERS II

Continue practicing number strategies by adding **RELATE IT** and **SEE** to your repertoire of memory techniques. **RELATE IT:** with this strategy, the idea is to associate, or "link," new information you are learning with a familiar concept. For example, you might link a string of numbers you need to remember to a date on the calendar. In that way, the string 1 0 2 4 would become October 24. **SEE:** this strategy requires you to visualize, or "see" in your mind, the information you are trying to learn. The more vivid and detailed the image, the better this technique will work for you.

Try using the **RELATE IT** and **SEE** strategies to remember the lists of numbers. First, go through the lists using the **RELATE IT** strategy. To test yourself, write down each number string after you've used the strategy for it. See how you did. Now do the same thing with the **SEE** strategy.

NUMBER LIST

5 2 9

2 5 1 8 6

4 2 9 5 0 1 4

3 1 7 4 9 2 7 0 6

1 5 2 8 4 6 9 5 3 7

CONTINUE TO NEXT PAGE →

■ YOGA/FLEXIBILTY EXERCISES

These flexibility moves are designed to increase your circulation, improve your range of motion, and strengthen your core muscles. Move in and out of the poses gradually and be sure to focus on your breathing: inhale deeply and slowly through your nose and exhale out of your mouth.

MOUNTAIN POSE

CLASPING LEG POSE

Ⓐ Stand erect with feet together and flat on floor, with weight evenly distributed and arms at sides. Imagine a string running through your spine that's pulling you upward, stretching knees, hamstrings, and hips. Pull in abdomen and keep chest high. Hold pose for 10 seconds and repeat 3 times. Practicing the mountain pose is a great way to improve posture.

Ⓐ Assume mountain pose. Ⓑ Now bend forward and bring arms behind knees, clasping hands together firmly. Ⓒ Slowly lower upper torso as far as you can without becoming uncomfortable. Head should also be lowered and directed toward knees. Hold this position for 10 seconds. Ⓓ Now lower hands to floor. Once again, draw body inward. Keep body close to legs and contract stomach muscles by pulling navel toward spine. Hold for 10 seconds. Ⓔ Unclasp hands, inhale deeply, and slowly raise trunk back to starting position.

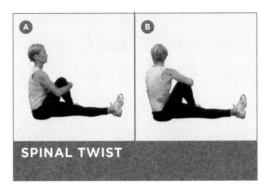

SPINAL TWIST

DOWNWARD-FACING DOG POSE

A Sit on floor. Place right heel against outside of left thigh. Cross right foot over left knee and place sole of foot firmly on floor. Position left hand in front of you. Bring right hand to left knee and firmly grasp it. **B** Slowly twist trunk and head to the left. Left arm should wrap around waist and rest on right side. Keep chin close to left shoulder. Hold for 10 seconds. Alternate leg positions and repeat on other side.

Start with hands and knees on exercise mat. Spread fingers so that pinkies are about an inch from sides of mat. Raise hips up and back, come off knees, and send heels toward mat. Your body should form an inverted V shape.

Breathe deeply and concentrate on slowly lowering heels closer to mat. Contract stomach muscles and lift bottom as high as possible. Look backward toward knees and make sure to keep head in line with spine. Hold position for about 30 seconds.

CHILD'S POSE

Kneel on exercise mat with bottom resting on heels. Bring chest toward mat and rest forehead on mat. Place arms at sides, palms facing up. Hold for 10 seconds. This pose releases tension in your back, shoulders, and neck.

END OF DAY 2

■ BREAKFAST

EGG SANDWICH

Fill 1 whole-wheat English muffin with 1 slice reduced-fat Swiss cheese, 1 egg fried in 1 teaspoon olive oil, 1 slice tomato, and 3 leaves baby spinach. Eat with 1 small apple.

calories: 375
protein: 19 g
carbohydrate: 44 g
dietary fiber: 8 g
total fat: 15.5 g
saturated fat: 5.5 g
cholesterol: 227 mg
sodium: 342 mg

■ LUNCH

VEGGIE BURGER WITH WHOLE-WHEAT PASTA SALAD

Fill whole-wheat English muffin with 1 veggie burger, 2 slices tomato, 1 slice red onion, 1 leaf romaine lettuce, and 2 teaspoons mustard, ketchup, or hummus. For salad: toss 1 cup cooked whole-wheat pasta with 1 teaspoon olive oil, 1 tablespoon red wine vinegar, 2 tablespoons sliced or chopped black olives, and ½ cup chopped broccoli.

calories: 528
protein: 26.6 g
carbohydrate: 81.8 g
dietary fiber: 17.9 g
total fat: 13.4 g
saturated fat: 2.3 g
cholesterol: 3.5 mg
sodium: 808 mg

■ DINNER

TURKEY TOSTADAS WITH BLACK BEAN SALAD

Lightly toast 2 corn tortillas in oven and top with 3 ounces 97% fat-free ground turkey cooked with ⅛ teaspoon cumin and ⅛ teaspoon turmeric, ¼ cup shredded reduced-fat cheese, ⅛ avocado, chopped, and ¼ cup salsa. For black bean salad: mix ¼ cup reduced-sodium black beans, rinsed and drained, with ¼ cup chopped tomato and red onion and 1 teaspoon olive oil.

calories: 532
protein: 32 g
carbohydrate: 57 g
dietary fiber: 12 g
total fat: 21.5 g
saturated fat: 5.5 g
cholesterol: 100 mg
sodium: 448 mg

■ BRAINPOWER SNACKS   *Choose 1 snack*   *Eat both snacks*

BERRIES AND CHOCOLATE

Top 1 cup berries with 1 tablespoon dark chocolate chips and 1 tablespoon chopped nuts.

calories: 184; protein: 3 g; carbohydrate: 29 g; dietary fiber: 5 g; total fat: 8.5 g; saturated fat: 2.4 g; cholesterol: 0 mg; sodium: 3 mg

CEREAL TRAIL MIX

Combine ½ cup whole-grain cereal, ¼ cup raisins or dried chopped apricots, cranberries, or cherries, and 1 tablespoon chopped walnuts or slivered almonds.

calories: 207; protein: 7 g; carbohydrate: 34 g; dietary fiber: 4 g; total fat: 7 g; saturated fat: 1.3 g; cholesterol: 0 mg; sodium: 111 mg

■ FIND IT

This brain booster will help hone your visual-searching skills—and help you spot a friend in a crowded room or even just find your keys. The table below features many different symbols. Your job is to count how many times each symbol appears. Here's the catch: you have only 30 seconds per symbol.

Turn to page 264 for the answer.

■ SAY THE WORD

Use the **REHEARSE** and **RESIZE** strategies to memorize the list of words below. Try the **REHEARSE** strategy first, then close the book and write down as many words from the list as you can recall. How did you do? Now try to remember the words using the **RESIZE** strategy.

ROCK	CANDLE	TOWEL
ADMIRE	POSTER	CHIME
SOAP	DIFFICULT	LOG

■ REARRANGE IT

Shake up your environment to give your brain a fresh challenge. It has probably been years since you reorganized your desk. Get out of the rut and rearrange your workspace. Now you'll have to think before you reach for the stapler.

CONTINUE TO NEXT PAGE

■ CARDIO | 30 MINUTES

If you don't belong to a gym, either do the Brainpower Walk from Day 1, swim, jog, or bike outside. Otherwise, follow the workout for the elliptical machine, treadmill, and stationary bicycle below.

ELLIPTICAL MACHINE | 10 MINUTES

Elliptical machines have controls that allow you to perform preset workouts that vary in intensity and difficulty or to create your own workouts. Set the level anywhere from 1–3, maintaining a moderate pace and pushing the pedals with a forward motion. If the machine you are using has moving handles (most do), grab hold and give your upper body a workout. If the handles are fixed in place, hold on to them but be sure to stand up straight and try not to lean into the machine.

TREADMILL | 10 MINUTES

Set the treadmill at a 3.5 mph pace. Keep abdominal muscles contracted by pulling navel inward toward spine. Buttocks should be clenched and tight. Breathing rate should increase, but you should still be able to maintain a conversation.

STATIONARY BIKE | 10 MINUTES

Most stationary bicycles allow you to set different levels of resistance—that is, how hard you have to pedal—and have controls that show how fast you're pedaling. Set your level anywhere from 1–3, aiming for 70 to 80 revolutions per minute (RPM). If you're pedaling faster than 100 RPM, set the resistance higher to challenge yourself.

■ STRENGTH TRAINING

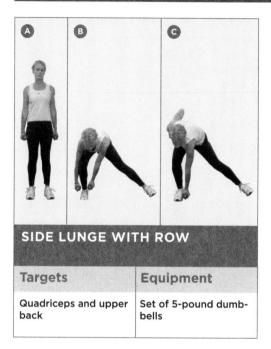

SIDE LUNGE WITH ROW

Targets	Equipment
Quadriceps and upper back	Set of 5-pound dumbbells

Ⓐ Hold a dumbbell in each hand, arms at your sides and palms facing inward. Ⓑ Lunge to the right, keeping right knee over toes. Bring dumbbells to each side of right foot. Ⓒ Lift right dumbbell, keeping elbow close to body. At the top of the move, elbow should be pointing toward ceiling. Return to starting position and repeat on left side. Do 2 sets of 12 reps on each side.

Make It Easier:
Use 3-pound dumbbells.
Make It Harder:
Use 8-pound dumbbells.

WALL SITS WITH FITNESS BALL

Targets	Equipment
Quadriceps	Fitness ball (optional)

HAMSTRING CURLS WITH FITNESS BALL

Targets	Equipment
Hamstrings, abdominals, and lower back	Fitness ball (optional) and exercise mat

Stand facing away from a wall with feet shoulder-width apart. Place fitness ball between lower back and wall, then move feet forward about 1 foot. **A** Slowly squat, rolling ball downward with back, keeping back straight and abdominal muscles contracted by pulling navel toward spine. Keep squatting until thighs are parallel with floor. **B** Pause, then reverse process by moving up wall. Do 2 sets of 12 reps.

Make It Easier:
Do 1 set of 12 reps.
Make It Harder:
Do 3 sets of 12 reps.
If You Don't Have A Ball:
Do 2 sets of 12 squats.

A Lie faceup on mat with fitness ball under heels, legs extended, arms by sides. Pull navel toward spine and slowly lift hips off mat, forming a diagonal line from shoulders to feet. **B** Keeping body still, pull ball closer to you with heels, then roll it back to starting position. Do 2 sets of 12 reps.

Make It Easier:
Do 1 set of 12 reps.
Make It Harder:
Do 3 sets of 12 reps.
If You Don't Have A Ball:
Place feet on ottoman or chair. Raise hips until you create a straight line between ankles, hips, and shoulders. Lower slowly. Repeat 12 times.

■ BREAKFAST

WAFFLE PARFAIT

Top 2 whole-grain waffles with ½ cup frozen berries (thawed), ½ cup low-fat plain yogurt, and 2 teaspoons ground flaxseed.

calories: 367
protein: 24 g
carbohydrate: 44 g
dietary fiber: 6 g
total fat: 11.5 g
saturated fat: 3.5 g
cholesterol: 79 mg
sodium: 367 mg

■ LUNCH

SALMON SALAD WRAP WITH
CUCUMBER AND ORANGE SALAD

Fill 8″ whole-wheat wrap with 3 ounces boneless, skinless, canned salmon packed in water, drained, 1 tablespoon low-fat mayonnaise, and ½ cup combined chopped tomato, red onion, and celery. Add 1 slice reduced-fat Swiss cheese and ½ cup chopped lettuce. Serve with salad made from ½ cup sliced cucumber topped with 1 teaspoon olive oil and ½ cup orange slices.

calories: 518
protein: 37 g
carbohydrate: 51 g
dietary fiber: 8 g
total fat: 20 g
saturated fat: 5.5 g
cholesterol: 74 mg
sodium: 808 mg

■ DINNER

WHOLE-WHEAT PASTA WITH TURKEY TOMATO SAUCE

Sauté 3 ounces 97% fat-free ground turkey until cooked. In separate pan sauté 1 cup combined chopped spinach, mushrooms, and onions in 2 teaspoons olive oil. Add cooked turkey and vegetables to ½ cup reduced-sodium marinara sauce and heat until warm. Serve over 1 ¼ cups cooked whole-wheat pasta and top with 2 tablespoons Parmesan cheese.

calories: 523
protein: 36 g
carbohydrate: 64 g
dietary fiber: 13 g
total fat: 17 g
saturated fat: 4.5 g
cholesterol: 94 mg
sodium: 333 mg

■ BRAINPOWER SNACKS   👩 *Choose 1 snack*   👨 *Eat both snacks*

HUMMUS AND VEGGIES

Serve ⅓ cup hummus with 1 ½ cups combined celery and baby carrots.

calories: 196; protein: 5 g; carbohydrate: 28 g; dietary fiber: 7 g; total fat: 7.4 g; saturated fat: 1 g; cholesterol: 0 mg; sodium: 336 mg

LÄRABAR®

1 LÄRABAR® (cherry pie, cocoa mole, pecan pie, cranberry almond, or Jŏcolat chocolate cherry).

calories: 190; protein: 4 g; carbohydrate: 27 g; dietary fiber: 5 g; total fat: 9 g; saturated fat: 2 g; cholesterol: 0 mg; sodium: 0 mg

LÄRABAR® nutrition facts may vary slightly depending on the flavor.

■ RHYTHM EXERCISE | 30 MINUTES

Consider signing up for a dance or aerobics class at your local gym or dance studio. Dancing in a group setting is fun and provides the added brain benefit of socialization. But if you don't have time, we've devised a rhythm workout that will challenge your memory by teaching you a few moves that you'll mix up each week. Find some upbeat music to dance to—and have a ball.

Write down each of the following exercise names on a separate index card. Do a combination of the exercises for 30 minutes. When you're ready to cool down, march in place for 1–2 minutes.

MARCHING IN PLACE

Pump arms, keeping them close to body, as though you were power-walking.

KNEES

Bring knees up as high as you can. Pump arms for more intensity.

JUMPING JACKS

Be sure to land softly on feet and try to keep arms moving.

PUSH-UPS

You can do modified (on knees) or full ones.

BALLROOM DANCING

Do this with a partner—real or imaginary. If you don't know how to ballroom dance, just act like you do.

STEP-UPS

Use a stair and step right foot up first, followed by left. Then step right foot back down, then left. Keep alternating feet. Use arms to drive you up.

JOGGING IN PLACE

Try to keep in time with the music.

Marching in place with high knees

BOXING MOVES

Pretend you're sparring in the ring. Punch arms forward and keep feet moving.

Boxing moves

SKI MOVES

Jump from side to side with feet together. Bend knees slightly and land softly on feet.

CONTINUE TO NEXT PAGE →

■ THINK-WALK

Do you ever feel like the noise in your head interferes with your focus and concentration? Learning to be mindful of the details in the world around you is a great way to strengthen your ability to sustain attention. (It's an effective stress buster too.) Take a 5-minute stroll in a familiar place. But instead of letting your thoughts drift to worries and daily concerns, focus on what's going on around you. At the end of your walk, write down five things you saw that you'd never noticed before.

1 _____

2 _____

3 _____

4 _____

5 _____

■ SAY THE WORD II

Use the **RELATE IT** and **SEE** strategies to memorize the list of words below. Try the **RELATE IT** strategy first, then close the book and write down as many words from the list as you can recall. How did you do? Now repeat with the **SEE** strategy.

GAME	EGG	HONOR
PEN	BENCH	STRIPE
WELT	FAN	PHONE

■ WORD WORLD

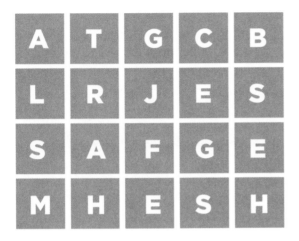

A	T	G	C	B
L	R	J	E	S
S	A	F	G	E
M	H	E	S	H

Find as many words as you can in the following letter grid in 3 minutes. Words can run in any direction—up, down, sideways, or diagonally—as long as each letter touches the following letter. For example, you can form the word LARGE by starting with L, moving up to A, diagonally to R, and so on.

■ BREAKFAST

SMOOTHIE WITH TOAST

Blend 8 ounces nonfat milk with ½ cup frozen berries, ¼ banana, 1 tablespoon ground flaxseed, and ⅓ cup high-fiber cereal. Serve with 1 slice whole-wheat toast topped with ¼ cup regular or no-salt-added 1% cottage cheese (whipped or regular), ¼ banana, sliced, and dash cinnamon.

calories: 361
protein: 23 g
carbohydrate: 64 g
dietary fiber: 17 g
total fat: 6.7 g
saturated fat: 1.4 g
cholesterol: 7.5 mg
sodium: 597 mg

■ LUNCH

EGG SALAD SANDWICH WITH CUCUMBER-TOMATO SALAD

Chop 1 hard-boiled egg and 2 hard-boiled egg whites. Mix eggs with 1 tablespoon low-fat mayonnaise, 1 teaspoon mustard, ⅛ teaspoon turmeric, 2 tablespoons chopped celery, ¼ cup shredded cheese, and freshly ground black pepper. Spread mixture on ½ whole-wheat English muffin. Add ¼ cup raw baby spinach and 2 medium slices tomato and top with other half of English muffin. For the side salad, mix ½ cup diced fresh tomatoes with ½ cup diced cucumber, 1 tablespoon olive oil, 1 tablespoon red-wine vinegar, and freshly ground black pepper.

calories: 503
protein: 29 g
carbohydrate: 36 g
dietary fiber: 7 g
total fat: 29 g
saturated fat: 7 g
cholesterol: 234 mg
sodium: 798 mg

■ DINNER

GRILLED STEAK SALAD WITH BEETS

Mix 2 cups baby spinach with ½ cup sliced canned beets and ¾ cup reduced-sodium canned corn. Top with 4 ounces sliced grilled top sirloin and 2 tablespoons reduced-fat feta cheese. Drizzle with 2 teaspoons olive oil and 1 tablespoon balsamic vinegar.

calories: 564
protein: 44 g
carbohydrate: 51.9 g
dietary fiber: 8 g
total fat: 24.6 g
saturated fat: 8.4 g
cholesterol: 117 mg
sodium: 401 mg

■ BRAINPOWER SNACKS   *Choose 1 snack*   *Eat both snacks*

BERRIES AND CHOCOLATE

Top 1 cup berries with 1 tablespoon dark chocolate chips and 1 tablespoon chopped nuts.
calories: 184; protein: 3 g; carbohydrate: 29 g; dietary fiber: 5 g; total fat: 8.5 g; saturated fat: 2.4 g; cholesterol: 0 mg; sodium: 3 mg

LÄRABAR®

1 LÄRABAR® (cherry pie, cocoa mole, pecan pie, cranberry almond, or Jŏcolat chocolate cherry).
calories: 190; protein: 4 g; carbohydrate: 27 g; dietary fiber: 5 g; total fat: 9 g; saturated fat: 2 g; cholesterol: 0 mg; sodium: 0 mg

LÄRABAR® nutrition facts may vary slightly depending on the flavor.

■ TRIPLE FIGURES

Here's a brain challenge that will help you discover the artist within. Using the space at right, draw as many objects as you can using three straight lines of the same length.

■ MOON WALK

Make like it's the '80s for a few minutes and give your brain a new perspective. Try walking backward through your home or office for at least 5 minutes every hour. Make sure to clear any obstacles—like ottomans or dozing pets—first.

■ PLAY FAVORITES

It's your choice—pick the memory strategy that works best for you. Try each strategy you've learned so far on these new lists. When you're done, commit to one strategy and make it a habit.

LIST A	LIST B	LIST C
3 7 4 9 7 0	RUT	TEST
U S 3 1 0 0 F	COVER	FABLE
5 T F 2 8 V W G	WEST	BOAT
	TABLE	POT
	TORN	FARM

CONTINUE TO NEXT PAGE

■ TOTAL BODY WORKOUT CIRCUIT

STEP-UPS WITH OVERHEAD PRESS	
Targets	**Equipment**
Quadriceps and shoulders	Set of 5-pound dumbbells and low step or bench

SQUAT THRUST	
Targets	**Equipment**
Quadriceps, shoulders, abdominals, and lower back	Exercise mat

A Stand in front of step or bench and hold a dumbbell in each hand with elbows bent at 90-degree angles, hands at shoulder height, and palms facing forward. **B** Put right foot on step; at the same time, lift weights above head in overhead press motion. **C** Slowly lower body and arms back to starting position and repeat with same leg. Do 2 sets of 12 reps with each leg.

Make It Easier:
Use 3-pound dumbbells.
Make It Harder:
Use 6- to 8-pound dumbbells.

This move combines strength and cardio training. Make sure to maintain good form for all the reps. **A** From standing position, **B** drop to a squat, placing hands on mat next to feet. **C** Thrust feet back, so that body is in push-up position. Bring feet back into squat position, keeping hands on floor. Stand back up to starting position and repeat. Do 2 sets of 12 squats.

Make It Easier:
Do 1 set of 12 squats.
Make It Harder:
Do 3 sets of 12 squats.

LUNGE WITH BICEPS CURL

Targets	Equipment
Quadriceps, buttocks, and biceps	Set of 5-pound dumbbells

FITNESS BALL ABS WORK

Targets	Equipment
Upper body and core muscles	Fitness ball (optional) and exercise mat

A Stand in a split stance: step forward with right foot and place it flat on floor. **B** Then stretch left leg back, resting on toes of left foot. Hold a weight in each hand, weights raised and elbows locked into your sides. Bend both knees, lowering into a lunge—be sure right knee stays over right toes. As you lower your body, lower arms to sides. Before your knee touches the ground, slowly resume starting position, raising arms up into a curl as you stand back up. Do 2 sets of 12 reps on each leg.

Make It Easier:
Do 1 set using 3-pound dumbbells.
Make It Harder:
Use 8- to 10-pound dumbbells.

A From kneeling position, clasp hands together and place forearms on fitness ball. Hips should be in line with knees. **B** Keeping abdominals tight and back straight, roll forward 6 to 8 inches or until you feel a tightening in lower back and abdominals. Pause, then slowly roll back to starting position and repeat. Do 2 sets of 12 reps.

Make It Really Easy:
Stand and push-up against wall with feet 3 feet from wall. Do 2 sets of wall push-ups.
Make It Easier:
Do 1 set of 12 reps.
Make It Harder:
Do 3 sets of 12 reps.
If You Don't Have A Ball:
Do 2 sets of push-ups on the floor and on your knees.

■ BREAKFAST

HARD-BOILED EGG SANDWICH

Fill 1 whole-wheat English muffin with 1 sliced hard-boiled egg, 1 slice tomato, 1 teaspoon olive oil, and 1 slice reduced-fat cheese. Serve with 4 ounces black cherry juice or black currant juice.

calories: 382
protein: 18 g
carbohydrate: 43 g
dietary fiber: 6 g
total fat: 16 g
saturated fat: 5.5 g
cholesterol: 227 mg
sodium: 327 mg

■ LUNCH

BLACK BEAN VEGGIE SOUP TOPPED WITH YOGURT AND SALSA

Heat 1 ¼ cups canned reduced-sodium black bean soup. Add ½ cup frozen or fresh vegetables while heating. Top with 2 tablespoons salsa and finish with ¼ cup low-fat plain yogurt. Serve with 1 whole-wheat pita and ¼ cup dried cherries served over ½ cup plain low-fat yogurt.

calories: 503
protein: 23.8 g
carbohydrate: 95 g
dietary fiber: 13.5 g
total fat: 6.5 g
saturated fat: 2.1 g
cholesterol: 11 mg
sodium: 925 mg

■ DINNER

SHRIMP AND VEGGIE STIR-FRY OVER BROWN RICE

Sauté 5 ounces peeled and deveined shrimp (about 6 medium to large shrimp) in 2 teaspoons olive oil or sesame oil and 1 teaspoon chopped garlic, until pink. Transfer to plate. Then sauté 1 ½ cups combined sliced red pepper, broccoli, onions, and mushrooms in 1 teaspoon olive oil (or sesame oil) for 5 minutes. Then add ¼ cup vegetable or chicken broth, 1 teaspoon low-sodium soy sauce, and 1 teaspoon fresh chopped ginger (optional). Simmer until vegetables are almost cooked, add shrimp, and cook another 2 minutes. Sprinkle with 1 tablespoon slivered almonds. Serve over ⅔ cup cooked brown rice.

calories: 554
protein: 46 g
carbohydrate: 43 g
dietary fiber: 6 g
total fat: 21.7 g
saturated fat: 3 g
cholesterol: 284 mg
sodium: 643 mg

■ BRAINPOWER SNACKS   Choose 1 snack   Eat both snacks

CEREAL TRAIL MIX

Combine ½ cup whole-grain cereal, ¼ cup raisins or dried chopped apricots, cranberries, or cherries, and 1 tablespoon chopped walnuts or slivered almonds.

calories: 207; protein: 7 g; carbohydrate: 34 g; dietary fiber: 4 g; total fat: 7 g; saturated fat: 1.3 g; cholesterol: 0 mg; sodium: 111 mg

HUMMUS AND VEGGIES

Serve ⅓ cup hummus with 1 ½ cups combined celery and baby carrots.

calories: 196; protein: 5 g; carbohydrate: 28 g; dietary fiber: 7 g; total fat: 7.4 g; saturated fat: 1 g; cholesterol: 0 mg; sodium: 336 mg

■ CARDIO | 30 MINUTES

If you don't belong to a gym, either do the Brainpower Walk from Day 1, swim, jog, or bike outside. Otherwise, follow the workout for the elliptical machine, treadmill, and stationary bicycle below.

ELLIPTICAL MACHINE | 10 MINUTES

Set the level anywhere from 2–4, maintaining a moderate pace and pushing the pedals with a forward motion.

TREADMILL | 10 MINUTES

Set the treadmill at a 3.5 mph pace and a 2% incline. Keep abdominal muscles contracted by pulling navel inward toward spine. Buttocks should be clenched and tight. Breathing rate should increase, but you should still be able to maintain a conversation.

STATIONARY BIKE | 10 MINUTES

Set your level anywhere from 2–4, aiming for 70 to 80 revolutions per minute (RPM). If you're pedaling faster than 100 RPM, set the resistance higher to challenge yourself. Make sure that the seat position is correct: adjust seat so knees are slightly bent even when legs are fully extended. Avoid sitting tall in the saddle and holding front of handlebars. Instead, round body over handlebars to take pressure off lower back and increase circulation in legs.

CONTINUE TO NEXT PAGE

■ ATTENTION ER

Everybody loses focus now and then. The trick is knowing how to get it back. Practice these Attention ER techniques. Try each a few times, then pick one that you can turn to the next time you need laser-sharp focus.

- Count backward from 20.

- Take several slow, deep breaths.

- Breathe into your heart: think of an image that makes you feel safe and happy—yourself sitting on a beach, perhaps, or the face of a loved one. Hold that picture in your mind and take several slow, deep breaths, as if you are trying to fill your heart with air each time you inhale.

■ PRACTICE YOUR PICK: NUMBERS

Use your favorite memory-maxing strategy to learn and remember numbers you must commit to memory. Use the worksheet below to make note of numbers you need to know—the phone number of an important new contact, or a friend's that you need to look up every time you dial it, for instance. Then practice your preferred memory technique to make those numbers more memorable.

FRIEND	FRIEND	FRIEND
home:	home:	home:
cell:	cell:	cell:
work:	work:	work:

■ **GET THE PICTURE**

Give your visual attention span a workout. Study this photograph for 1 minute. Then close the book and write down as many of the items in the photo as you can remember. How did you do? Try a second time, but before you start, take a deep breath and actively focus on the photo. Did you do any better the second time?

Turn to page 264 for the answer.

■ BREAKFAST

CEREAL WITH PEACHES AND MILK

Mix ¾ cup whole-grain cereal with ½ cup high-fiber cereal. Top with 4 teaspoons chopped walnuts, 1 sliced medium peach, and 8 ounces nonfat milk.

calories: 348
protein: 18 g
carbohydrate: 75 g
dietary fiber: 21 g
total fat: 6.5 g
saturated fat: 1 g
cholestrol: 4.9 g
sodium: 248 mg

■ LUNCH

BABY SPINACH SALAD WITH GRILLED SHRIMP

Grill 4 ounces peeled and deveined shrimp. Toss with 1 ½ cups baby spinach, add ¼ cup tomato and ¼ cup carrots, ½ cup reduced-sodium canned white beans, rinsed and drained, and ¼ cup reduced-fat feta cheese. Dress with 1 teaspoon olive oil and 2 tablespoons balsamic vinegar. Serve with ½ whole-grain English muffin and 1 medium apple, sliced.

calories: 493
protein: 37 g
carbohydrate: 70 g
dietary fiber: 18 g
total fat: 8.5 g
saturated fat: 1.5 g
cholesterol: 173 mg
sodium: 338 mg

■ DINNER

BROILED SALMON WITH ROASTED ROSEMARY FENNEL AND POTATOES

Broil 3 ounces salmon for about 6 minutes on each side or until salmon flakes with a fork. Serve with 1 cup small red potatoes, halved and roasted (at 350°F for about 30 minutes, or until tender), with 1 ½ cups sliced fennel bulb, 2 teaspoons olive oil, 1 tablespoon fresh or 1 teaspoon dried rosemary, and salt and pepper to taste. **FOR DESSERT:** ¾ cup fat-free plain Greek-style yogurt topped with 1 tablespoon dried cherries or cranberries and ¼ cup frozen blueberries, thawed.

calories: 520
protein: 37.8 g
carbohydrate: 58.8 g
dietary fiber: 8.2 g
total fat: 15.3 g
saturated fat: 2.3 g
cholesterol: 46.8 mg
sodium: 310 mg

■ BRAINPOWER SNACKS   👤 *Choose 1 snack*   👤 *Eat both snacks*

BERRIES AND CHOCOLATE

Top 1 cup berries with 1 tablespoon dark chocolate chips and 1 tablespoon chopped nuts.

calories: 184; protein: 3 g; carbohydrate: 29 g; dietary fiber: 5 g; total fat: 8.5 g; saturated fat: 2.4 g; cholesterol: 0 mg; sodium: 3 mg

LÄRABAR®

1 LÄRABAR® (cherry pie, cocoa mole, pecan pie, cranberry almond, or Jŏcolat chocolate cherry).

calories: 190; protein: 4 g; carbohydrate: 27 g; dietary fiber: 5 g; total fat: 9 g; saturated fat: 2 g; cholesterol: 0 mg; sodium: 0 mg

LÄRABAR® nutrition facts may vary slightly depending on the flavor.

Reshuffle your index cards from Day 4, turn on some music, and get moving.

Marching in place

Ski moves

Jumping jacks

Marching in place with high knees

Boxing moves

Jogging in place

Step-ups

Push-ups

Ballroom dancing

CONTINUE TO NEXT PAGE →

■ GO ELECTRONIC

Playing a game on your cell phone or computer puts your powers of attention to the test. Find a game for your cell phone, PDA, or computer that you can play for 5 minutes at a time.

■ IN JUST SEVEN WORDS

Test your creativity with this verbal challenge. Write a short story. And I mean really short—use just seven words to tell your tale.

■ PRACTICE YOUR MEMORY STRATEGY: DIRECTIONS

Use one of the memory techniques from the past week to memorize words you need to remember. Jot down some information you want to remember on the worksheet below, such as a set of directions. Now practice your newly honed strategy for learning words to commit the information to memory.

■ USE THIS SPACE TO TAKE NOTES

EAT WELL

MY WEIGHT:

EXERCISE

CHAPTER 2: Brainpower Game Plan

PLAY BRAIN GAMES

■ GROCERY LIST

VEGETABLES

- ☐ Acorn squash, 1 small
- ☐ Arugula, 1 small package
- ☐ Asparagus, 1 small bunch
- ☐ Broccoli, 1 small bunch
- ☐ Celery, 1 small bunch
- ☐ Cucumber, 1 large
- ☐ Kale, 1 small bunch
- ☐ Mushrooms, 5–8 oz package
- ☐ Parsley, 1 small bunch
- ☐ Red bell pepper, 1
- ☐ Sweet potatoes, 2 medium

FRUIT

- ☐ Apple, 1 medium
- ☐ Avocado, 1
- ☐ Black currant juice, 8 oz bottle
- ☐ Grapefruit, 1 medium
- ☐ Lemon, 1
- ☐ Nectarine, 1 medium
- ☐ Oranges, 3 medium
- ☐ Strawberries, 1 pt
- ☐ Tomatoes, 4 medium

OTHER

- ☐ Hummus, 10 oz container

DAIRY

- ☐ 1% reduced-sodium cottage cheese, 8 oz container
- ☐ Eggs, 3
- ☐ Grated Parmesan cheese, 4 oz package
- ☐ Low-fat plain yogurt, 32 oz container
- ☐ Nonfat milk, 1 quart
- ☐ Reduced-fat feta cheese, 1 small package
- ☐ Reduced-fat sliced Swiss cheese, ¼ lb
- ☐ Reduced-fat string cheese, 4 sticks

BAKERY

- ☐ 8″ diameter, whole-wheat tortillas, 1 package
- ☐ Baked tortilla chips, 1 small bag
- ☐ Whole-wheat bread, 1 loaf

FROZEN FOODS

- ☐ Frozen cauliflower, 10 oz bag
- ☐ Frozen whole-grain waffles, 1 package

DRY GOODS

- ☐ Artichoke hearts, in water, 1 can
- ☐ Chopped walnuts, 1 small bag
- ☐ Dark chocolate chips, 12 oz bag
- ☐ No-salt-added corn, 11 oz can
- ☐ Olives, 1 can
- ☐ Quinoa, 1 box
- ☐ Raisins, 1 small box
- ☐ Reduced-sodium chickpeas/ garbanzo beans, 1 can
- ☐ Reduced-sodium tomato soup, 1 can
- ☐ Reduced-sodium white beans, 1 can
- ☐ Slivered almonds, 1 small bag
- ☐ Whole-wheat melba toasts, 1 box
- ☐ Whole-wheat pancake mix, 1 box
- ☐ Whole-wheat pasta, 16 oz box

MEAT/SEAFOOD

- ☐ Canadian bacon, 1 package
- ☐ Extra-firm tofu, 14 oz block
- ☐ Raw 97% fat-free ground turkey, 5 oz
- ☐ Raw salmon filet, 7 oz
- ☐ Raw shrimp, 6 oz
- ☐ Raw skinless, boneless chicken breast, 8 oz
- ☐ Silken (soft) tofu, 14 oz package
- ☐ Skinless, boneless salmon, 6 oz can
- ☐ Sliced deli turkey breast, 6 oz
- ☐ Smoked salmon, 4 oz package

■ GRAB AND GO MEALS

These meals can be substituted for any of the designated meals for this week, for example: breakfast for breakfast, lunch for lunch, or dinner for dinner. However, try not to substitute more than one meal per day.

BREAKFAST

COTTAGE CHEESE, WAFFLE, AND FRUIT
Toast 1 frozen whole-wheat waffle and top with ¾ cup 1% cottage cheese, 1 chopped small apple, and 2 tablespoons slivered almonds.

calories: 359; protein: 27 g; carbohydrate: 28 g; dietary fiber: 4 g; total fat: 16.4 g; saturated fat: 3.6 g; cholesterol: 46 mg; sodium: 173 mg

LUNCH

CHILI WRAP
1 Guiltless Gourmet Four Bean Chili Wrap®, microwaved. Serve with 1 cup frozen broccoli and ½ cup frozen corn, microwaved and topped with 1 teaspoon olive oil and 2 tablespoons grated Parmesan cheese.

calories: 496; protein: 21 g; carbohydrate: 78 g; dietary fiber: 13 g; total fat: 13.4 g; saturated fat: 2.5 g; cholesterol: 9 mg; sodium: 453 mg

DINNER

CHICKEN PIZZA
Top each half of a toasted whole-wheat English muffin with ¼ cup marinara sauce, 2 ounces pre-grilled chicken strips, and 2 tablespoons shredded part-skim mozzarella cheese. Heat in oven or toaster until cheese melts.

calories: 539; protein: 50 g; carbohydrate: 48 g; dietary fiber: 9 g; total fat: 17.2 g; saturated fat: 5.9 g; cholesterol: 110 mg; sodium: 700 mg

■ BREAKFAST

LOX TOAST

Top 2 slices whole-wheat toast with ¼ cup regular or no-salt-added 1% cottage cheese (whipped or regular), 2 slices red onion, and 2 ounces smoked salmon. Serve with 1 medium orange or 6 ounces orange juice.

calories: 338
protein: 24 g
carbohydrate: 52 g
dietary fiber: 9 g
total fat: 4.5 g
saturated fat: 1 g
cholesterol: 15 mg
sodium: 523 mg

■ LUNCH

EGG SALAD AND ENDIVE

Fill 2 endive cups with mixture of 1 hard-boiled egg, 2 hard-boiled egg whites, 1 tablespoon low-fat mayonnaise, 1 teaspoon mustard, ⅛ teaspoon turmeric, and ¼ cup diced celery. Top with ¼ cup sliced red bell pepper. Serve with 4 Wasa® fiber crispbreads spread with 2 Laughing Cow® Light cheese wedges and 1 medium orange.

calories: 456
protein: 27 g
carbohydrate: 60 g
dietary fiber: 12 g
total fat: 13.4 g
saturated fat: 4.2 g
cholesterol: 235 mg
sodium: 948 mg

■ DINNER

GRILLED SHRIMP WITH ROASTED VEGETABLES

Mix 1 teaspoon olive oil, 2 teaspoons freshly squeezed lemon juice, ½ teaspoon minced garlic, 1 to 2 teaspoons fresh parsley, and pinch of freshly ground black pepper and crushed red pepper. Add 4 ounces peeled and deveined shrimp and toss to coat. Marinate 30 minutes and grill on skewers or in grill pan. Serve with 1 cup combined broccoli and cauliflower, and 1 ½ cups sweet potato, cubed and roasted with 2 teaspoons olive oil. **FOR DESSERT:** ½ cup low-fat plain yogurt drizzled with 1 teaspoon honey.

calories: 543
protein: 35 g
carbohydrate: 64 g
dietary fiber: 9 g
total fat: 17.5 g
saturated fat: 3.5 g
cholesterol: 179 mg
sodium: 366 mg

■ BRAINPOWER SNACKS   👩 *Choose 1 snack*   👨 *Eat both snacks*

CHIPS, SALSA, AND CHEESE

Serve 1 ounce (about 7) baked tortilla chips with ¼ cup salsa and 1 piece reduced-fat string cheese.

calories: 217; protein: 11 g; carbohydrate: 27 g; dietary fiber: 3 g; total fat: 7.4 g; saturated fat: 3.8 g; cholesterol: 15 mg; sodium: 434 mg

PEANUT BUTTER AND TOAST

Spread 1 slice whole-wheat toast with ½ tablespoon peanut butter. Serve with 1 medium apple.

calories: 204; protein: 5 g; carbohydrate: 36 g; dietary fiber: 5 g; total fat: 6 g; saturated fat: 1.1 g; cholesterol: 0.3 mg; sodium: 177 mg

■ SPEEDY MATH

Think fast: how well do you know your multiplication tables? Beginning with 0 x 0, see how far you can get in 3 minutes. (Stop if you reach 12 x 12.) Repeat three times and time yourself.

■ HAIKU, ANYONE?

A haiku is a three-line poem in which the first line has five syllables, the second line has seven syllables, and the third line has five syllables. And yes, that's syllables, not words. Select a common object on your desk—a letter opener, maybe, or the phone—and write an ode to it in the form of a haiku.

■ REMEMBERING A LIST: RECORD IT

Sometimes the best thing you can do for your memory is to forget. Stop trying to recall every grocery item or conversation and get in the habit of taking notes. The **RECORD IT** strategy requires you simply to write down the list of items you need to recall. Take a few minutes to write down a list you need to get something done. It could be a grocery list, to-do list, packing list, or checklist for a project at work.

CONTINUE TO NEXT PAGE

■ CARDIO | 30 MINUTES

If you don't belong to a gym, either do the Brainpower Walk from Day 1, swim, jog, or bike outside. Otherwise, follow the workout for the elliptical machine, treadmill, and stationary bicycle below.

ELLIPTICAL MACHINE | 10 MINUTES

Set the level anywhere from 2–4, maintaining a moderate pace and pushing the pedals with a forward motion.

TREADMILL | 10 MINUTES

Set the treadmill at a 3.5 mph pace and a 2% incline. Keep abdominal muscles contracted by pulling navel inward toward spine. Buttocks should be clenched and tight. Breathing rate should increase, but you should still be able to maintain a conversation.

STATIONARY BIKE | 10 MINUTES

Set your level anywhere from 2–4, aiming for 70 to 80 revolutions per minute (RPM). If you're pedaling faster than 100 RPM, set the resistance higher to challenge yourself.

■ STRENGTH TRAINING

OVERHEAD PRESS ON FITNESS BALL

Targets	Equipment
Deltoids, lower back, and abdominals	Set of 5-pound dumbbells and fitness ball (optional)

A Sit on fitness ball with feet flat on floor and 5-pound dumbbell in each hand. Hold dumbbells up, keeping elbows parallel to shoulders, palms facing out. **B** Extend arms and lift dumbbells over head, keeping head steady and back straight. The dumbbells should almost touch each other at the extension. Pause, then lower arms back to starting position. Make sure not to lock elbows or arch lower back. Do 2 sets of 12 reps.

Make It Easier:
Do 1 set of 12 reps using 3-pound dumbbells.
Make It Harder:
Use 8- to 10-pound dumbbells.
If You Don't Have A Ball:
Place feet on ottoman or chair. Raise hips until you create a straight line between ankles, hips, and shoulders. Lower slowly. Repeat 12 times.

LUNGES

Targets	Equipment
Butt and legs	None

TRADE-OFFS

Targets	Equipment
Core muscles	Fitness ball (optional) and exercise mat

A While standing, take a lunging step forward with right foot, ending with right knee bent and lined up over right toe. Left knee should go straight down toward floor, keeping left heel up and weight on toes. **B** Step back up into starting position. **C** Repeat move, this time stepping forward with left foot. Do 1 set of 24 lunges (12 steps on each leg).

Make It Easier:
Do 1 set of 12 lunges.
Make It Harder:
Do 2 sets of 24 lunges.

A Lie on back on mat and place fitness ball between feet. Extend legs toward ceiling, squeezing ball with insides of feet. Place arms behind head. **B** Slowly rise from mat, reaching for ball with hands. **C** Grab ball and slowly bring it down behind head, keeping shoulder blades off mat. Just before ball touches mat, contract abs and reach back up with ball, returning it between feet. Slowly lower arms and body back down, keeping shoulder blades off mat. Do 2 sets of 12 reps.

Make It Easier:
Do 1 set of 12 reps.
Make It Harder:
Do 3 sets of 12 reps.
If You Don't Have A Ball:
Use a pillow.

END OF DAY 8

■ BREAKFAST

BACON, TOMATO, AND CHEESE SANDWICH

Top 1 slice whole-wheat bread with 1 slice reduced-fat Swiss cheese, 2 slices Canadian bacon, and 2 slices tomato. Top with another slice of whole-wheat bread. Serve with 1 grapefruit, sliced in half and drizzled with 1 teaspoon honey.

calories: 355
protein: 19 g
carbohydrate: 56 g
dietary fiber: 9 g
total fat: 8.5 g
saturated fat: 4 g
cholesterol: 28 mg
sodium: 620 mg

■ LUNCH

ARUGULA SALAD WITH GRILLED SHRIMP

Grill 4 ounces peeled and deveined shrimp. Toss with 1 ½ cups arugula, add ¼ cup tomato and ¼ cup cucumber, ½ cup reduced-sodium canned white beans, rinsed and drained, and ¼ cup reduced-fat feta cheese. Dress with 2 teaspoons olive oil and 2 tablespoons balsamic vinegar. Serve with 1 slice whole-wheat bread and 1 small orange.

calories: 506
protein: 36 g
carbohydrate: 60 g
dietary fiber: 14 g
total fat: 14 g
saturated fat: 2 g
cholesterol: 173 mg
sodium: 341 mg

■ DINNER

VEGETARIAN SAUTÉ

Sauté 4 ounces extra-firm tofu in 1 teaspoon olive oil, 1 teaspoon garlic, and ½ teaspoon chopped fresh ginger, or ⅛ teaspoon ground ginger. Add salt and pepper to taste. Add 2 cups chopped kale, 1 teaspoon garlic, and 1 teaspoon olive oil. Once kale wilts, add ¼ cup canned reduced-sodium white beans, rinsed and drained. Cook until ingredients are mixed. Serve with 1 cup steamed cubed acorn squash topped with 2 tablespoons Parmesan cheese. **FOR DESSERT:** ½ cup low-fat plain yogurt drizzled with 1 teaspoon honey.

calories: 524
protein: 34 g
carbohydrate: 51 g
dietary fiber: 16 g
total fat: 25.5 g
saturated fat: 5 g
cholesterol: 9 mg
sodium: 234 mg

■ BRAINPOWER SNACKS   👩 *Choose 1 snack*   👨 *Eat both snacks*

CHIPS, SALSA, AND CHEESE

Serve 1 ounce (about 7) baked tortilla chips with ¼ cup salsa and 1 piece reduced-fat string cheese.

calories: 217; protein: 11 g; carbohydrate: 27 g; dietary fiber: 3 g; total fat: 7.4 g; saturated fat: 3.8 g; cholesterol: 15 mg; sodium: 434 mg

CHOCOLATE AND NUTS

Mix 2 tablespoons chopped walnuts with 2 tablespoons dark chocolate chips.

calories: 199; protein: 3 g; carbohydrate: 15 g; dietary fiber: 2 g; total fat: 16 g; saturated fat: 4.6 g; cholesterol: 0 mg; sodium: 3 mg

■ HOME CARDIO | 15-30 MINUTES

Here are three home cardio exercises that are fun and easy to do (even in front of the TV—no excuses!). Do each exercise for 5 minutes. If you still feel energized afterward, repeat the circuit.

HOPSCOTCH

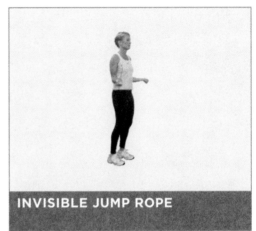

INVISIBLE JUMP ROPE

Ⓐ Begin with feet shoulder-width apart. Ⓑ Start by hopping forward onto right foot, then hop forward landing on both feet. Continue by hopping forward onto left foot, then hop forward landing on both feet again. Repeat at least 5 times.

Start in an upright position, with feet shoulder-width apart and hands at sides. Begin by jumping, pushing off with toes and swinging arms in a circular motion, as if there were a jump rope in hands. If you have a jump rope, use it!

MOUNTAIN CLIMBERS

Begin in a push-up position, making sure hands are in line with shoulders. Keep head in line with body and stomach muscles contracted throughout exercise. Bring right knee to chest and then quickly switch to left knee to chest. Continue movement for 30 seconds. Rest for 15 seconds, then repeat.

CONTINUE TO NEXT PAGE

■ **ART APPRECIATION**

Study this painting for a few minutes. What details do you notice? Close the book, do something else for a while, then return and study the painting again. Are there any details you didn't notice the first time?

■ DOMINO

Sometimes remembering all of the items on a list isn't enough—you need to know them in order. For example, say you need to memorize the key talking points for a speech or presentation at work. Or you need to recall a set of directions. The **DOMINO** technique lets the information fall into place. To use the **DOMINO** technique, mentally connect one item on the list with the item that follows it by creating a visual image or phrase. For instance, if you had the list: *calendar*, *gloves*, *shoelaces*, and *plate*, you might start by connecting *calendar* to *gloves* by picturing a calendar with photographs of gloves as illustrations. To hook *gloves* to *shoelaces*, you might imagine a pair of gloved hands tying a shoe. To connect the last two words, you might visualize the shoelaces being placed on a plate.

WORD LIST

HUT
CANDLE
RECORD
FOOT
POUR
BRUSH
CANDY

Now try using the **DOMINO** technique to remember the list of words at right:

■ SING IT!

Today you'll sing for your synapses with a brain stretch that lets you show off your musical side. Create a jingle by putting the following words to music. Don't worry—this isn't a contest. The goal is simply to challenge your brain (and let you get in the groove).

HEART	SUGAR	PUFF
BOX	RAW	HAIR
MATTER	DANDELION	FOREST

END OF DAY 9

■ BREAKFAST

WHOLE-WHEAT WAFFLE SANDWICH

Cover toasted frozen whole-grain waffle with ½ tablespoon almond butter, ½ small banana, sliced, 1 teaspoon honey or maple syrup, and 4 ounces low-fat yogurt. Top with second toasted frozen whole grain waffle.

calories: 372
protein: 13 g
carbohydrate: 50 g
dietary fiber: 4 g
total fat: 14.6 g
saturated fat: 3.9 g
cholesterol: 81 mg
sodium: 353 mg

■ LUNCH

GRILLED CHEESE AND MUSHROOM SANDWICH WITH TOMATO SOUP

On 2 slices whole-wheat bread, place 1 slice reduced-fat Swiss cheese, ¾ cup cooked mushrooms, and 1 teaspoon olive oil. Serve with 2 cups tomato soup topped with 2 tablespoons Parmesan cheese.

calories: 512
protein: 21 g
carbohydrate: 70 g
dietary fiber: 5 g
total fat: 19.5 g
saturated fat: 6.5 g
cholesterol: 24 mg
sodium: 644 mg

■ DINNER

MUSTARD DILL SALMON WITH QUINOA

Steam 1 cup asparagus spears. Roast 5 ounces of wild salmon. Place salmon and asparagus over 1 ¼ cups cooked quinoa mixed with 1 teaspoon olive oil. For mustard-dill sauce: blend together 1 ounce soft tofu, 2 teaspoons freshly squeezed lemon juice, 1 teaspoon honey, 1 tablespoon Dijon mustard, ⅛ teaspoon freshly ground black pepper, and ¼ cup water. Pour sauce over cooked salmon and asparagus.

calories: 551
protein: 42 g
carbohydrate: 54 g
dietary fiber: 9 g
total fat: 18.5 g
saturated fat: 2 g
cholesterol: 78 mg
sodium: 145 mg

■ BRAINPOWER SNACKS   Choose 1 snack   Eat both snacks

PEANUT BUTTER AND TOAST

Spread 1 slice whole-wheat toast with ½ tablespoon peanut butter. Serve with 1 medium apple.

calories: 204; protein: 5 g; carbohydrate: 36 g; dietary fiber: 5 g; total fat: 6 g; saturated fat: 1.1 g; cholesterol: 0.3 mg; sodium: 177 mg

CHOCOLATE AND NUTS

Mix 2 tablespoons chopped walnuts with 2 tablespoons dark chocolate chips.

calories: 199; protein: 3 g; carbohydrate: 15 g; dietary fiber: 2 g; total fat: 16 g; saturated fat: 4.6 g; cholesterol: 0 mg; sodium: 3 mg

RESIZE AND LABEL

Practice the **RESIZE** technique and learn how to use the **LABEL** technique. **RESIZE:** As you learned last week, resizing a long list of items makes it easier to remember by breaking it down into several shorter lists. **LABEL:** this technique is similar to **RESIZING** but adds an element. Often, some items on a long list are related to one another, which makes them easy to group into categories. So instead of randomly breaking up information on a long list, divide it into natural groupings and give each one a label, like produce, dry goods, fish, baked goods. These labels act as hints to help you recall the items on each smaller list. Try using these two techniques to memorize the grocery list at right. First, read the list of items once, close the book, and write down as many as you can remember. How did you do?

GROCERY LIST

- ☐ Apples
- ☐ Salt
- ☐ Flour
- ☐ Cod
- ☐ Oatmeal
- ☐ Muffins
- ☐ Bagels
- ☐ Celery
- ☐ Quinoa
- ☐ Trout
- ☐ Shrimp
- ☐ Pears
- ☐ Spinach
- ☐ Biscuits
- ☐ Salmon
- ☐ Cookies

SCENT WALK

Go for a stroll around your office, your neighborhood, or a local park. Focus on the various scents that you encounter along the way.

JUGGLING

Challenge how quickly you can think on your feet and practice juggling for 5 minutes. Start out with one ball, slowly tossing it in the air from one hand to the other to form a large loop. When you've mastered one ball, add another. Now try three. Don't worry if you find it too hard; try juggling scarves instead (they are easier to grab and fall more gracefully). Having fun? Keep at it: a recent study showed that juggling may build brain volume, which could mean an increase in new connections between synapses and stronger cognitive reserve.

CONTINUE TO NEXT PAGE

■ CARDIO | 30 MINUTES

If you don't belong to a gym, either do the Brainpower Walk from Day 1, swim, jog, or bike outside. Otherwise, follow the workout for the elliptical machine, treadmill, and stationary bicycle below.

ELLIPTICAL MACHINE | 10 MINUTES

Set the level anywhere from 3–5, maintaining a moderate pace and pushing the pedals with a forward motion.

TREADMILL | 10 MINUTES

Set the treadmill at a 4.0 mph pace and a 2% incline. Keep abdominal muscles contracted by pulling navel inward toward spine. Buttocks should be clenched and tight. Breathing rate should increase, but you should still be able to maintain a conversation.

STATIONARY BIKE | 10 MINUTES

Set your level anywhere from 2–4, aiming for 70 to 80 revolutions per minute (RPM). If you're pedaling faster than 100 RPM, set the resistance higher to challenge yourself.

■ STRENGTH TRAINING

SIDE PLANK/SHOULDER RAISE

Targets	Equipment
Upper back, shoulders, and core	Set of 3-pound dumbbells and exercise mat

Ⓐ Place left hand on floor, so that it is aligned with left shoulder. Then extend both legs to one side, placing left foot behind right. Tighten abs so body forms a straight line from head to feet. Ⓑ Hold dumbbell in right hand, arm extended, palm facing inward and resting on hip. Keep head steady, looking forward. Keeping right arm straight, lift it until arms form a T, then slowly lower right arm to starting position. Do 2–3 sets, 12 reps each arm.

Make It Easier:
Put your inside knee down for extra support.
Make It Harder:
Use 5-pound dumbbells.

REVERSE LUNGE/LAT RAISE

Targets	Equipment
Quadriceps, deltoids, and glutes	Set of 5-pound dumbbells

TRICEPS DIPS ON CHAIR

Targets	Equipment
Triceps	Sturdy chair or bench

Ⓐ Stand holding a dumbbell in each hand, palms facing inward. Ⓑ As you step backward with right foot, extend both arms straight up, with weights parallel to shoulders. Lock wrists and keep arms straight. As you lunge, make sure to keep right knee over right toes. Return to starting position and repeat using left leg. Do 2 sets of 12 reps on each leg.

Make It Easier:
Do 1 set of 12 reps using 3-pound dumbbells.
Make It Harder:
Do 3 sets of 12 reps.

Sit on chair with hands behind you and grip front edge of seat. Knees should be bent and feet flat on floor. Ⓐ Keeping legs together, move forward until hips and buttocks are off seat. Ⓑ Slowly bend elbows and lower buttocks toward floor, keeping abs tight and elbows pointing behind you (don't let them flare out to the sides). When elbows are bent at 90-degree angles, slowly raise body back to starting position. Do 2 sets of 12 reps.

Make It Easier:
Do 1 set of 12 reps.
Make It Harder:
Do 3 sets of 12 reps.

END OF DAY 10

■ **BREAKFAST**

HOMEMADE MUESLI

Mix ½ cup raw oats with 2 tablespoons raisins, ¼ cup chopped apple, 1 tablespoon slivered almonds (or 6 almonds, chopped), 4 ounces low-fat plain yogurt, 2 ounces nonfat milk, and ½ teaspoon brown sugar or honey (if desired).

calories: 361
protein: 17 g
carbohydrate: 57 g
dietary fiber: 6 g
total fat: 8.6 g
saturated fat: 2 g
cholesterol: 9 mg
sodium: 114 mg

■ **LUNCH**

CUCUMBER, TOMATO, AND CHICKPEA SALAD

Toss ½ cup canned chickpeas, rinsed and drained, with ½ cup chopped tomato and ½ cup cucumber slices. Top with 2 teaspoons olive oil, 1 tablespoon freshly squeezed lemon juice, and salt and pepper to taste. Serve with 2 slices whole-wheat bread, toasted, with ¼ cup hummus and ½ cup strawberries.

calories: 518
protein: 18 g
carbohydrate: 74 g
dietary fiber: 16 g
total fat: 19.5 g
saturated fat: 2.5 g
cholesterol: 0 mg
sodium: 628 mg

■ **DINNER**

TURKEY TACO SALAD

Cook 4 ounces 97% fat-free ground turkey seasoned with cumin, turmeric, and chili powder to taste in a large, deep skillet over medium-high heat until turkey is browned. Serve over 1½ cups romaine lettuce mixed with ¼ cup canned corn, ¼ cup reduced-sodium canned garbanzo beans, rinsed and drained, ¼ cup chopped tomato, and 5 olives, chopped. Top with ¼ cup shredded reduced-fat cheese, 2 tablespoons low-fat plain yogurt, and 2 tablespoons salsa. Serve with 8″ whole-wheat tortilla.

calories: 538
protein: 41 g
carbohydrate: 55 g
dietary fiber: 12 g
total fat: 19 g
saturated fat: 6.5 g
cholesterol: 112 mg
sodium: 1112 mg

■ **BRAINPOWER SNACKS**   👩 *Choose 1 snack*   👨 *Eat both snacks*

HUMMUS AND VEGGIES

Serve ⅓ cup hummus with 1½ cups combined celery and baby carrots.

calories: 196; protein: 5 g; carbohydrate: 28 g; dietary fiber: 7 g; total fat: 7.4 g; saturated fat: 1 g; cholesterol: 0 mg; sodium: 336 mg

PEANUT BUTTER AND TOAST

Spread 1 slice whole-wheat toast with ½ tablespoon peanut butter. Serve with 1 medium apple.

calories: 204; protein: 5 g; carbohydrate: 36 g; dietary fiber: 5 g; total fat: 6 g; saturated fat: 1.1 g; cholesterol: 0.3 mg; sodium: 177 mg

■ NAME IT

Using scrap paper, write down as many types of animals as you can think of in 1 minute. How did you do? Now try this exercise again, only this time with types of fruit. When you're done, try the exercise one more time, choosing your own category—car models, perhaps, or dog breeds.

■ ORIGINAL ORIGAMI

Take a blank square piece of paper and fold it into an interesting shape. Now start over with a fresh sheet of paper. Try to come up with two more origami creations. Stumped? Try making a boat or house.

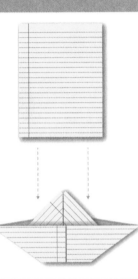

■ REMEMBERING A LIST: TALES AND VIDEOS

Tap your creativity as a way of making lists easier to recall. These techniques aren't for everyone, but if **TALES** and **VIDEOS** appeal to your sensibilities, they can be a great addition to your memory arsenal. **TALES:** who doesn't love a good story? You can make a list more memorable by turning it into a fun, creative tale. The stranger and more outlandish, the better—it will be attention-grabbing and meaningful, making you more likely to remember the information. **VIDEOS:** videos are simply the YouTube version of **TALES**. Use items on a list to create a short movie in your mind. Again, putting the items into an offbeat, funny, or bizarre story will make them more memorable. Try using both the **TALES** and **VIDEOS** techniques with the list of words at right.

WORD LIST

BOY
PADDOCK
TOWER
CLUB
WIND
METHOD
JUMP
VINE
STEAM
DECK

CONTINUE TO NEXT PAGE

■ YOGA/FLEXIBILITY EXERCISES

CAT/COW

COBRA

Start on all fours, bringing wrists underneath shoulders and knees underneath hips. Think of spine as a straight line connecting shoulders to hips.

Ⓐ Cat pose: round spine by dropping head and looking toward navel.

Ⓑ Cow pose: drop belly while looking toward ceiling. Let the motion in spine start from tailbone, so that neck is the last part to move.

Alternate between cat and cow pose with each inhale and exhale, matching movement to breath. Continue for 5–10 breaths, moving whole spine. After final exhale, return to neutral position.

Start by lying facedown, flat on floor with feet together. Place hands on floor next to shoulders, palms down. Gently push upper body off floor a few inches at a time, while keeping legs on floor. It should feel like you're doing a push-up but with relaxed stomach and back muscles. Keep looking up at all times and push slowly until you feel the stretch in stomach and lower back muscles. If stretch feels uncomfortable, just push a few inches off floor. Hold for 10–15 seconds.

HAMSTRING STRETCH

SEATED POSE

Sit on floor with right leg extended and left leg bent so that left heel is against inner part of right knee. Try to keep both legs as flat as possible. Keep torso upright, abs in, and shoulders down. Place hands on straight leg (or on floor on either side of it) and lean forward from waist. Keep chin up, as if reaching chin toward toes of straightened leg. Hold for 15–30 seconds. Repeat on other side.

Sit on floor and open legs as wide as possible while remaining in a comfortable position. Keep quads tight and toes pointing toward ceiling. Press backs of legs into floor, feeling the stretch in hamstrings, back, and calves. Focus on sitting up straight. Hold for 15–30 seconds.

■ BREAKFAST

CRUNCHY PEANUT BUTTER YOGURT

Mix 1 cup low-fat plain yogurt with ½ tablespoon peanut butter, ½ cup Wheat Chex®, and ½ cup sliced apples. Add cinnamon to taste.

calories: 330
protein: 18 g
carbohydrate: 49 g
dietary fiber: 6 g
total fat: 8.5 g
saturated fat: 3.5 g
cholesterol: 15 mg
sodium: 399 mg

■ LUNCH

MEDITERRANEAN PASTA AND VEGGIE SALAD

Mix 1 cup cooked whole-wheat pasta with 2 ounces grilled chicken breast, ¼ cup cooked broccoli, ¼ cup red bell peppers, ½ cup chopped artichoke hearts, 1 tablespoon chopped red onion, and 5 chopped black olives. Dress with 1 teaspoon olive oil, 1 tablespoon freshly squeezed lemon juice, and 1 tablespoon grated Parmesan cheese. Serve with ⅓ cup plain low-fat yogurt drizzled with 1 teaspoon honey, and ½ cup nectarine slices sprinkled with cinnamon.

calories: 506
protein: 35 g
carbohydrate: 71 g
dietary fiber: 13 g
total fat: 12 g
saturated fat: 3.3 g
cholesterol: 57 mg
sodium: 663 mg

■ DINNER

OPEN-FACED SALMON SANDWICH WITH SIDE SALAD

Top 2 slices toasted whole-wheat bread with ⅓ cup (4 ounces) boneless, skinless, canned salmon, packed in water, drained. Mix with 1 tablespoon low-fat mayonnaise, ¼ cup chopped tomato, and ½ cup chopped cucumber. Cut bread into squares or triangles. Serve with 1 cup arugula topped with 1 tablespoon chopped walnuts and drizzled with 1 tablespoon balsamic vinegar and 1 teaspoon olive oil. **FOR DESSERT:** ¾ cup strawberries topped with 1 teaspoon honey.

calories: 543
protein: 31 g
carbohydrate: 56 g
dietary fiber: 6.5 g
total fat: 23 g
saturated fat: 4 g
cholesterol: 61 mg
sodium: 911 mg

■ BRAINPOWER SNACKS   *Choose 1 snack*   *Eat both snacks*

HUMMUS AND VEGGIES

Serve ⅓ cup hummus with 1 ½ cups combined celery and baby carrots.

calories: 196; protein: 5 g; carbohydrate: 28 g; dietary fiber: 7 g; total fat: 7.4 g; saturated fat: 1 g; cholesterol: 0 mg; sodium: 336 mg

CHOCOLATE AND NUTS

Mix 2 tablespoons chopped walnuts with 2 tablespoons dark chocolate chips.

calories: 199; protein: 3 g; carbohydrate: 15 g; dietary fiber: 2 g; total fat: 16 g; saturated fat: 4.6 g; cholesterol: 0 mg; sodium: 3 mg

■ STAIRS WORKOUT

Here's a good way to break up the day and sneak in a workout.

STAIR CLIMBING | 10 MINUTES

Here's a great workout you can do in virtually any building with a second floor. Keep your feet moving and arms pumping to help pull you up each step. For safety's sake, don't be afraid to hold the railing on your way back down.

PUSH-UPS

Try a push-up with hands shoulder-width apart on second or third step and toes on floor at the bottom of the stairs, hip-width apart. Slowly lower chest by bending elbows at 90-degree angles. Go down as far as you can, then slowly return to starting position. If you're a beginner, you can do a modified version by starting with knees on the floor. Do 2 sets of 12 push-ups.

Make It Easier:
Do 2 sets of 12 modified push-ups.
Make It Harder:
Do 3 sets of 12 push-ups.

TRICEPS DIPS

Sit on edge of a step with hands at sides. Feet should be flat on floor. Push butt off step, bend elbows, and slowly lower body toward floor. Butt should stay close to step, brushing it on the way down. Return to starting position. Do 2 sets of 12 dips.

Make It Easier
Do 1 set of 12 dips.
Make It Harder
Do 3 sets of 12 dips.

STEP-UPS

Stand on floor facing stairs. Leading with left foot, step up on first step while driving right knee up as though trying to hit chest. Return both feet to floor. Do 12 consecutive steps, then switch lead foot to the right, driving up with left knee. Do 2 sets of 12 step-ups with each leg.

Make It Easier
Do 1 set of 12 step-ups.
Make It Harder
Do 3 sets of 12 step-ups.

CONTINUE TO NEXT PAGE →

■ ARCADE ACTION

Go online or visit the arcade at your local shopping mall and find brain-boosting games that require quick thinking and lightning-fast reactions. Play them several times and watch your score improve—proof that your brain skills are revving up. Want more brain games? Check out *prevention.com/braingames*.

■ CHOREOGRAPH YOURSELF

Learning new dance steps has been linked to building cognitive reserve in some studies. It's also just a good way to cut loose and shake away the day's stress and tension. Put on some music and create a new dance. This is no time to be a wallflower—hitting the dance floor is good for your brain. Want an added boost? Teach your new moves to someone else.

■ STRAIGHT STORY

Here's a simple yet effective brain workout that will help focus your mind on the point of a story.

- **Pause.** Stop for a few seconds and focus your thoughts. Bring your attention to the story you are trying to remember.

- **Identify the main point.** All stories are hierarchical. That means that some information in a narrative is more important than other information—and that at some point in the story you discover the most essential ingredient. How can you find it? Figure out what phrase or point of the story is so critical that the rest of the tale makes no sense without it. I like to use the movie *Titanic* to illustrate this point. The main point, of course, is that the boat hit an iceberg and sank. Think about it: if the boat stays afloat, none of the romantic intrigue or other subplots really matter.

- **Ignore the details.** Don't let minor details sidetrack you. Let your mantra be "Just the facts, ma'am—and only the really important ones." Trust me, you'll remember the details anyway once you've got the main point down.

- **Get to the heart.** When you have identified the main point, go back and add a few of the major details to get to the heart of the story. Using *Titanic* again, you would add to the main point—the boat sank—by focusing on how many lives were lost. You still wouldn't focus on the romantic intrigue—but I bet you would remember that detail anyway.

Try the **STRAIGHT STORY** technique with stories you read today in the newspaper.

END OF DAY 12

■ BREAKFAST

BREAKFAST QUESADILLA

Fill 8″ whole-wheat tortilla with 1 egg and 2 egg whites, scrambled in 1 teaspoon of olive oil, and ¼ cup shredded reduced-fat feta cheese. Fold in half and microwave (or heat in a skillet) until cheese melts. Top with 2 tablespoons low-fat plain yogurt and ¼ cup salsa. Serve with 4 ounces black currant juice or orange juice.

calories: 352
protein: 23 g
carbohydrate: 35 g
dietary fiber: 5 g
total fat: 15 g
saturated fat: 5 g
cholesterol: 221 mg
sodium: 590 mg

■ LUNCH

TURKEY AVOCADO WRAP

In 8″ whole-wheat tortilla, spread 2 teaspoons low-fat mayonnaise, place ⅛ avocado, sliced, 3 ounces turkey breast, ½ cup fresh spinach, 2 slices tomato, and 1 slice reduced-fat Swiss cheese, and roll up wrap. Serve with ½ cup bite-size shredded wheat and 2 tablespoons raisins.

calories: 526
protein: 34 g
carbohydrate: 72 g
dietary fiber: 20 g
total fat: 13.5 g
saturated fat: 4.5 g
cholesterol: 49 mg
sodium: 939 mg

■ DINNER

BROILED SCALLOPS WITH
STEAMED VEGGIES AND QUINOA

Brush 5 ounces scallops with 1 teaspoon olive oil. Place in shallow baking dish with 2 tablespoons white wine, 1 tablespoon fresh parsley, ½ teaspoon paprika, and freshly ground pepper and freshly squeezed lemon juice to taste. Sprinkle with 2 tablespoons crushed whole-wheat melba toast or crackers and broil until scallops are opaque. Serve with 1 cup steamed cauliflower and 1 ¼ cups cooked quinoa tossed with 1 teaspoon olive oil.

calories: 581
protein: 38 g
carbohydrate: 70 g
dietary fiber: 10 g
total fat: 15 g
saturated fat: 1.4 g
cholesterol: 47 mg
sodium: 359 mg

■ BRAINPOWER SNACKS   Choose 1 snack   Eat both snacks

HUMMUS AND VEGGIES

Serve ⅓ cup hummus with 1 ½ cups combined celery and baby carrots.

calories: 196; protein: 5 g; carbohydrate: 28 g; dietary fiber: 7 g; total fat: 7.4 g; saturated fat: 1 g; cholesterol: 0 mg; sodium: 336 mg

CHOCOLATE AND NUTS

Mix 2 tablespoons chopped walnuts with 2 tablespoons dark chocolate chips.

calories: 199; protein: 3 g; carbohydrate: 15 g; dietary fiber: 2 g; total fat: 16 g; saturated fat: 4.6 g; cholesterol: 0 mg; sodium: 3 mg

■ RHYTHM EXERCISE | 30 MINUTES

Reshuffle your index cards from Day 4, turn on some music, and get moving.

Marching in place

Ski moves

Jumping jacks

Ballroom dancing

Marching in place with high knees

Jogging in place

Boxing moves

Push-ups

Step-ups

CONTINUE TO NEXT PAGE →

■ A GOOD SIGN

Learning a foreign language is a challenge, but using sign language requires your brain to work in new ways since you must express yourself using your hands instead of spoken language. Teach yourself the following sign language alphabet.

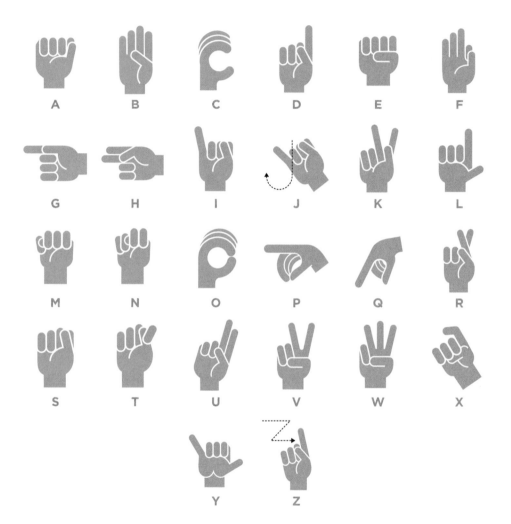

■ HAPPY TRAILS

Remember those connect-the-dots puzzles you did as a kid? See how much of this puzzle you can complete in 1 minute. Then erase your work, take a break, and try it again. Did you get further the second time?

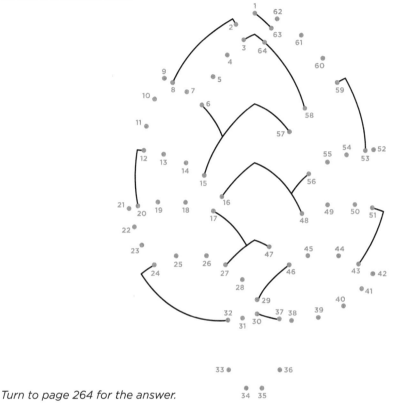

Turn to page 264 for the answer.

■ STRAIGHT STORY

Practice may not always make perfect, but it can improve your memory, as you'll no doubt discover by using the **STRAIGHT STORY** technique again. Read the story below, then apply the principles of the **STRAIGHT STORY** technique. (If you need a quick refresher, refer back to Day 12.)

Tom Barber lives near a large river that sometimes floods in the spring. Last summer, two girls were swinging from a rope tied to the branch of a tree hanging over the river. One of the girls fell off the swing and landed in the shallow water close to shore, injuring herself. A fisherman nearby saw the accident and took the girls to the local doctor. Luckily, the girl had only sprained her ankle and recovered quickly.

Now write down on a piece of paper as much of the story as you can remember. How did you do?

END OF DAY 13

■ BREAKFAST

PANCAKES WITH BERRIES

Top two 6″ whole-wheat pancakes with ½ cup berries, ½ cup low-fat plain yogurt, and 2 teaspoons chopped walnuts.

calories: 354
protein: 15 g
carbohydrate: 47 g
dietary fiber: 3 g
total fat: 12.9 g
saturated fat: 4.2 g
cholesterol: 73 mg
sodium: 595 mg

■ LUNCH

TURKEY AND RED PEPPER SANDWICH

Spread 1 teaspoon mustard on 2 slices whole-wheat bread. Top 1 slice with 3 ounces roasted turkey breast, ¼ cup sliced red peppers, 1 slice reduced-fat Swiss cheese, and ¼ cup baby spinach. Top with other slice. Serve with ½ cup fresh fruit and 2 tablespoons walnuts.

calories: 482
protein: 33 g
carbohydrate: 46 g
dietary fiber: 6 g
total fat: 19 g
saturated fat: 4.5 g
cholesterol: 46 mg
sodium: 950 mg

■ DINNER

CHICKEN AND VEGGIE FAJITAS

Sauté ¼ cup sliced red onion and ½ cup combined sliced red and green peppers in 1 tablespoon olive oil. Add ½ teaspoon minced garlic, ½ teaspoon cumin, and ¼ cup salsa. Place mixture in 8″ whole-wheat tortilla and top with 4 ounces cooked, thinly sliced chicken strips, ¼ cup chopped tomatoes, lettuce, and reduced-fat shredded cheese.

calories: 530
protein: 43 g
carbohydrate: 44 g
dietary fiber: 8 g
total fat: 22 g
saturated fat: 5.5 g
cholesterol: 86 mg
sodium: 701 mg

■ BRAINPOWER SNACKS   👩 *Choose 1 snack*   🧑 *Eat both snacks*

CHIPS, SALSA, AND CHEESE

Serve 1 ounce (about 7) baked tortilla chips with ¼ cup salsa and 1 piece reduced-fat string cheese.

calories: 217; protein: 11 g; carbohydrate: 27 g; dietary fiber: 3 g; total fat: 7.4 g; saturated fat: 3.8 g; cholesterol: 15 mg; sodium: 434 mg

CHOCOLATE AND NUTS

Mix 2 tablespoons chopped walnuts with 2 tablespoons dark chocolate chips.

calories: 199; protein: 3 g; carbohydrate: 15 g; dietary fiber: 2 g; total fat: 16 g; saturated fat: 4.6 g; cholesterol: 0 mg; sodium: 3 mg

■ CARDIO | 30 MINUTES

If you don't belong to a gym, either do the Brainpower Walk from Day 1, swim, jog, or bike outside. Otherwise, follow the workout for the elliptical machine, treadmill, and stationary bicycle below.

ELLIPTICAL MACHINE | 10 MINUTES

Set the level anywhere from 3–5, maintaining a moderate pace and pushing the pedals with a forward motion.

TREADMILL | 10 MINUTES

Set the treadmill at a 4.0 mph pace and a 2% incline. Keep abdominal muscles contracted by pulling navel inward toward spine. Buttocks should be clenched and tight. Breathing rate should increase, but you should still be able to maintain a conversation.

STATIONARY BIKE | 10 MINUTES

Set your level anywhere from 2–4, aiming for 70 to 80 revolutions per minute (RPM). If you're pedaling faster than 100 RPM, set the resistance higher to challenge yourself.

CONTINUE TO NEXT PAGE →

■ MAZE MASTERY

Give your visual speed a workout with this a-maze-ing task. Using a pencil, trace your way through the following maze. How far did you get in 3 minutes? This is a particularly challenging maze. Don't be discouraged if you can't finish the maze in time. Simply erase your marks and give it another try.

Turn to page 265 for the answer.

CHAPTER 2: Brainpower Game Plan

■ SELF-PORTRAIT

Everyone has some artistic skill, even if it's hidden. Find yours by forcing your brain to think in a totally new way. Draw a portrait of yourself. One catch: your pen can only touch the paper five times.

■ STRAIGHT STORY

Today, practice using the **STRAIGHT STORY** technique as part of your daily routine. Turn on your radio while driving to work or doing errands or household chores. Listen to a news program or talk show. At the end of a segment, apply the **STRAIGHT STORY** technique to the information you just heard, then write down as much as you can remember. How did you do?

END OF WEEK 2

WEEK 3

■ USE THIS SPACE TO TAKE NOTES

EAT WELL

MY WEIGHT:

EXERCISE

CHAPTER 2: Brainpower Game Plan

PLAY BRAIN GAMES

■ GROCERY LIST

VEGETABLES

- ☐ Baby spinach, 1 bag
- ☐ Bell pepper, 1
- ☐ Broccoli, 1 small bunch
- ☐ Celery, 1 small bunch
- ☐ Cucumber, 1 medium
- ☐ Eggplant, 1 small
- ☐ Garlic, 1 small head
- ☐ Potato, 1 medium
- ☐ Romaine lettuce, 1 small head
- ☐ Sweet potatoes, 2 small
- ☐ Yellow onion, 1 small

FRUIT

- ☐ Apples, 7 medium
- ☐ Banana, 1 medium
- ☐ Lemon, 1 small
- ☐ Pears, 2 small
- ☐ Strawberries, 2 pt
- ☐ Tangerines, 3 small
- ☐ Tomatoes, 5 medium

DAIRY

- ☐ 1% reduced-sodium cottage cheese, 16 oz container
- ☐ Eggs, ½ dozen
- ☐ Fat-free blueberry yogurt, 6 oz container
- ☐ Fat-free ricotta cheese, 15 oz container
- ☐ Grated Parmesan cheese, 4 oz container
- ☐ Low-fat plain yogurt, 32 oz container
- ☐ Nonfat milk, 1 qt
- ☐ Reduced-fat cream cheese, 8 oz block
- ☐ Reduced-fat shredded cheddar cheese, 8 oz bag
- ☐ Reduced-fat shredded Monterey Jack cheese, 8 oz bag

BAKERY

- ☐ Corn tortillas, 1 small package
- ☐ WASA® Fiber Crispbread, 1 small box
- ☐ Whole-wheat bread, 1 loaf
- ☐ Whole-wheat bread crumbs, 1 small bag
- ☐ Whole-wheat English muffins, 1 package
- ☐ Whole-wheat hamburger buns, 1 package

FROZEN FOODS

- ☐ Frozen cauliflower, 16 oz bag
- ☐ Frozen veggie burgers, 1 box

DRY GOODS

- ☐ Barley, 1 box
- ☐ Black olives, 15 oz can
- ☐ Bulgur wheat, 1 box
- ☐ Chopped walnuts, 1 small bag
- ☐ Cooking spray, 1 can
- ☐ Dark chocolate chips, 12 oz bag
- ☐ Golden raisins, 1 box
- ☐ LÄRABARs®, 4
- ☐ Lentil soup, 1 can
- ☐ Marinara sauce, 26 oz jar
- ☐ No-salt-added corn, 15 oz can
- ☐ Pineapple in its own juice, 20 oz can
- ☐ Reduced-sodium vegetable broth, 1 can
- ☐ Reduced-sodium vegetable soup, 1 can
- ☐ Slivered almonds, 1 small bag
- ☐ Sun-dried tomatoes, oil-packed, 1 jar
- ☐ Whole-wheat rotini (spiral) pasta, 16 oz box

MEAT/SEAFOOD

- ☐ Firm tofu, 14 oz block
- ☐ Raw 97% fat-free ground turkey, 9 oz
- ☐ Raw salmon filet, 3 oz
- ☐ Raw shrimp, 7 oz
- ☐ Raw skinless, boneless chicken breast, 12 oz
- ☐ Skinless, boneless salmon, 6 oz can
- ☐ Turkey bacon, 8 oz package

■ GRAB AND GO MEALS

These meals can be substituted for any of the designated meals for this week, for example: breakfast for breakfast, lunch for lunch, or dinner for dinner. However, try not to substitute more than one meal per day.

BREAKFAST

CEREAL WITH FRUIT AND NUTS

1 cup whole-grain cereal (like Kashi® GoLean®) with 1 cup nonfat milk, ½ cup chopped fruit, 2 tablespoons raisins, and 2 tablespoons slivered almonds.

calories: 356; protein: 15 g; carbohydrate: 60 g; dietary fiber: 6 g; total fat: 8.6 g; saturated fat: 1.2 g; cholesterol: 5 mg; sodium: 341 mg

LUNCH

TURKEY AND CHEESE ROLL-UPS WITH WASA® CRACKERS

3 ounces (3 slices) turkey rolled up with 3 ounces (3 slices) reduced-fat Swiss cheese. Eat with 5 WASA® crispbread crackers and 1 large orange.

calories: 509; protein: 47 g; carbohydrate: 69 g; dietary fiber: 11 g; total fat: 6.8 g; saturated fat: 3.3 g; cholesterol: 64 mg; sodium: 813 mg

DINNER

AMY'S® LASAGNA

1 Amy's® Organic Light in Sodium Vegetable Lasagna, microwaved. Serve with a side salad topped with 2 teaspoons olive oil and ½ tablespoon balsamic vinegar. Serve with 1 slice whole-grain toast with 2 teaspoons trans-free margarine.

calories: 543; protein: 19 g; carbohydrate: 63 g; dietary fiber: 7 g; total fat: 25 g; saturated fat: 7 g; cholesterol: 0.5 mg; sodium: 568 mg

■ BREAKFAST

BREAKFAST SANDWICH
Scramble 1 egg and 1 egg white with 2 tablespoons each of diced yellow onions and tomato sautéed in 1 teaspoon olive oil. Place on half a whole-wheat English muffin and top with ¼ cup reduced-fat cheddar cheese and remaining half of English muffin. Serve with a tangerine.

calories: 359
protein: 23 g
carbohydrate: 40 g
dietary fiber: 7 g
total fat: 13 g
saturated fat: 3.8 g
cholesterol: 217 mg
sodium: 473 mg

■ LUNCH

BLT WITH VEGETABLE SOUP
Toast 2 slices whole-wheat bread. Top 1 slice with 1 tablespoon reduced-fat mayonnaise, 2 thin slices turkey bacon, 4 slices tomato, and 2 large leaves romaine lettuce. Top with second slice of toast. Serve with 1 cup reduced-sodium vegetable soup topped with ⅓ cup reduced-fat Monterey jack cheese.

calories: 485
protein: 24 g
carbohydrate: 53 g
dietary fiber: 7 g
total fat: 20 g
saturated fat: 7.5 g
cholesterol: 44 mg
sodium: 1407 mg

■ DINNER

PASTA WITH GRILLED CHICKEN AND SUN-DRIED TOMATOES
Toss 1 ¾ cup cooked whole-wheat spiral pasta with 3 tablespoons chopped oil-packed sun-dried tomatoes, ½ cup frozen cauliflower, cooked, and 3 ounces grilled chicken breast. **FOR DESSERT:** 1 cup cubed watermelon.

calories: 552
protein: 43 g
carbohydrate: 85 g
dietary fiber: 15 g
total fat: 7.8 g
saturated fat: 1.6 g
cholesterol: 71 mg
sodium: 575 mg

■ BRAINPOWER SNACKS   👩 *Choose 1 snack*   👨 *Eat both snacks*

BERRIES AND CHOCOLATE
Top 1 cup berries with 1 tablespoon dark chocolate chips and 1 tablespoon chopped nuts.
calories: 184; protein: 3 g; carbohydrate: 29 g; dietary fiber: 5 g; total fat: 8.5 g; saturated fat: 2.4 g; cholesterol: 0 mg; sodium: 3 mg

CEREAL TRAIL MIX
Combine ½ cup whole-grain cereal, ¼ cup raisins or dried chopped apricots, cranberries, or cherries, and 1 ½ tablespoons chopped walnuts or slivered almonds.
calories: 207; protein: 4 g; carbohydrate: 33 g; dietary fiber: 5 g; total fat: 8.5 g; saturated fat: 1 g; cholesterol: 0 mg; sodium: 109 mg

■ REBUS RALLY

Each of the word combinations below represents a common phrase. Can you figure out all 10? To get you started, I'll give you the first one: "Big bad wolf." Can you see why?

1. **B A D   wolf**

2. **S**
   L
   O
   W

3. **R | E | A | D**

4. **Thought Clever**

5. **M**
   R
   A
   W

6. **E G G S**
   E A S Y

7. **T O U K E E P C H**

8. **S C O T C H**
   R O C K S

9. **T**
   A
   B L E

10. **E V I L**
    - - - - - - - - - > evil

Turn to page 265 for the answers.

■ REMAP

If you take the same route to work or the gym every day, get out a map and find a new pathway. Want to give your mind a greater challenge? Forget the map and find your own way.

■ GET THE NAME: REHEARSE

One of the most effective ways to remember names is to adopt the **REHEARSE** technique: that is, repeat a person's name as soon as you hear it. Not just once, but several times (but don't repeat it so often that you seem weird). For instance, if you're at a party and a woman tells you her name, you might say, "Eliza? Hello, Eliza, it's a pleasure to meet you. Tell me, Eliza, how is the punch?"

CONTINUE TO NEXT PAGE

■ **STRENGTH TRAINING**

VERTICAL JUMP

Targets	Equipment
Lower body strength and power	None

Ⓐ Stand with knees bent and arms at sides. Ⓑ Jump as high as you can, reaching toward the ceiling with arms. Do 2 sets of 12 jumps.

Make It Easier:
Do 1 set of 12 jumps.
Make It Harder:
Do 3 sets of 12 jumps.

DUMBBELL KICK-OUTS

Targets	Equipment
Legs, butt, and core	Set of 5-pound dumbbells

Ⓐ Stand up straight holding dumbbells at sides. Ⓑ Bend at knees until weights touch floor. Ⓒ Kick feet behind you into plank position. Hands should be resting on dumbbells. Then bring feet back underneath you and jump up. Do 2 sets of 12 reps.

Make It Easier:
Do 1 set of 12 reps.
Make It Harder:
Do 3 sets of 12 reps.

DUMBBELL SQUAT PRESS

Targets	Equipment
Shoulders, glutes, hamstrings, and quads	Set of 5-pound dumbbells

QUICK FEET

Targets	Equipment
Agility	None

(A) Stand with feet hip-width apart. (B) Place a dumbbell on the floor at each side of feet. With hands at sides, squat until thighs are almost parallel to floor. (C) Grab dumbbells and, using legs, stand up while pressing dumbbells over head. Go back down to a squat and place dumbbells back on floor. Do 2 sets of 12 reps.

Make It Easier:
Do 1 set of 12 reps using 3-pound dumbbells.
Make It Harder:
Do 3 sets of 12 reps.

With knees slightly bent and feet about hip-width apart, bend elbows about 90 degrees with hands making fists and facing each other. (A) Lift left knee and foot; return foot to floor. (B) Repeat with right knee and foot. Maintain this quick up-and-down motion for about 30 seconds, then rest for 10 seconds. Repeat for 2 minutes.

END OF DAY 15

■ BREAKFAST

TRAIL MIX AND YOGURT
Mix ½ cup Kashi® GoLean® cereal with a ¼ cup bite-size shredded wheat, 2 teaspoons chopped walnuts, and 1½ tablespoons golden raisins. Serve with 6 ounces fat-free blueberry yogurt.

calories: 349
protein: 17 g
carbohydrate: 69 g
dietary fiber: 7 g
total fat: 4 g
saturated fat: 0.7 g
cholesterol: 3 mg
sodium: 144 mg

■ LUNCH

GRILLED CHICKEN AND SUN-DRIED TOMATO SANDWICH
Top whole-wheat hamburger bun with 3 ounces grilled chicken, 3 tablespoons oil-packed sun-dried tomatoes, 2 leaves romaine lettuce, and 2 slices yellow onion. Serve with ½ cup baked sweet potato fries (or small baked sweet potato). Enjoy with an apple.

calories: 504
protein: 35 g
carbohydrate: 80 g
dietary fiber: 13 g
total fat: 7.7 g
saturated fat: 1.6 g
cholesterol: 71 mg
sodium: 780 mg

■ DINNER

PINEAPPLE-POACHED SALMON WITH BARLEY AND SPINACH
In a saucepan, poach 3 ounces salmon in ½ cup pineapple juice (reserved from canned pineapple), ½ cup reduced-sodium vegetable or chicken broth, 1 teaspoon reduced-sodium soy sauce, and freshly ground pepper (discard poaching liquid after cooking) with cover on for approximately 5 minutes or until cooked through. Mix 1¼ cups cooked barley with ⅓ cup chopped canned pineapple, drained, 1 tablespoon chopped walnuts, and freshly ground black pepper. Place poached salmon on top of barley/pineapple mixture and serve with 1 cup baby spinach sautéed in 1 teaspoon olive oil and 1 teaspoon chopped garlic.

calories: 548
protein: 27 g
carbohydrate: 78 g
dietary fiber: 10 g
total fat: 15.5 g
saturated fat: 2.5 g
cholesterol: 38 mg
sodium: 626 mg

■ BRAINPOWER SNACKS   *Choose 1 snack*   *Eat both snacks*

LÄRABAR®
1 LÄRABAR® (cherry pie, cocoa mole, pecan pie, cranberry almond, or Jŏcolat chocolate cherry).
calories: 190; protein: 4 g; carbohydrate: 27 g; dietary fiber: 5 g; total fat: 9 g; saturated fat: 2 g; cholesterol: 0 mg; sodium: 0 mg

LÄRABAR® nutrition facts may vary slightly depending on the flavor.

PEANUT BUTTER AND TOAST
Spread 1 slice whole-wheat toast with ½ tablespoon peanut butter. Serve with 1 medium apple.
calories: 204; protein: 5 g; carbohydrate: 36 g; dietary fiber: 5 g; total fat: 6 g; saturated fat: 1.1 g; cholesterol: 0.3 mg; sodium: 177 mg

■ CARDIO | 30 MINUTES

If you don't belong to a gym, either do the Brainpower Walk from Day 1, swim, jog, or bike outside. Otherwise, follow the workout for the elliptical machine, treadmill, and stationary bicycle below.

ELLIPTICAL MACHINE | 10 MINUTES

Set the level anywhere from 3–5, maintaining a moderate pace and pushing the pedals with a forward motion.

TREADMILL | 10 MINUTES

Set the treadmill at a 4.0 mph pace and a 2% incline. Keep abdominal muscles contracted by pulling navel inward toward spine. Buttocks should be clenched and tight. Breathing rate should increase, but you should still be able to maintain a conversation.

STATIONARY BIKE | 10 MINUTES

Set your level anywhere from 2–4, aiming for 70 to 80 revolutions per minute (RPM). If you're pedaling faster than 100 RPM, set the resistance higher to challenge yourself.

CONTINUE TO NEXT PAGE

■ WORD MAKER

Using one set of information in different ways tests your brain's flexibility. How many words can you make out of each of the following words?

BALDERDASH	CACOPHONY	ONOMATOPOEIA

CHAPTER 2: Brainpower Game Plan

■ WRITE A LIMERICK

A limerick is a humorous, five-line poem in which the first, second, and fifth lines rhyme with one another and have the same number of syllables (typically eight or nine). The third and fourth lines rhyme with each other and are shorter in length (typically five or six syllables). I'll give you the first line: "there once was a gal who was brainy . . ." Can you finish the limerick?

■ GET THE NAME: RELATE IT

The **RELATE IT** technique I introduced in Week 1 is one of my favorite strategies for learning and remembering names. Why? Because we tend to associate new names we learn with names we already know. Use the **RELATE IT** technique to learn the following names. Keep in mind that a link can be the name of a friend or other acquaintance, a celebrity or famous historical figure, or an object that you connect with the name.

OLIVIA FROND	**OMANI ASHE**	**SUSAN GONZALES**
WALTER SMYTHE	**DAVID STARWOOD**	**LAUREN BAKER**

END OF DAY 16

■ BREAKFAST

GRILLED PEANUT BUTTER AND BANANA SANDWICH

Top 1 slice whole-grain bread with 1 tablespoon peanut butter, half a banana, sliced, and dash of cinnamon. Top with another slice of bread and place in nonstick skillet (coated with cooking spray) over medium heat. Heat on both sides until golden brown. Serve with a café au lait (8 ounces hot nonfat milk added to 2 ounces of strong coffee).

calories: 369
protein: 20 g
carbohydrate: 52 g
dietary fiber: 6 g
total fat: 10.3 g
saturated fat: 2.3 g
cholesterol: 5 mg
sodium: 371 mg

■ LUNCH

VEGGIE BURGER WITH BARLEY PILAF

To make barley pilaf, combine 1 cup cooked barley, 1 small sweet potato, cooked and cubed, 2 tablespoons golden raisins, and 1 tablespoon chopped walnuts. Place cooked veggie burger on top of pilaf and serve with 1 cup steamed broccoli.

calories: 512
protein: 22 g
carbohydrate: 89 g
dietary fiber: 16 g
total fat: 10 g
saturated fat: 1.2 g
cholesterol: 0 mg
sodium: 689 mg

■ DINNER

SHRIMP TACOS

Sauté 4 ounces shrimp, peeled and deveined, in 1 teaspoon olive oil, 1 teaspoon chopped garlic, and $\frac{1}{8}$ teaspoon turmeric. Fill 2 corn tortillas with sautéed shrimp and top with $\frac{1}{4}$ cup shredded reduced-fat Monterey Jack cheese, $\frac{1}{4}$ cup chopped Romaine lettuce, and $\frac{1}{4}$ cup salsa. Add dash of turmeric, garlic powder, and cumin to 1 cup lentil soup and heat. Top with 1 tablespoon low-fat plain yogurt and serve with shrimp tacos. **FOR DESSERT:** Eat 2 small tangerines.

calories: 565
protein: 44 g
carbohydrate: 64 g
dietary fiber: 12 g
total fat: 15.9 g
saturated fat: 5.6 g
cholesterol: 191 mg
sodium: 985 mg

■ BRAINPOWER SNACKS   👩 *Choose 1 snack*   👨 *Eat both snacks*

CEREAL TRAIL MIX

Combine $\frac{1}{2}$ cup whole-grain cereal, $\frac{1}{4}$ cup raisins or dried chopped apricots, cranberries, or cherries, and 1 $\frac{1}{2}$ tablespoons chopped walnuts or slivered almonds.

calories: 207; protein: 4 g; carbohydrate: 33 g; dietary fiber: 5 g; total fat: 8.5 g; saturated fat: 1 g; cholesterol: 0 mg; sodium: 109 mg

LÄRABAR®

1 LÄRABAR® (cherry pie, cocoa mole, pecan pie, cranberry almond, or Jŏcolat chocolate cherry).

calories: 190; protein: 4 g; carbohydrate: 27 g; dietary fiber: 5 g; total fat: 9 g; saturated fat: 2 g; cholesterol: 0 mg; sodium: 0 mg

LÄRABAR® nutrition facts may vary slightly depending on the flavor.

■ HOW SYMBOLIC

To solve the puzzle, substitute the following letters for the symbols with which they are paired. Want an even greater challenge? Try solving this puzzle against the clock—give yourself 1 minute.

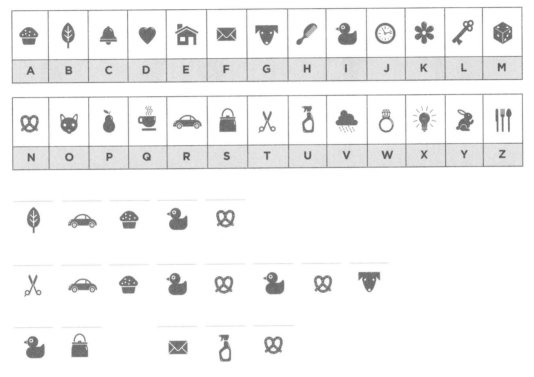

Turn to page 265 for the answer.

■ SOUND WALK

Continue to explore the role your senses play in how your brain perceives the world. Go for a stroll around your office, your neighborhood, or a local park. Notice the various sounds that you hear along the way.

■ GET THE NAME: SEE

Most of us have strong visual memory, but too few people use this skill to their full advantage. If you learn information best visually—for instance, if you would rather look at a map than read a set of directions—this technique is for you. Use the **SEE** technique, which you learned in Week 1, to memorize the following names:

ROBYN FOSTER **EBONY REYNOLDS** **TAYLOR FISHMAN**

JOY ARMSTRONG **IRIS SAYLOR** **OLIVIA JENKINS**

CONTINUE TO NEXT PAGE

■ STRENGTH TRAINING

BICEP CURLS ON ONE FOOT

Targets	Equipment
Biceps, butt, and core	Set of 5-pound dumbbells

Stand with feet shoulder-width apart and hold a dumbbell in each hand, palms facing inward. **A** Lift right foot off the floor so knee is at 45-degree angle. **B** While balancing on left leg, curl arms up toward shoulders. At the top of the movement, palms should be facing up. Make sure to keep elbows pressed to sides. Slowly lower to starting position, maintaining balance on left foot. Do 2 sets of 12 reps on each leg.

Make It Easier:
Use 3-pound dumbbells.
Make It Harder:
Use 8- to 10-pound dumbbells.

2-WAY SHOULDER RAISE

Targets	Equipment
Front and middle of deltoids	Set of 5-pound dumbbells

Stand with feet shoulder-width apart, making sure that you're not locking knees. **A** Hold a dumbbell in each hand, with arms at sides and palms facing inward. **B** Lift arms up **C** and out to the side to shoulder height. Lower arms to sides. Repeat with palms facing up and elbows slightly bent. Lower arms again, turn palms inward, and continue alternating these two moves. Do 2 sets of 12 reps.

Make It Easier:
Use 3-pound dumbbells.
Make It Harder:
Use 6- to 10-pound dumbbells.

BRIDGE ABDUCTOR

Targets	Equipment
Butt and abs	Exercise mat

PULSING SQUAT

Targets	Equipment
Butt and quads	None

Ⓐ Lie on back with knees bent and press hips up, creating a 90-degree angle with knees. Ⓑ Extend left leg and Ⓒ bring it out to the side while keeping hips up. Do 2 sets of 12 reps on each leg.

Make It Easier:
Use 3-pound dumbbells.
Make It Harder:
Use 8- to 10-pound dumbbells.

Ⓐ Stand with feet spread apart to twice shoulder width. Keep toes pointed out at 45-degree angle. Ⓑ Squat back and down as if you're sitting in a chair. Slowly lower your butt about 2 inches, then return to starting position. Keep pulsing up and down for 25 reps, then hold squat position for 25 seconds.

Make It Easier:
Use 3-pound dumbbell.
Make It Harder:
Use 6- to 10-pound dumbbell.

END OF DAY 17

■ BREAKFAST

NUTTY ENGLISH MUFFIN

Fill whole-wheat English muffin with ⅔ cup 1% reduced-sodium cottage cheese, 1 tablespoon slivered almonds, and 1 small pear, sliced.

calories: 360
protein: 26 g
carbohydrate: 53 g
dietary fiber: 10 g
total fat: 6.6 g
saturated fat: 1.6 g
cholesterol: 6 mg
sodium: 193 mg

■ LUNCH

SHRIMP SALAD

Top 1 cup mixed chopped Romaine lettuce with ½ cup chopped tomatoes, ½ cup cooked barley, and 3 ounces shrimp, peeled, deveined, and sautéed in 1 teaspoon olive oil. Top with 1 teaspoon olive oil, 2 tablespoons shredded reduced-fat Monterey Jack cheese, and freshly ground black pepper. Serve with 1 slice whole-wheat toast and 1 medium apple.

calories: 484
protein: 28 g
carbohydrate: 62 g
dietary fiber: 11 g
total fat: 15.7 g
saturated fat: 3.9 g
cholesterol: 138 mg
sodium: 386 mg

■ DINNER

STUFFED BELL PEPPER

Cut stem end off 1 bell pepper and remove seeds. Mix 1 cup cooked bulgur wheat with ¼ cup Parmesan cheese, ¼ cup chopped black olives, and ¼ cup diced tomatoes. Stuff pepper with bulgur mixture and bake at 325°F until browned. Sauté 1 cup no-salt-added canned corn with 2 teaspoons olive oil, ½ teaspoon chopped garlic, and freshly ground black pepper. Serve with stuffed bell peppers.

calories: 530
protein: 21 g
carbohydrate: 74 g
dietary fiber: 15 g
total fat: 22 g
saturated fat: 6.4 g
cholesterol: 22 mg
sodium: 698 mg

■ BRAINPOWER SNACKS   👩 Choose 1 snack   🧍 Eat both snacks

BERRIES AND CHOCOLATE

Top 1 cup berries with 1 tablespoon dark chocolate chips and 1 tablespoon chopped nuts.

calories: 184; protein: 3 g; carbohydrate: 29 g; dietary fiber: 5 g; total fat: 8.5 g; saturated fat: 2.4 g; cholesterol: 0 mg; sodium: 3 mg

LÄRABAR®

1 LÄRABAR® (cherry pie, cocoa mole, pecan pie, cranberry almond, or Jŏcolat chocolate cherry).

calories: 190; protein: 4 g; carbohydrate: 27 g; dietary fiber: 5 g; total fat: 9 g; saturated fat: 2 g; cholesterol: 0 mg; sodium: 0 mg

LÄRABAR® nutrition facts may vary slightly depending on the flavor.

■ YOGA/FLEXIBILITY EXERCISES

Today, go through all the moves from Day 11 twice: Cat/Cow, Cobra, Hamstring Stretch, and Seated Pose.

CAT/COW

COBRA

HAMSTRING STRETCH

SEATED POSE

CONTINUE TO NEXT PAGE →

■ PICTURE/RE-PICTURE IT

Hone your brain's visual flexibility by learning to look at the same object from different perspectives. Can you picture this? And that? Each of these three pictures depicts two very different images, depending on how you look at it. Can you see both?

①

②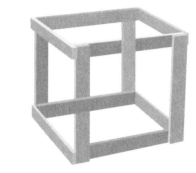

③

■ INVENT IT

Do you have a practical problem that's making you crazy? Spend 10 minutes brainstorming a solution. Write down any and all ideas that come to mind. If your solution requires a newly invented gadget, sketch what it might look like. This approach is what led to the creation of everything from the potato peeler to the Post-it note.

■ GET THE NAME: RELATE IT

Use the **TALES** technique, from Week 2, to memorize the following names. Again, the odder and sillier the tale, the better. For example, you might turn the first name on the list into "Jay's son barked at Lee."

JASON BARKLEY	**JESSICA HUNTER**	**JOMBI MUGAWI**
PEDRO ROMAN	**FLORENCE CONE**	**SHARON MAXX**

■ BREAKFAST

CREAM OF BULGUR WHEAT WITH APPLES

Mix 1 cup cooked bulgur wheat with 1 cup fat-free milk and ¼ cup chopped red apple and heat for 2 minutes in microwave (stirring halfway through). Top with pinch of cinnamon, 1 teaspoon honey, 2 tablespoons plus 1 teaspoon slivered almonds, and ¼ cup chopped red apple.

calories: 342
protein: 16 g
carbohydrate: 54 g
dietary fiber: 9 g
total fat: 8.9 g
saturated fat: 1.0 g
cholesterol: 5 mg
sodium: 135 mg

■ LUNCH

CRACKER TARTINES WITH BROCCOLI AND CHICKEN

Spread 2 tablespoons low-fat cream cheese on 2 whole-grain crisp breads. Top with 4 slices tomato and ¼ cup sliced olives. Serve with ½ cup steamed broccoli and 3 ounces chopped grilled chicken tossed with ½ cup cooked bulgur wheat and topped with freshly ground black pepper and 1 teaspoon freshly squeezed lemon juice.

calories: 484
protein: 40 g
carbohydrate: 57 g
dietary fiber: 16 g
total fat: 13.1 g
saturated fat: 4.8 g
cholesterol: 88 mg
sodium: 741 mg

■ DINNER

PUMPKIN RICOTTA PASTA

In saucepan, combine 1 ½ cups cooked whole-wheat rotini pasta, ½ cup canned pumpkin, ¼ cup fat-free ricotta cheese, 3 ounces canned salmon, and 1 cup baby spinach. Stir over low heat until spinach is wilted. Serve with ½ cup frozen cauliflower, thawed and sautéed in 1 teaspoon olive oil and ¼ teaspoon chopped garlic. **FOR DESSERT:** ½ cup sliced strawberries with 1 teaspoon lemon juice (if desired).

calories: 543
protein: 36 g
carbohydrate: 80 g
dietary fiber: 17 g
total fat: 11.5 g
saturated fat: 2.4 g
cholesterol: 50 mg
sodium: 528 mg

■ BRAINPOWER SNACKS   Choose 1 snack   Eat both snacks

CEREAL TRAIL MIX

Combine ½ cup whole-grain cereal, ¼ cup raisins or dried chopped apricots, cranberries, or cherries, and 1 ½ tablespoons chopped walnuts or slivered almonds.

calories: 207; protein: 4 g; carbohydrate: 33 g; dietary fiber: 5 g; total fat: 8.5 g; saturated fat: 1 g; cholesterol: 0 mg; sodium: 109 mg

LÄRABAR®

1 LÄRABAR® (cherry pie, cocoa mole, pecan pie, cranberry almond, or Jŏcolat chocolate cherry).

calories: 190; protein: 4 g; carbohydrate: 27 g; dietary fiber: 5 g; total fat: 9 g; saturated fat: 2 g; cholesterol: 0 mg; sodium: 0 mg

LÄRABAR® nutrition facts may vary slightly depending on the flavor.

■ RHYTHM EXERCISE | 30 MINUTES

Reshuffle your index cards from Day 4, turn on some music, and get moving.

Marching in place

Ski moves

Jumping jacks

Marching in place
with high knees

Boxing moves

Jogging in place

Step-ups

Push-ups

Ballroom dancing

CONTINUE TO NEXT PAGE

■ **TRIANGLES**

See how many triangles you can find in the following picture.

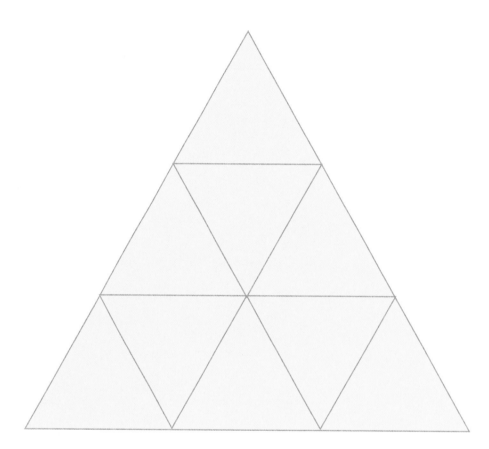

Turn to page 265 for the answer.

CHAPTER 2: Brainpower Game Plan

■ RIDDLE ME THIS

Use your noggin to solve this riddle.

Three men are captured by cannibals in the jungle. The cannibals decide to give the men one chance to escape with their lives. They bind the men to stakes in such a way that one man can see the backs of the other two, the middle man can see the back of the front man, and the front man can't see anybody. The cannibals show the men five hats. Three of them are black; the other two are white. Then they blindfold the men and place one of the five hats on each man's head, hiding the two remaining hats. After removing the blindfolds, the cannibals tell the men that if one of them can guess what color hat he's wearing, they can all go free. Time passes. Finally, the front man, who can't see anyone, correctly guesses the color of his hat. What color was the hat? How did he know?

Turn to page 265 for the answer.

■ GET THE NAME: VIDEO

Use the **VIDEO** technique from Week 2 to learn and remember the following names:

FRANCIS KORN	**CAROLE SANDERSON**	**HANNAH MARTINS**
BLAKE GALLO	**CARMENZA FIELDS**	**STEVEN GESTLER**

■ BREAKFAST

PUMPKIN YOGURT CRUNCH
Stir ¼ cup canned pumpkin, ½ small pear, chopped, and 1 teaspoon honey into ¾ cup low-fat plain yogurt. Top with ½ cup Kashi® GoLean® cereal, 1 tablespoon chopped walnuts, and remaining half pear, chopped.

calories: 362
protein: 19 g
carbohydrate: 61 g
dietary fiber: 12 g
total fat: 8.6 g
saturated fat: 2.5 g
cholesterol: 11 mg
sodium: 177 mg

■ LUNCH

STUFFED TOMATO WITH WHOLE-WHEAT PASTA
Mash 4 ounces firm tofu, drained, with 1 tablespoon reduced-fat mayonnaise, 1 teaspoon mustard, ⅛ teaspoon turmeric, 1 teaspoon chopped black olives, and ¼ cup chopped celery. Add salt and pepper to taste. Remove stem end of medium tomato, scoop out seeds, and stuff with tofu salad. Serve with 1 cup cooked whole-wheat rotini topped with ¼ cup fat-free ricotta and ¼ cup marinara sauce.

calories: 505
protein: 31 g
carbohydrate: 64 g
dietary fiber: 13 g
total fat: 17.3 g
saturated fat: 2.1 g
cholesterol: 10 mg
sodium: 264 mg

■ DINNER

TURKEY BURGER WITH CUCUMBER SALAD
Top 1 whole-wheat hamburger bun with 4-ounce cooked 97% fat-free turkey burger, ¼ cup reduced-fat cheddar cheese, 2 slices tomato, and 1 leaf romaine lettuce. Serve with ½ medium baked potato topped with 1 tablespoon low-fat plain yogurt and black pepper. Drizzle 1 teaspoon olive oil and 1 tablespoon balsamic vinegar over ½ cup thinly sliced cucumber. Salt and pepper to taste. **FOR DESSERT:** 1 cup apple slices with 1 teaspoon chopped walnuts.

calories: 560
protein: 34 g
carbohydrate: 65 g
dietary fiber: 9 g
total fat: 20 g
saturated fat: 7 g
cholesterol: 68 mg
sodium: 611 mg

■ BRAINPOWER SNACKS   *Choose 1 snack*   *Eat both snacks*

BERRIES AND CHOCOLATE
Top 1 cup berries with 1 tablespoon dark chocolate chips and 1 tablespoon chopped nuts.
calories: 184; protein: 3 g; carbohydrate: 29 g; dietary fiber: 5 g; total fat: 8.5 g; saturated fat: 2.4 g; cholesterol: 0 mg; sodium: 3 mg

PEANUT BUTTER AND TOAST
Spread 1 slice whole-wheat toast with ½ tablespoon peanut butter. Serve with 1 medium apple.
calories: 204; protein: 5 g; carbohydrate: 36 g; dietary fiber: 5 g; total fat: 6 g; saturated fat: 1.1 g; cholesterol: 0.3 mg; sodium: 177 mg

■ LOOK, MA—NO VOWELS!

Every day you use a brain skill known as deductive reasoning: the ability to reach a correct conclusion based on just a few existing facts. Here's an exercise that gives your powers of deductive reasoning a good stretch.

Can you read this message? Bet you can!

GT N GRT SHP BY USNG THE BRN PWR BK. SRPRSE YRSLF

AND YR FRNDS WTH YR PWRS OF DDCTV RSONNG. SM

FMLIAR? PRHPS YOU OR YR KDS LK TO TXT MSSGE.

Turn to page 265 for the answer.

■ GET THE NAME: TIME TO PICK!

Memory techniques work best when they become habit, so three steps are critical: practice, practice, practice. Choose from the various techniques you have learned, then use the list of names below to practice your skill.

ZACHARY MENKEN   **AMY MENENDEZ**   **MUSHTER WELLSTONE**

TIM SLATKIN   **VALERIE HOPKINS**   **KATE ELDON**

■ READING BACKWARD

Anyone can read backward. But understanding what you read requires some well-toned mental muscles. Give yours a flex. Choose an article in today's newspaper and read it backward, beginning with the last word in the story and working your way to the first. Can you make sense of what you read?

CONTINUE TO NEXT PAGE

■ STRENGTH TRAINING

Warm up with 30 minutes of any kind of cardio, including the Brainpower Walk (see Day 1), jogging, swimming, biking, or using equipment at the gym.

TRADEOFFS		RIGHT ARM/LEFT LEG CRUNCH	
Targets	**Equipment**	**Targets**	**Equipment**
Most of your midsection	Fitness ball (optional) and exercise mat	Upper abs and shoulders	Set of 3-pound dumbbells and exercise mat

Lie on exercise mat and place fitness ball between feet. **A** Extend legs toward the ceiling, squeezing ball with insides of feet. Place arms over head. **B** Slowly crunch up, reaching for ball with hands. **C** Grab ball with hands and slowly bring it down behind head, keeping shoulder blades off floor. Just before ball touches the floor, contract abs and reach back up with ball, placing it between feet. Slowly lower arms and body back down, again keeping shoulder blades off ground. Do 2 sets of 12 reps.

Make It Easier:
Do 1 set of 12 reps.
Make It Harder:
Do 3 sets of 12 reps.
If You Don't Have A Ball:
Use a pillow.

Lie on mat with legs extended, feet slightly apart. **A** Place a dumbbell in each hand. Raise arms over head and place on ground. **B** Slowly sit up, and bring right arm and left leg to meet each other while keeping both straight. Once dumbbell meets left shin, slowly return to starting position. **C** Repeat move, sitting up so that left arm meets right shin. Do 2 sets of 12 reps.

Make It Easier:
Do exercise without dumbbells.
Make It Harder:
Use 5-pound dumbbells.

FITNESS BALL AB PULL/PUSH-UP

Targets	Equipment
Abs and upper body	Fitness ball (optional) and exercise mat

FITNESS BALL WEIGHTED TWIST

Targets	Equipment
Upper and lower abs and obliques	Fitness ball (optional) and 5-pound dumbbell

A Get into push-up position with shins resting on ball. **B** Keeping abs tight, bend knees, bringing ball toward chest with shins, then roll it back out. **C** Slowly bend elbows and lower body to perform a push-up, being sure to keep abs contracted. Do 2 sets of 12 reps.

Make It Really Easy:
Stand and push-up against wall with feet 3 feet from wall. Do 2 sets of wall push-ups.
Make It Easier:
Place ball closer to hips and rest weight on ball.
Make It Harder:
Do 3 sets of 12 reps.
If You Don't Have A Ball:
Do 2 sets of push-ups on the floor and on your knees.

Sit on ball with feet flat on floor. **A** Roll forward until ball is at lower-middle back (small of back). Hold dumbbell by ends with both hands, arms straight out in front. Lean back slowly; be careful not to go too far. Contract abs. **B** Twist torso as far as you can to one side and **C** then to other side to complete 1 rep. Do 2 sets of 12 reps.

Make It Easier:
Use 3-pound dumbbells.
Make It Harder:
Do 3 sets of 12 reps.
If You Don't Have A Ball:
Place feet on ottoman or chair. Raise hips until you create a straight line between ankles, hips, and shoulders. Lower slowly. Repeat 12 times.

END OF DAY 20

■ BREAKFAST

STUFFED FRENCH TOAST
Spread 2 slices whole-grain bread each with ½ tablespoon reduced-fat cream cheese. Top 1 slice with ¼ cup sliced strawberries, and cover with remaining bread slice. Press slices together to seal in contents. In shallow bowl mix 1 egg white with ¼ cup fat-free milk, ½ teaspoon vanilla, and dash of cinnamon. Place sandwich in egg mixture for 1 minute on each side. Cook over medium heat, pouring remaining egg mixture over top, in nonstick skillet until golden brown. Top with ¼ cup low-fat plain yogurt, ¼ cup sliced strawberries, and 1 ½ teaspoons honey.

calories: 341
protein: 16 g
carbohydrate: 54 g
dietary fiber: 4 g
total fat: 7.4 g
saturated fat: 2.9 g
cholesterol: 14 mg
sodium: 453 mg

■ LUNCH

PASTA WITH GROUND TURKEY MARINARA
Mix 1 ¼ cups cooked whole-wheat pasta with 3 ounces 97% fat-free cooked ground turkey (cook until browned). Sauté 1 cup baby spinach in 1 teaspoon olive oil, add ⅓ cup marinara sauce, and pour over pasta mixture.

calories: 482
protein: 27 g
carbohydrate: 61 g
dietary fiber: 11 g
total fat: 16.6 g
saturated fat: 3.3 g
cholesterol: 68 mg
sodium: 134 mg

■ DINNER

EGGPLANT MINI-PIZZAS
Mix 1 egg white and 1 tablespoon water in shallow, wide dish. In another dish, mix ½ cup whole-grain bread crumbs with dash of pepper and garlic powder. Cut 1 eggplant into half-inch slices. Dip 4 slices into egg mixture and coat with bread crumb mixture. Bake at 375°F for 25 minutes or until tender and golden. Top each slice with 2 tablespoons marinara sauce and 1 tablespoon Parmesan cheese. **FOR DESSERT:** Top ⅔ cup 1% reduced-sodium cottage cheese with cinnamon and 1 teaspoon honey.

calories: 551
protein: 35 g
carbohydrate: 77 g
dietary fiber: 11 g
total fat: 12 g
saturated fat: 3.4 g
cholesterol: 10.3 mg
sodium: 587 mg

■ BRAINPOWER SNACKS *Choose 1 snack* *Eat both snacks*

CEREAL TRAIL MIX
Combine ½ cup whole-grain cereal, ¼ cup raisins or dried chopped apricots, cranberries, or cherries, and 1 ½ tablespoon chopped walnuts or slivered almonds.
calories: 207; protein: 4 g; carbohydrate: 33 g; dietary fiber: 5 g; total fat: 8.5 g; saturated fat: 1 g; cholesterol: 0 mg; sodium: 109 mg

PEANUT BUTTER AND TOAST
Spread 1 slice whole-wheat toast with ½ tablespoon peanut butter. Serve with 1 medium apple.
calories: 204; protein: 5 g; carbohydrate: 36 g; dietary fiber: 5 g; total fat: 6 g; saturated fat: 1.1 g; cholesterol: 0.5 mg; sodium: 177 mg

■ CARDIO | 30 MINUTES

If you don't belong to a gym, either do the Brainpower Walk from Day 1, swim, jog, or bike outside. Otherwise, follow the workout for the elliptical machine, treadmill, and stationary bicycle below.

ELLIPTICAL MACHINE | 10 MINUTES

Set the level anywhere from 3–5, maintaining a moderate pace and pushing the pedals with a forward motion.

STATIONARY BIKE | 10 MINUTES

Set your level anywhere from 2–4, aiming for 70 to 80 revolutions per minute (RPM). If you're pedaling faster than 100 RPM, set the resistance higher to challenge yourself.

TREADMILL | 10 MINUTES

Set the treadmill at a 4.0 mph pace and a 2% incline. Keep abdominal muscles contracted by pulling navel inward toward spine. Buttocks should be clenched and tight. Breathing rate should increase, but you should still be able to maintain a conversation.

CONTINUE TO NEXT PAGE

■ **TEASERS**

Solve the following brainteasers. If you enjoy this type of mental challenge, keep the brain bene-fits coming by picking up a puzzle-a-day calendar. Or find a Web site that offers a daily puzzle.

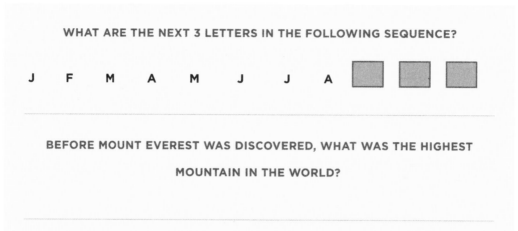

WHAT ARE THE NEXT 3 LETTERS IN THE FOLLOWING SEQUENCE?

J   F   M   A   M   J   J   A   ☐   ☐   ☐

BEFORE MOUNT EVEREST WAS DISCOVERED, WHAT WAS THE HIGHEST MOUNTAIN IN THE WORLD?

A PLANE CRASHES ON THE BORDER OF THE U.S. AND CANADA. WHERE DO THEY BURY THE SURVIVORS?

Turn to page 265 for the answers.

■ **HONING THE HABIT**

Write down the names of five people you met in the past 2 weeks. Apply your favorite memory technique to help you remember their names.

■ JIGSAWS

Can you assemble the following puzzles? Before you break out the scissors, wait: solve these jigsaws using only your mental muscles.

Turn to page 265 for the answer.

WEEK 4

■ USE THIS SPACE TO TAKE NOTES

EAT WELL

MY WEIGHT:

EXERCISE

CHAPTER 2: Brainpower Game Plan

PLAY BRAIN GAMES

■ GROCERY LIST

VEGETABLES

- ☐ Baby carrots, 1 large bag
- ☐ Baby spinach, 1 large bag
- ☐ Celery, 1 large bunch
- ☐ Garlic, 1 small head
- ☐ Mixed greens, 1 bag
- ☐ Portobello mushroom caps, 2
- ☐ Red onion, 1 large
- ☐ Shredded purple cabbage, 1 small bag

FRUIT

- ☐ Avocado, 1
- ☐ Banana, 1 medium
- ☐ Black currant juice, 16 oz bottle
- ☐ Grapefruit, 1
- ☐ Kiwi fruit, 4
- ☐ Lemon, 1 small
- ☐ Orange, 1 small
- ☐ Peaches (if not in season choose 1 pear or apple), 2
- ☐ Red apples, 4 medium
- ☐ Red grapes, 1 small bunch
- ☐ Tomatoes, 2 large

OTHER

- ☐ Hummus, 16 oz container

BAKERY

- ☐ 8" diameter, whole-wheat tortillas, 1 package
- ☐ Baked tortilla chips, 1 bag
- ☐ Whole-wheat bread, 1 loaf
- ☐ Whole-wheat pita bread, 1 package

DAIRY

- ☐ 1% reduced-sodium cottage cheese, 16 oz container
- ☐ Eggs, 1/2 dozen
- ☐ Grated Parmesan cheese, 4 oz container
- ☐ Low-fat plain yogurt, 32 oz container
- ☐ Nonfat milk, 1 qt
- ☐ Reduced-fat Mexican-blend cheese, 8 oz bag
- ☐ Reduced-fat shredded mozzarella cheese, 8 oz bag
- ☐ Reduced-fat string cheese, 4 sticks
- ☐ Reduced-fat Swiss cheese (from deli), 2 slices

FROZEN

- ☐ Frozen blueberries, 8 oz bag
- ☐ Frozen broccoli, 16 oz bag
- ☐ Frozen veggie burgers, 1 box
- ☐ Whole-grain waffles, 1 box

MEAT/SEAFOOD

- ☐ Chunk light tuna, in water, 6 oz can
- ☐ Firm tofu, 14 oz block
- ☐ Raw beef tenderloin, 8 oz
- ☐ Raw boneless and skinless chicken breast, 19 oz
- ☐ Raw salmon filet, 3 oz
- ☐ Raw tilapia filet, 3 oz
- ☐ Sliced reduced-sodium deli turkey breast, 3 oz

DRY GOODS

- ☐ Almonds, 1 small bag
- ☐ Black olives, 15 oz can
- ☐ Cheerios®, 1 small box
- ☐ Chopped walnuts, 1 small bag
- ☐ Golden raisins, 1 box
- ☐ Marinara sauce, 26 oz jar
- ☐ No-salt-added corn, 15 oz can
- ☐ Quinoa, 1 small box
- ☐ Reduced-sodium vegetable soup, 1 can
- ☐ Reduced-sodium white beans, 15 oz can
- ☐ Refried beans, 15 oz can
- ☐ Roasted red peppers packed in water, 1 jar
- ☐ Whole-wheat penne pasta, 16 oz box

■ GRAB AND GO MEALS

These meals can be substituted for any of the designated meals for this week, for example: breakfast for breakfast, lunch for lunch, or dinner for dinner. However, try not to substitute more than one meal per day.

BREAKFAST

GRANOLA BAR WITH YOGURT
Kashi® TLC granola bar. Serve with 6-ounce container of low-fat fruit yogurt.
calories: 347; protein: 15 g; carbohydrate: 58 g; dietary fiber: 6 g; total fat: 8.2 g; saturated fat: 2.1 g; cholesterol: 10 mg; sodium: 206 mg

LUNCH

MCDONALD'S SOUTHWEST SALAD WITH GRILLED CHICKEN
1 salad, ½ packet of Newman's Own® Low-Fat Balsamic Vinaigrette dressing. Serve with 1 yogurt parfait.
calories: 490; protein: 34 g; carbohydrate: 62 g; dietary fiber: 7 g; total fat: 12.5 g; saturated fat: 4 g; cholesterol: 80 mg; sodium: 1780 mg

DINNER

VEGETABLE SOUP WITH A CHEESE SANDWICH
Stir ¼ cup salsa into 1 ½ cups canned vegetable soup and heat until warmed through. Serve with a cheese sandwich (2 slices whole-wheat bread, two slices reduced-fat cheese, and 1 tablespoon hummus) and medium apple.
calories: 553; protein: 24 g; carbohydrate: 81 g; dietary fiber: 10 g; total fat: 17 g; saturated fat: 7.5 g; cholesterol: 30 mg; sodium: 1086 mg

■ BREAKFAST

COTTAGE CHEESE AND FRUIT WITH PEANUT BUTTER TOAST

Top ½ cup 1% reduced-sodium cottage cheese with ½ cup frozen blueberries, thawed. Eat with a piece of whole-wheat toast spread with 1 ½ tablespoons peanut butter.

calories: 372
protein: 25 g
carbohydrate: 38 g
dietary fiber: 7 g
total fat: 15 g
saturated fat: 3.6 g
cholesterol: 5 mg
sodium: 336 mg

■ LUNCH

GRILLED CHICKEN AND AVOCADO SANDWICH

Place 3 ounces grilled chicken, ½ cup roasted red peppers, ½ cup baby spinach, ¼ cup shredded (or 1-ounce slice) reduced-fat mozzarella cheese, and ¼ avocado, sliced, on a piece of whole-wheat bread. Drizzle with 2 teaspoons olive oil, 1 teaspoon balsamic vinegar, and top with remaining slice of bread.

calories: 505
protein: 40 g
carbohydrate: 32
dietary fiber: 8 g
total fat: 25 g
saturated fat: 6.5 g
cholesterol: 89 mg
sodium: 724 mg

■ DINNER

BEEF TENDERLOIN SALAD

Sauté ½ cup sliced portobello mushrooms in 1 teaspoon olive oil. Place mushrooms with 3 ounces cooked beef tenderloin strips on top of 2 cups baby spinach and ¼ cup no-salt-added canned corn. Drizzle with 1 tablespoon low-fat vinaigrette and top with 2 tablespoons reduced-fat Mexican-blend cheese. Serve with ½ whole-wheat pita bread. **FOR DESSERT:** 15 red grapes with 1 cup low-fat plain yogurt drizzled with 1 teaspoon honey.

calories: 566
protein: 47 g
carbohydrate: 52 g
dietary fiber: 5 g
total fat: 20 g
saturated fat: 7.9 g
cholesterol: 92 mg
sodium: 618 mg

■ BRAINPOWER SNACKS   👩 *Choose 1 snack*   👨 *Eat both snacks*

CHIPS, SALSA, AND CHEESE

Serve 1 ounce (about 7) baked tortilla chips with ¼ cup salsa and 1 piece reduced-fat string cheese.

calories: 217; protein: 11 g; carbohydrate: 27 g; dietary fiber: 3 g; total fat: 7.4 g; saturated fat: 3.8 g; cholesterol: 15 mg; sodium: 434 mg

CEREAL TRAIL MIX

Combine ½ cup whole-grain cereal, ¼ cup raisins or dried chopped apricots, cranberries, or cherries, and 1 ½ tablespoon chopped walnuts or slivered almonds.

calories: 207; protein: 4 g; carbohydrate: 33 g; dietary fiber: 4.5 g; total fat: 8.5 g; saturated fat: 1 g; cholesterol: 0 mg; sodium: 109 mg

If your daily workouts are starting to seem too easy, take these steps to be sure you keep challenging yourself.

CARDIO

INCREASE THE INTENSITY

If you work out on a treadmill, increase the incline. If you walk or jog outdoors, add some hills or stadium steps to your route.

AMP UP YOUR SPEED

If you walk or jog on a treadmill, increase the speed. If you walk or jog outdoors, time how long it takes you to complete a section of your usual route, say four laps around the block. Now quicken your pace and try to do five laps in the same amount of time.

INCREASE THE DURATION

A 30-minute cardio workout burns calories and boosts production of important brain chemicals—but pushing yourself to go for 45 minutes increases your benefits by 50%. Think of ways to sneak in exercise in addition to your normal workouts. For instance, instead of meeting a friend for drinks or dinner, invite your pal to go for a walk (or at least meet early and take a walk before dinner).

STRENGTH

INCREASE THE WEIGHT

If you've been using 5-pound weights for most strength exercises—and you usually finish the last rep with ease—increase the weight of your dumbbells by 2-3 pounds during your next workout.

ADD REPETITIONS

If you've been stopping at 8 or 10 reps, consider doing 12 reps on the easier moves.

■ HIGH-ENERGY DANCE ROUTINE | 30 MINUTES

Grab your index cards, shuffle them, and get to work.

Boxing moves

Push-ups

Ballroom dancing

CONTINUE TO NEXT PAGE

■ RAISIN MEDITATION

This exercise in "mindfulness," adapted from the work of Dr. Jon Kabat-Zinn (see page 93), teaches you how to use all of your senses to experience more every day.

When was the last time you really thought about . . . a raisin? Take a raisin and, instead of popping it into your mouth, spend time observing its appearance. How does it feel? How would you describe its aroma? Now put it in your mouth and chew slowly. What sensations do you experience?

■ TOOL CHECK

One of the best ways to improve your level of organization is to begin with a review of what you currently do. At a minimum, you should be using a scheduler, such as a PDA or appointment book, and a to-do list. A few other memory tools could nicely round out your list, and we'll review some of them over this week.

I USE:

☐ Scheduler
☐ To-do list
☐ Reminder file
☐ Memory logs
☐ Project notes
☐ Memory place (box or container for use by the door)
☐ Packet of sticky notes and pen
☐ Whiteboard calendar/ chart and dry-erase markers

■ **GET THE GROUP**

This game challenges your ability to identify similarities and differences within a group. Each of the symbols in the following set has three different characteristics in color, shape, and pattern. Find as many groups of three symbols as you can in which all three are either the same or different with respect to each of these characteristics.

Turn to page 265 for the answer.

■ BREAKFAST

SMOOTHIE AND TOAST

Blend ³/₄ cup low-fat plain yogurt, ¹/₃ cup frozen blueberries, ¹/₃ banana, and 4 ounces black currant juice (or pomegranate juice). Enjoy with 1 slice whole-wheat toast spread with 2 teaspoons peanut butter.

calories: 369
protein: 17 g
carbohydrate: 58 g
dietary fiber: 6 g
total fat: 10 g
saturated fat: 3 g
cholesterol: 11 mg
sodium: 270 mg

■ LUNCH

BEEF BURRITO

Fill one 8″ whole-wheat tortilla with 3 ounces cooked beef tenderloin, ¹/₃ cup cooked quinoa, ¹/₂ cup baby spinach, ¹/₄ cup chopped tomato, ¹/₄ cup salsa, ¹/₄ cup shredded reduced-fat Mexican-blend cheese, and 1 tablespoon low-fat plain yogurt.

calories: 513
protein: 42 g
carbohydrate: 49 g
dietary fiber: 8 g
total fat: 17 g
saturated fat: 7.5 g
cholesterol: 91 mg
sodium: 662 mg

■ DINNER

PENNE WITH WHITE BEANS AND BROCCOLI

Toss 1 cup cooked whole-wheat penne pasta with 1 teaspoon olive oil, 2 teaspoons chopped garlic, ¹/₄ cup canned reduced-sodium white beans, rinsed and drained, 4 ounces cubed firm tofu sautéed in 1 teaspoon olive oil, and 1 cup frozen broccoli, cooked. Top with 2 tablespoons Parmesan cheese.

calories: 556
protein: 36 g
carbohydrate: 60 g
dietary fiber: 14 g
total fat: 23 g
saturated fat: 4.7 g
cholesterol: 9 mg
sodium: 606 mg

■ BRAINPOWER SNACKS   Choose 1 snack   Eat both snacks

CEREAL TRAIL MIX

Combine ¹/₂ cup whole-grain cereal, ¹/₄ cup raisins or dried chopped apricots, cranberries, or cherries, and 1 ¹/₂ tablespoons chopped walnuts or slivered almonds.

calories: 207; protein: 4 g; carbohydrate: 33 g; dietary fiber: 5 g; total fat: 8.5 g; saturated fat: 1 g; cholesterol: 0 mg; sodium: 109 mg

HUMMUS AND VEGGIES

Serve ¹/₃ cup hummus with 1 ¹/₂ cups combined celery and baby carrots.

calories: 196; protein: 5 g; carbohydrate: 28 g; dietary fiber: 7 g; total fat: 7.4 g; saturated fat: 1 g; cholesterol: 0 mg; sodium: 336 mg

■ GET SOME GAME

Visit your local toy store and check out the different brands of handheld electronic games. My favorite? Hasbro's™ Simon, which provides a great cross-training workout at a low cost. Get into the habit of playing whichever game you choose several times a week for at least 10 minutes. Also, look into purchasing brain fitness software products, which are available online. Before you buy, make sure a product challenges your attention span, speed, and flexibility—and becomes more challenging as your skills improve.

■ HELLO, FRIEND

Call a friend you haven't spoken to in at least 3 years. As you reminisce, you'll probably end up talking about mutual friends you knew in the old days—a great booster for your memory bank.

■ GETTING A TOOL HABIT

Adopting the following steps will guarantee that you're using your memory tools to their greatest potential:

WEEKLY MATTERS
At the beginning of each week, set aside 10 minutes for the following: first, review your appointments for the upcoming week. Then compose a to-do list for the week. Finally, take information from your Reminder File (which you'll learn about on Day 24) and add important dates to your calendar.

MORNING MINUTE
Every morning, take a minute to look at your calendar and to-do list. This simple step forces you to review and pay more attention to your appointments and errands. Most important, it makes you more likely to remember them.

CONTINUE TO NEXT PAGE

■ CARDIO | 30 MINUTES

If you don't belong to a gym, either do the Brainpower Walk from Day 1, swim, jog, or bike outside. Otherwise, follow the workout for the elliptical machine, treadmill, and stationary bicycle below.

ELLIPTICAL MACHINE | 10 MINUTES

Set the level anywhere from 3–5, maintaining a moderate pace and pushing the pedals with a forward motion.

TREADMILL | 10 MINUTES

Set the treadmill at a 4.0 mph pace and a 2% incline. Keep abdominal muscles contracted by pulling navel inward toward spine. Buttocks should be clenched and tight. Breathing rate should increase, but you should still be able to maintain a conversation.

STATIONARY BIKE | 10 MINUTES

Set your level anywhere from 2–4, aiming for 70 to 80 revolutions per minute (RPM). If you're pedaling faster than 100 RPM, set the resistance higher to challenge yourself.

■ POWER MOVES

POWER LUNGE AND TWIST

Targets	Equipment
Legs, shoulders, and core	5-pound dumbbell

Pick up dumbbell in right hand. Let it hang at side, palm facing in. Put left hand on hip. **A** Lunge forward with left leg until knee is bent at about 90 degrees. **B** Straighten left leg and bend right elbow, pulling dumbbell toward ribs as you rotate torso to the right. Lower weight and return to lunge position. Repeat, alternating sides. Do 2 sets of 12 reps on each side.

Make It Easier:
Do 1 set of 12 reps on each side.
Make It Harder:
Do 3 sets of 12 reps on each side.

STANDING OBLIQUE ROTATIONS

Targets	Equipment
Obliques and shoulders	5-pound dumbbell

Hold dumbbell with both hands and place feet shoulder-width apart. **A** Extend dumbbell straight out in front of you at shoulder height. Keep hips pointing forward and arms straight. **B** Rotate torso and arms to the right. Pause, then rotate torso and arms to the left. Do 2 sets of 12 reps.

Make It Easier:
Do 1 set of 12 reps using 3-pound dumbbell.
Make It Harder:
Do 3 sets of 12 reps.

PALM ROTATION ROW

Targets	Equipment
Back and shoulders	Set of 5-pound dumbbells

Grasp a dumbbell in each hand with an overhand grip and straighten arms. **A** Bend over and bend knees, keeping lower back straight and chest out. **B** Lift dumbbells to each side of torso, twisting palms as you lift so that palms face forward at top of motion. Elbows should be moving backward as they bend. Now reverse the movement, twisting hands back into overhand grip. Do 2 sets of 12 reps.

Make It Easier:
Do 1 set of 12 reps using 3-pound dumbbells.
Make It Harder:
Do 3 sets of 12 reps.

END OF DAY 23

■ BREAKFAST

BREAKFAST WRAP

Scramble 1 egg and 2 egg whites in 1 teaspoon olive oil with ¼ cup combined chopped red onions and tomato and 2 tablespoons shredded reduced-fat mozzarella cheese. Place in an 8″ whole-wheat tortilla and roll up. Serve with ½ grapefruit.

calories: 369
protein: 23 g
carbohydrate: 41 g
dietary fiber: 5 g
total fat: 13 g
saturated fat: 4 g
cholesterol: 216 mg
sodium: 509 mg

■ LUNCH

HEARTY VEGETABLE SOUP

Add 1 crumbled veggie burger, sautéed in 1 teaspoon olive oil, ½ cup reduced-sodium canned white beans, rinsed and drained, and ½ cup frozen and thawed broccoli to 1 cup vegetable soup and heat until steaming. Top with ¼ cup reduced-fat Mexican-blend cheese. Serve with ½ small whole-wheat pita and ½ grapefruit.

calories: 522
protein: 33 g
carbohydrate: 66 g
dietary fiber: 13 g
total fat: 16.5 g
saturated fat: 5.2 g
cholesterol: 19 mg
sodium: 667 mg

■ DINNER

GRILLED CHICKEN TORTILLA PIZZA

Place an 8″ whole-wheat tortilla on baking sheet (greased with small amount of cooking spray) and top with ¼ cup marinara sauce, ½ cup baby spinach sautéed in 1 teaspoon olive oil, 2 ounces diced grilled chicken breast, ¼ cup reduced-sodium canned white beans, rinsed and drained, and ¼ cup shredded reduced-fat mozzarella cheese. Bake at 375°F until cheese is melted and tortilla is crisp. Eat a small orange, sliced, for dessert.

calories: 573
protein: 46 g
carbohydrate: 63 g
dietary fiber: 11 g
total fat: 16.3 g
saturated fat: 5.1 g
cholesterol: 86 mg
sodium: 691 mg

■ BRAINPOWER SNACKS ⚲ *Choose 1 snack* ⚲ *Eat both snacks*

HUMMUS AND VEGGIES

Serve ⅓ cup hummus with 1 ½ cups combined celery and baby carrots.

calories: 196; protein: 5 g; carbohydrate: 28 g; dietary fiber: 7 g; total fat: 7.4 g; saturated fat: 1 g; cholesterol: 0 mg; sodium: 336 mg

PEANUT BUTTER AND TOAST

Spread 1 slice whole-wheat toast with ½ tablespoon peanut butter. Serve with 1 medium apple.

calories: 204; protein: 5 g; carbohydrate: 36 g; dietary fiber: 5 g; total fat: 6 g; saturated fat: 1.1 g; cholesterol: 0.3 mg; sodium: 177 mg

■ WORK BETTER

Complex, intellectually challenging work may keep dementia at bay. Think of five improvements you could make at work, either for your own position or for the company in general. Now take this idea to the next level: try to execute at least two of the improvements.

■ REMINDER FILE

Keep better track of all those dates and times that you need to remember. Get a large manila envelope and label it **"REMINDER FILE."** Put the envelope in a convenient place, such as on your desk or the table where you sort mail. As you come up with things you need to remember—such as attending a lecture at the local library or getting tickets for a concert—write yourself a note and put it in your **REMINDER FILE**. Then, when you run through your **WEEKLY MATTERS**, from Day 23, simply go through your **REMINDER FILE** and log all of that information into your appointment book. Stick with this plan and you'll never miss another event.

■ CONCENTRATION

Lay out a deck of playing cards facedown on a table. Turning over two cards at a time, try to find matching pairs. If the two you turn over don't match, return them to the table facedown. If you make a match, remove the cards. Obviously, at first you won't make many pairs, but trying to remember where cards are located will help you clear the table. (If you want to start out by making the game easier, use only half the deck, leaving one pair of each number and face card.) Use a stopwatch and see how long it takes to find all of the pairs.

CONTINUE TO NEXT PAGE ⟶

■ YOGA/FLEXIBILITY EXERCISES

CAT/COW

COBRA

Start on all fours, bringing wrists underneath shoulders and knees underneath hips. Think of spine as a straight line connecting shoulders to hips.

Ⓐ Cat pose: round spine by dropping head and looking toward navel.

Ⓑ Cow pose: drop belly while looking toward ceiling. Let the motion in spine start from tailbone, so that neck is the last part to move.

Alternate between cat and cow pose with each inhale and exhale, matching movement to breath. Continue for 5–10 breaths, moving whole spine. After final exhale, return to neutral position.

Start by lying facedown, flat on floor with feet together. Place hands on floor next to shoulders, palms down. Gently push upper body off floor a few inches at a time, while keeping legs on floor. It should feel like you're doing a push-up but with relaxed stomach and back muscles. Keep looking up at all times and push slowly until you feel the stretch in stomach and lower back muscles. If stretch feels uncomfortable, just push a few inches off floor. Hold for 10–15 seconds.

HAMSTRING STRETCH

SEATED POSE

Sit on floor with right leg extended and left leg bent so that left heel is against inner part of right knee. Try to keep both legs as flat as possible. Keep torso upright, abs in, and shoulders down. Place hands on straight leg (or on floor on either side of it) and lean forward from waist. Keep chin up, as if reaching chin toward toes of straightened leg. Hold for 15–30 seconds. Repeat on the other side.

Sit on floor and open legs as wide as possible while remaining in a comfortable position. Keep quads tight and toes pointing toward ceiling. Press backs of legs into floor, feeling the stretch in hamstrings, back, and calves. Focus on sitting up straight. Hold for 15–30 seconds.

END OF DAY 24

■ BREAKFAST

CEREAL WITH PEACHES AND MILK

Mix 1 cup Cheerios® with ¼ cup Kashi® GoLean® cereal. Top with 4 teaspoons slivered almonds, 1 medium peach, sliced, and 8 ounces nonfat milk.

calories: 324
protein: 18 g
carbohydrate: 54 g
dietary fiber: 8 g
total fat: 7 g
saturated fat: 1 g
cholesterol: 5 mg
sodium: 360 mg

■ LUNCH

CHICKEN, APPLE, AND WALNUT SALAD

Over 2 cups mixed field greens, place 3 ounces grilled chicken, ½ cup sliced apples, ¼ cup shredded reduced-fat mozzarella cheese, and 1 tablespoon chopped walnuts. Dress with 2 teaspoons olive oil and 1 tablespoon balsamic vinegar. Serve with 1 whole-wheat pita.

calories: 487
protein: 39 g
carbohydrate: 32 g
dietary fiber: 7 g
total fat: 23.3 g
saturated fat: 6.3 g
cholesterol: 86 mg
sodium: 548 mg

■ DINNER

HONEY MUSTARD SALMON WITH SAUTÉED VEGGIE MELANGE

Sauté 2 cups baby spinach in skillet with 2 teaspoons olive oil, 1 teaspoon chopped garlic, ½ cup Portobello mushroom slices, and ¼ cup red onion until greens are wilted. Mix 1 tablespoon Dijon mustard with 2 teaspoons honey and 1 teaspoon dried dill. Spread mixture over a 3-ounce salmon filet. Broil for 3–5 minutes or until fish is no longer translucent. Serve veggie mixture and salmon over 1 ½ cups cooked quinoa.

calories: 536
protein: 29 g
carbohydrate: 67 g
dietary fiber: 7 g
total fat: 19 g
saturated fat: 2.5 g
cholesterol: 43 mg
sodium: 559 mg

■ BRAINPOWER SNACKS   *Choose 1 snack*   *Eat both snacks*

CHIPS, SALSA, AND CHEESE

Serve 1 ounce (about 7) baked tortilla chips with ¼ cup salsa and 1 piece reduced-fat string cheese.

calories: 217; protein: 11 g; carbohydrate: 27 g; dietary fiber: 3 g; total fat: 7.4 g; saturated fat: 3.8 g; cholesterol: 15 mg; sodium: 434 mg

PEANUT BUTTER AND TOAST

Spread 1 slice whole-wheat toast with ½ tablespoon peanut butter. Serve with 1 medium apple.

calories: 204; protein: 5 g; carbohydrate: 36 g; dietary fiber: 5 g; total fat: 6 g; saturated fat: 1.1 g; cholesterol: 0.3 mg; sodium: 177 mg

■ DECK OF CARDS WORKOUT | 45 MINUTES

Adding some brain-stimulating variety—to say nothing of a little fun—to your workout is as simple as shuffling the deck. Get some playing cards and assign the following exercises to the suits:

Spades	Hearts	Clubs	Diamonds	Joker
jumping jacks	push-ups	your favorite dance move	crunches or sit-ups on fitness ball	1-minute rest

NUMBER OF REPS: The number on each card represents the number of reps you should perform. Count jacks, queens, and kings as 12 reps. Aces equal 1 rep.

Turn over the top card and make your way through the entire deck for an unusual and unpredictable 45-minute workout.

CONTINUE TO NEXT PAGE

■ TRAIL BLAZER

This simple yet effective exercise trains your attention, speed, and flexibility. Connect the following dots in order, alternating between the two different sets of information (for example, A, I, B, II, C, and so on), working as quickly as you can. Be careful—your mind needs to move back and forth between two different sets of information to complete the puzzle.

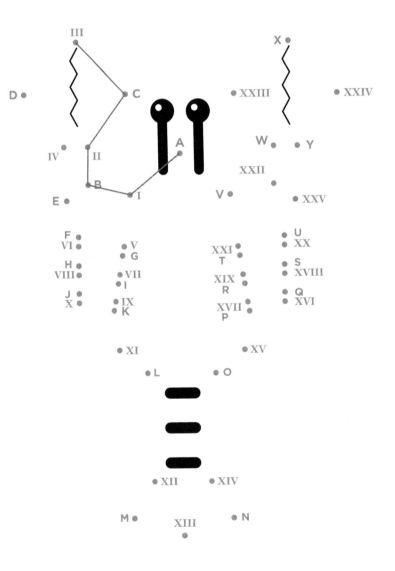

Turn to page 265 for the answer.

CHAPTER 2: Brainpower Game Plan

■ MEMORY LOGS

It can be difficult to track down information you use infrequently in your mind, so try storing it in a **MEMORY LOG**. A small address book works well for this purpose. For example, if you want to keep track of where you keep your will, turn to the "W" page, jot down "will," and note its location.

■ MYSTERY WRITER

Here's another opportunity to stretch your mind with a new and unusual challenge. Write a mystery novel—in 10 words or less.

END OF DAY 25

■ BREAKFAST

EGGS, TOAST, AND CRUNCHY YOGURT

Top 1 piece whole-wheat toast with 1 hard-cooked egg, sliced, drizzled with 1 teaspoon olive oil, and sprinkled with salt and pepper. On the side, top ¾ cup low-fat plain yogurt with ¼ cup Kashi® GoLean® cereal, 1 tablespoon golden raisins, sliced, and 1 teaspoon chopped walnuts.

calories: 369
protein: 22 g
carbohydrate: 39 g
dietary fiber: 5 g
total fat: 15.4 g
saturated fat: 4.4 g
cholesterol: 221 mg
sodium: 418 mg

■ LUNCH

TURKEY AND SWISS SANDWICH WITH PURPLE CABBAGE COLESLAW

Place 3 ounces reduced-sodium deli turkey breast, 2 teaspoons Dijon mustard, 1 teaspoon reduced-fat mayonnaise, 2 slices reduced-fat Swiss cheese, and 2 slices tomato between 2 slices whole-grain bread. To prepare coleslaw, toss 1 cup shredded purple cabbage with 1 tablespoon golden raisins, 1 tablespoon balsamic vinegar, 2 teaspoons olive oil, and freshly ground pepper.

calories: 514
protein: 43 g
carbohydrate: 36 g
dietary fiber: 6 g
total fat: 23 g
saturated fat: 8 g
cholesterol: 96 mg
sodium: 672 mg

■ DINNER

TILAPIA PARMESAN

Sauté 3-ounce tilapia filet in 1 teaspoon olive oil. Place on top of ½ cup cooked whole-wheat penne pasta. Top with ½ cup marinara sauce and 2 tablespoons Parmesan cheese. Serve with 1 piece whole-wheat toast. **FOR DESSERT:** 2 kiwi fruit.

calories: 560
protein: 32 g
carbohydrate: 76 g
dietary fiber: 14 g
total fat: 17 g
saturated fat: 4 g
cholesterol: 51 mg
sodium: 410 mg

■ BRAINPOWER SNACKS   *Choose 1 snack*   *Eat both snacks*

CHIPS, SALSA, AND CHEESE

Serve 1 ounce (about 7) baked tortilla chips with ¼ cup salsa and 1 piece reduced-fat string cheese.

calories: 217; protein: 11 g; carbohydrate: 27 g; dietary fiber: 3 g; total fat: 7.4 g; saturated fat: 3.8 g; cholesterol: 15 mg; sodium: 434 mg

HUMMUS AND VEGGIES

Serve ⅓ cup hummus with 1 ½ cups combined celery and baby carrots.

calories: 196; protein: 5 g; carbohydrate: 28 g; dietary fiber: 7 g; total fat: 7.4 g; saturated fat: 1 g; cholesterol: 0 mg; sodium: 336 mg

■ CARDIO | 45 MINUTES

If you don't belong to a gym, either do the Brainpower Walk from Day 1, swim, jog, or bike outside. Otherwise, follow the workout for the elliptical machince, treadmill, and stationary bike below.

ELLIPTICAL MACHINE | 15 MINUTES

Set the level anywhere from 4–6, maintaining a moderate pace and pushing the pedals with a forward motion.

STATIONARY BIKE | 15 MINUTES

Set your level anywhere from 3–5, aiming for 70 to 80 revolutions per minute (RPM). If you're pedaling faster than 100 RPM, set the resistance higher to challenge yourself.

TREADMILL | 15 MINUTES

Set the treadmill at a 4.0 mph pace and a 2% incline. Keep abdominal muscles contracted by pulling navel inward toward spine. Buttocks should be clenched and tight. Breathing rate should increase, but you should still be able to maintain a conversation.

CONTINUE TO NEXT PAGE

■ FIND IT II

Give your visual searching skills another workout—only this time with a twist that will boost your brain challenge even more. Remember this game from Week 1? This time around, you will be searching for two symbols in a specific order at a time. Start with Pair 1 and see how many you can find in 1 minute. We've given you three different pairs of symbols. Did your score improve on the final pair?

Turn to page 265 for the answer.

■ JACKS

Test your reaction time—and have some fun acting like a kid again—by playing a favorite game from your youth. Remember jacks? This simple children's game poses a great challenge for your brain. Toss 10 jacks onto your playing surface. Toss the ball in the air. Using the same hand, pick up 1 jack from the floor and catch the ball in the same hand. Continue by picking up one more jack each time. For example, next you would try to pick up 2 at the same time, then 3, and so on.

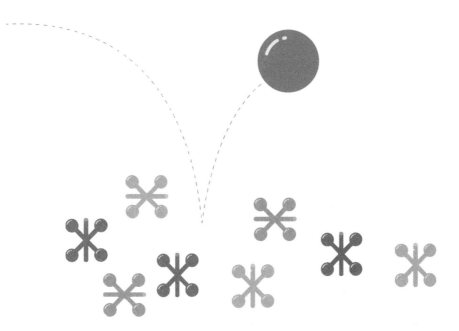

■ PROJECT NOTES

Get into the habit of taking notes whenever you receive critical information. Taking notes is particularly important when you are meeting with a doctor, lawyer, or financial planner, or in any other circumstance that may cause stress and anxiety—which can cloud your memory. Note-taking is always a good idea on the job, too. Try this: staple several sheets of blank paper to the inside of a project folder and use them to take notes during meetings or client calls. Later on you can go back to these notes for a record of what you discussed.

◼ BREAKFAST

WAFFLE WITH COTTAGE CHEESE AND FRUIT

Top 1 frozen whole-wheat waffle (toasted) with ¼ cup 1% reduced-sodium cottage cheese, ¼ cup frozen blueberries, thawed, and 2 tablespoons chopped almonds. Serve with an additional ¼ cup cottage cheese topped with ¼ cup blueberries, on the side, and café au lait (add 1 cup hot nonfat milk to 2 ounces strong coffee).

calories: 355
protein: 28 g
carbohydrate: 40 g
dietary fiber: 4 g
total fat: 10 g
saturated fat: 2.9 g
cholesterol: 49 mg
sodium: 295 mg

◼ LUNCH

TUNA SALAD SANDWICH

Top 1 slice toasted whole-wheat bread with 3 ounces water-packed chunk light tuna, drained, and mixed with 1 tablespoon reduced-fat mayonnaise, and 1 tablespoon chopped black olives. Top with remaining slice of bread. Serve with 22 baked tortilla chips and 1 cup baby carrots.

calories: 500
protein: 33 g
carbohydrate: 69 g
dietary fiber: 8 g
total fat: 11 g
saturated fat: 2 g
cholesterol: 31 mg
sodium: 1038 mg

◼ DINNER

WHOLE-WHEAT PENNE AND CHEESE WITH TOMATOES

Sauté ¼ cup diced red onion in 2 teaspoons olive oil. Add ½ cup chopped tomatoes, 1 cup cooked whole-wheat penne, and ⅓ cup reduced-fat Mexican-blend cheese. Season with freshly ground pepper. Serve with ½ cup celery sticks with 2 tablespoons hummus. **FOR DESSERT:** eat 2 kiwi fruit.

calories: 551
protein: 24 g
carbohydrate: 73 g
dietary fiber: 17 g
total fat: 22 g
saturated fat: 7 g
cholesterol: 25 mg
sodium: 383 mg

SNACKS   Choose 1 snack   Eat both snacks

CHIPS, SALSA, AND CHEESE

Serve 1 ounce (about 7) baked tortilla chips with ¼ cup salsa and 1 piece reduced-fat string cheese.

calories: 217; protein: 11 g; carbohydrate: 27 g; dietary fiber: 3 g; total fat: 7.4 g; saturated fat: 3.8 g; cholesterol: 15 mg; sodium: 434 mg

CEREAL TRAIL MIX

Combine ½ cup whole-grain cereal, ¼ cup raisins or dried chopped apricots, cranberries, or cherries, and 1 ½ tablespoons chopped walnuts or slivered almonds.

calories: 207; protein: 4 g; carbohydrate: 33 g; dietary fiber: 5 g; total fat: 8.5 g; saturated fat: 1 g; cholesterol: 0 mg; sodium: 109 mg

■ JUNK DRAWER JAM

Take inventory of your junk drawer for a visual memory workout. Open your junk drawer and study the contents for 1 minute. Then close the drawer and write down as many items inside as you can recall.

Want a brain-boosting bonus? Reorganize the drawer and toss out the genuine junk.

■ MEMORY PLACES

Today, set up a **MEMORY PLACE**. Find a bowl, dish, or other container large enough to hold your keys, wallet, glasses, cell phone—any important object that you are constantly picking up and putting down. Set up your **MEMORY PLACE** near the front door or whichever entry you use most often. Now cultivate the positive habit of always putting those frequently lost objects in your **MEMORY PLACE**. Here's another useful idea—keep a pad of sticky notes and a pen in your **MEMORY PLACE**. That way, when you remember something you need to take with you (like the dry cleaning or a DVD to return), you can write yourself a note and stick it on the door.

■ HOUSE OF CARDS

Today you will try a deceptively simple task that requires attention, ingenuity, creativity, and—perhaps above all— a steady hand. Get a deck of playing cards and use them to build a house. (You might want to close the window first—a breeze could be destructive.) Not as easy as it looks, is it?

CONTINUE TO NEXT PAGE

■ **STRENGTH TRAINING**

SIDE LUNGE WITH ROW

Targets	Equipment
Quadriceps and upper back	Set of 5-pound dumbbells

WALL SITS WITH FITNESS BALL

Targets	Equipment
Quadriceps	Fitness ball (optional)

A Hold a dumbbell in each hand with arms straight and palms facing inward. **B** Lunge to the right, keeping right knee over toes. Bring dumbbells to each side of right foot. **C** Lift right dumbbell upward, keeping elbow close to body. Return to starting position and repeat on left side. Do 1 set of 12 reps on each side.

Make It Easier:
Do the exercise without dumbbells.
Make It Harder:
Do 2 sets of 12 reps on each side.

Stand with feet shoulder-width apart facing away from a wall. Place fitness ball between lower back and wall, then move feet forward about 1 foot. **A** Slowly squat, rolling ball downward with back, keeping back straight and abdominal muscles contracted by pulling navel toward spine. Keep squatting until thighs are parallel with floor. **B** Pause, then reverse process by rising upward. Do 2 sets of 12 reps.

Make It Easier:
Do 1 set of 12 reps.
Make It Harder:
Do 3 sets of 12 reps.
If You Don't Have A Ball:
Do 2 sets of 12 squats.

HAMSTRING CURLS WITH FITNESS BALL

Targets	Equipment
Hamstrings and core (abdominals and lower back)	Fitness ball (optional) and exercise mat

Ⓐ Lie face up on exercise mat with fitness ball under heels, legs extended, arms by sides. Pull navel toward spine and slowly lift hips off floor, forming diagonal line from shoulders to feet. Ⓑ Keeping body still and hips up, pull ball closer to you with heels, then roll it back to starting position. Do 2 sets of 12 reps.

Make It Easier:
Do 1 set of 12 reps.
Make It Harder:
Do 3 sets of 12 reps.
If You Don't Have A Ball:
Place feet on ottoman or chair. Raise hips until you create a straight line between ankles, hips, and shoulders. Lower slowly. Repeat 12 times.

END OF DAY 27

■ BREAKFAST

SHREDDED WHEAT WITH FRUIT AND NUTS
Top 1 cup bite-size shredded wheat with 1 cup warmed non-fat milk, 1 tablespoon golden raisins, 1 large peach, chopped, 2 teaspoons chopped walnuts, and dash of cinnamon.

calories: 347
protein: 16 g
carbohydrate: 68 g
dietary fiber: 8 g
total fat: 4.8 g
saturated fat: 0.8 g
cholesterol: 5 mg
sodium: 133 mg

■ LUNCH

GRILLED CHICKEN WRAP
Fill 8″ whole-wheat tortilla with 3 ounces grilled chicken breast, 1 tablespoon hummus, ½ cup baby spinach, ¼ cup roasted red peppers, and 2 tablespoons shredded reduced-fat mozzarella cheese. Serve with salad of ¼ cup reduced-sodium canned white beans, rinsed and drained, ¼ cup no-salt-added canned corn, ¼ cup diced tomatoes, and ¼ cup diced celery. Dress with 1 teaspoon olive oil, 1 tablespoon salsa, and freshly ground black pepper.

calories: 503
protein: 42 g
carbohydrate: 57 g
dietary fiber: 10 g
total fat: 13 g
saturated fat: 3.5 g
cholesterol: 79 mg
sodium: 662 mg

■ DINNER

VEGGIE BURGER STEW
Add 1 crumbled veggie burger to 1 cup vegetable soup along with ¾ cup no-salt-added canned corn and ¾ cup cooked quinoa. Top with 2 tablespoons diced avocado and 2 table-spoons low-fat plain yogurt.

calories: 537
protein: 26 g
carbohydrate: 86 g
dietary fiber: 12 g
total fat: 13 g
saturated fat: 1.7 g
cholesterol: 2 mg
sodium: 475 mg

■ BRAINPOWER SNACKS   *Choose 1 snack*   *Eat both snacks*

HUMMUS AND VEGGIES
Serve ⅓ cup hummus with 1 ½ cups combined celery and baby carrots.
calories: 196; protein: 5 g; carbohydrate: 28 g; dietary fiber: 7 g; total fat: 7.4 g; saturated fat: 1 g; cholesterol: 0 mg; sodium: 336 mg

PEANUT BUTTER AND TOAST
Spread 1 slice whole-wheat toast with ½ tablespoon peanut butter. Serve with 1 medium apple.
calories: 204; protein: 5 g; carbohydrate: 36 g; dietary fiber: 5 g; total fat: 6 g; saturated fat: 1.1 g; cholesterol: 0.3 mg; sodium: 177 mg

■ CARDIO | 45 MINUTES

If you don't belong to a gym, either do the Brainpower Walk from Day 1, swim, jog, or bike outside. Otherwise, follow the workout for the elliptical machince, treadmill, and stationary bike below.

ELLIPTICAL MACHINE | 15 MINUTES

Set the level anywhere from 4–6, maintaining a moderate pace and pushing the pedals with a forward motion.

STATIONARY BIKE | 15 MINUTES

Set your level anywhere from 3–5, aiming for 70 to 80 revolutions per minute (RPM). If you're pedaling faster than 100 RPM, set the resistance higher to challenge yourself.

TREADMILL | 15 MINUTES

Set the treadmill at a 4.0 mph pace and a 2% incline. Keep abdominal muscles contracted by pulling navel inward toward spine. Buttocks should be clenched and tight. Breathing rate should increase, but you should still be able to maintain a conversation.

CONTINUE TO NEXT PAGE ➔

■ COLOR WITH CRAYONS

Recapture the joy of pure creativity. When was the last time you had some fun with crayons—with or without a coloring book? Crack open a box, get a few sheets of blank paper, and start coloring. You may be surprised by what you come up with.

■ FAMILY TRACKS

Are you in charge of organizing your own life as well as that of everyone else under your roof? Today you'll learn a great strategy for keeping track of the whole family—and you may even teach them better memory habits while you're at it.

Set up a large whiteboard in a highly visible location in the house that gets plenty of traffic, such as the kitchen. (You can even buy whiteboards that attach to the fridge.) Make a chart, listing days of the week on one side and the names of all family members on the other. Then pick a quiet time on the weekend when the whole family is around. Assign a different color marker to each family member. Have everyone write his or her schedule for the week on the whiteboard. With a little help, even the youngest family members can get into the act. Make filling in the whiteboard a weekly family routine and be sure everyone knows that it's his or her job to stay on the family track.

■ DECODE THIS

One last brain challenge! Using the following cipher, decode the message below.

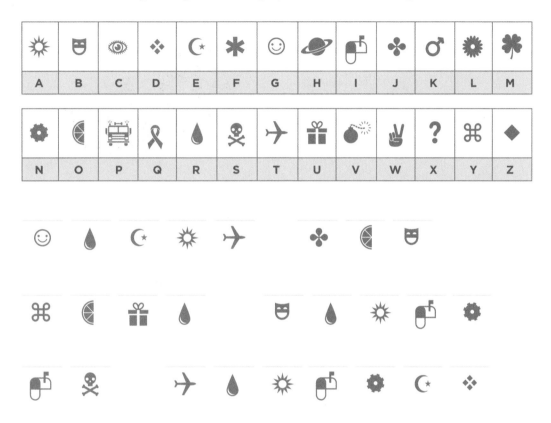

Turn to page 265 for the answer.

END OF WEEK 4

237

CHAPTER 3
A Sharper Mind and Healthier Brain—for Life!

A Sharper Mind and Healthier Brain— for Life!

Nice job! You just spent the past 4 weeks giving your mind the ultimate makeover—it's as though you sent your brain to a world-class spa.

You learned healthier ways to move and eat that will nurture and support your brain cells. The daily Brain Train exercises you've been doing have strengthened the connections between your neurons, making them more efficient and durable. And I bet you can feel the difference. The panelists who tried the Brainpower Game Plan consistently told us that it left them feeling mentally sharper and more on the ball. Many said that their moods brightened and stress levels dropped. The message we heard over and over was "I feel more control over my life."

Let's see just how much you improved by testing your Brain Q one more time. You'll see that the layout of Quiz 2 is the same as the first one you took, but the stories, names, numbers, and photography have been changed here. This is so that your new Brain Q score won't be based on remembering the answers from the first quiz, but will accurately reflect any progress you've made by following the Brainpower Game Plan. Once again, all you need is a pen, some scrap paper, a timer (a stopwatch is great, but any watch or clock with a second hand will do), and a quiet space where you won't be disturbed. Ready? Let's get started!

NO. 1

Set your stopwatch for 2 minutes and write down as many words that begin with B as you can. Do not repeat words and avoid using proper names. Stop when 2 minutes are up.

NO. 2

Fill in the blanks with the numbers, letters, or symbols that come next in each sequence.

ROW

1	1	6	11	16	21			
2	4	10	16	22	28			
3	B	D	F	H	J			
4	2	B	4	D	6	F		
5	**	+	\\	*	++	\		

NO. 3 | PART 1

Read the following paragraph. When you finish reading, turn the page.

Mike Brown and his wife, Judy, plan to open a children's shoe store. They looked for a location near the center of town in Clarkston. They first saw a basement-level site on Oak Street, but it was too dark. On Thursday, they found a place on Mission Street. It is at street level, with large windows facing the sidewalk. It has a storage area in the rear. There is a playground across the street that is always filled with parents and small children. After signing the lease, Mike and Judy went to their favorite restaurant, Jimmy's, to celebrate and eat lunch. Judy, who had worked for 13 years at "If the Shoe Fits" in the nearby city of Hartsville, decided to have a play area in the front of the store with a large bin for dress-up clothes. They named the store "Brown's Shoes."

Set your stopwatch for 2 minutes and write down as much of the story you just read as you can remember. Include all the details you can recall, in any order. No peeking—rely only on your memory. Stop when 2 minutes are up.

NO. 4

Set your stopwatch for 3 minutes and solve as many of the following math problems as you can. Feel free to use a separate sheet of paper for your calculations. Stop when 3 minutes are up.

ROW

1	7 x 4 =	21 + 32 =	149 – 45 =	542 – 56 =
2	135 ÷ 5 =	40 x 8 =	3 x 8 =	46 ÷ 4 =
3	120 ÷ 10 =	24 + 5 =	70 – 7 =	24 ÷ 8 =
4	11 x 4 =	79 – 38 =	48 ÷ 2 =	235 – 43 =
5	30 ÷ 2 =	53 – 11 =	32 – 7 =	75 x 3 =
6	12 – 4 =	33 x 2 =	10 – 7 =	350 ÷ 50 =
7	4 + 17 =	27 x 5 =	85 ÷ 5 =	532 – 67 =
8	92 – 5 =	66 ÷ 11 =	16 – 8 =	85 – 32 =
9	101 – 40 =	209 + 12 =	81 ÷ 9 =	112 – 32 =
10	54 + 21 =	40 – 3 =	43 + 29 =	24 ÷ 2 =
11	40 – 3 =	27 + 99 =	24 ÷ 2 =	456 x 10 =
12	43 – 9 =	23 – 7 =	12 + 6 =	46 x 8 =
13	38 + 9 =	5 + 43 =		

NO. 5 | PART 1

Read the following list. When you finish reading, turn the page.

Pears	Cereal	Buns	Oranges
Cheese	Onions	Peas	Squash
Tuna	Pretzels	Bread	Ice cream
Beets	Waffles	Cabbage	Tape
Paper	Hot dogs	Yogurt	Plums

Set your stopwatch for 2 minutes and write down as many items from the list as you can remember, in any order. Stop when 2 minutes are up.

_____   _____   _____   _____

_____   _____   _____   _____

_____   _____   _____   _____

_____   _____   _____   _____

_____   _____   _____   _____

NO. 6

At the beginning of this quiz, you read a brief story. Set your stopwatch for 2 minutes and write down as many details of that story as you can remember, in any order. Stop when 2 minutes are up.

_____

_____

_____

_____

_____

_____

_____

_____

_____

_____

Set your stopwatch for 2 minutes and examine this group of photographs, which feature 9 different people and their first and last names. When 2 minutes are up, turn the page.

BEVERLY HOWE

JOSHUA THOMAS

ASTRID ROGERS

TIM KNOWLES

NOAH BRIGHTLEY

HOLLY FERNANDEZ

MICHAEL ROTHFIELD

HANNAH TORTORIELLO

ANNA BOWER

Now look again at the photographs, this time not matched with names. Set your stop-watch for 2 minutes and fill in as many of the first and last names as you can remember. Stop when 2 minutes are up.

A short time ago you read a list of words. How well do you remember the list now? Set your stopwatch for 2 minutes and write down as many of the words as you can remember. Stop when 2 minutes are up.

_____	_____	_____	_____
_____	_____	_____	_____
_____	_____	_____	_____
_____	_____	_____	_____
_____	_____	_____	_____

Set your stopwatch for 1 minute and study the photograph below. When time is up, turn to the next page.

NO. 9 | PART 2

Write down as many objects as you can remember from the photograph you just studied.

_____   _____

_____   _____

_____   _____

_____   _____

_____   _____

_____   _____

_____   _____

_____   _____

A short time ago you studied a group of photographs of different people and their names. Set your stopwatch for 2 minutes and fill in as many first and last names as you can remember. Stop when 2 minutes are up.

SECTION 2: Diet

Read each statement and circle the answer that most accurately describes you.

1	I eat fish—especially fatty varieties, such as salmon.	never	rarely	sometimes	often	always
2	I eat at least 3 servings of vegetables a day.	never	rarely	sometimes	often	always
3	I eat breakfast.	never	rarely	sometimes	often	always
4	I watch my sodium intake.	never	rarely	sometimes	often	always
5	I eat at least one serving of fruit a day.	never	rarely	sometimes	often	always
6	I eat foods that are rich in vitamin E, such as avocados, olive oil, sunflower seeds, and nuts	never	rarely	sometimes	often	always
7	I eat fast food.	never	rarely	sometimes	often	always
8	I wait until I'm starving to eat.	never	rarely	sometimes	often	always
9	I snack on candy and cookies when I'm hungry.	never	rarely	sometimes	often	always
10	I eat packaged foods such as crackers and cookies.	never	rarely	sometimes	often	always

SECTION 3: Exercise

Read each statement and circle the answer that most accurately describes you.

11	I take a brisk walk during the day.	never	rarely	sometimes	often	always
12	I dance—either in a class or just for fun.	never	rarely	sometimes	often	always
13	I exercise strenuously enough to work up a sweat.	never	rarely	sometimes	often	always
14	I practice yoga, tai chi, Pilates, or some other type of flexibility and form-specific training.	never	rarely	sometimes	often	always
15	When I'm feeling stressed out, I exercise to clear my mind.	never	rarely	sometimes	often	always
16	I include strength training in my workout.	never	rarely	sometimes	often	always
17	I incorporate a new exercise into my workout.	never	rarely	sometimes	often	always
18	I work out with friends or colleagues.	never	rarely	sometimes	often	always
19	Regular old walking is a part of my routine—that is, I walk to work, to school, or around the neighborhood.	never	rarely	sometimes	often	always
20	I would describe myself as a very active person.	never	rarely	sometimes	often	always

SECTION 4: Memory Fitness, Stress, and Socializing

Read each statement and circle the answer that most accurately describes you.

21	I feel burned out and overwhelmed.	never	rarely	sometimes	often	always
22	I feel really bored and unchallenged at work. I watch the clock.	never	rarely	sometimes	often	always
23	I worry that I am going to forget someone's name.	never	rarely	sometimes	often	always
24	I spend most of the day alone.	never	rarely	sometimes	often	always
25	I enter a room and forget what I went in there to do.	never	rarely	sometimes	often	always
26	I lose my train of thought in conversation.	never	rarely	sometimes	often	always
27	I have no trouble relaxing—I know how to unwind and put a chaotic day behind me.	never	rarely	sometimes	often	always
28	I go out with friends.	never	rarely	sometimes	often	always
29	I enjoy having a new experience, whether it's taking a class, traveling to a foreign country, or simply taking a different route to or from work.	never	rarely	sometimes	often	always
30	I enter my appointments into a calendar, day planner, or personal digital assistant (PDA). What would I do without it?	never	rarely	sometimes	often	always

YOU'RE FINISHED!

READ A BRAINPOWER SUCCESS STORY

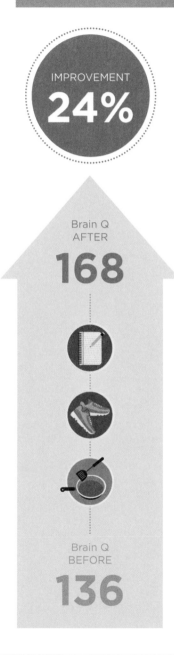

IMPROVEMENT
24%

Brain Q
AFTER
168

Brain Q
BEFORE
136

PANELIST: **Diane Cox**

AGE: **41**

I could honestly feel my brain atrophying. I was mourning the death of my brain cells! It wasn't that long ago that I felt that my memory was "leak proof"—I never had to look up a phone number a second time. But for the last couple of years, I've been frustrated by my forgetfulness. As a result, my kids missed doctors' appointments, bills were paid late, and library books went unreturned. Once I even forgot to attend a PTA meeting—which I was supposed to run. I'm not an airhead. I'm a very competent person. But that day sent me over the edge.

I signed up for the Brainpower Game Plan and became especially dedicated to the organizational tools that Dr. Green recommended. Among the many changes I made, I created a daily calendar—known in my household as the "hot spot"—that spells out everyone's individual schedule. I'm now devoted to to-do lists and I keep them, along with emergency numbers, coupons, reminders, and other essential family information, in a three-ring notebook.

There were days when I found myself spinning in the family room, wondering Oh my gosh, where do I start? **Now our whole life has a sense of calm and control. It's been really nice to gain it back.**

Everyday Brain Skills

NO. 1

If you wrote down:	Give yourself:
Zero words =	0
1–5 words =	1
6–10 words =	2
11–15 words =	3
16–20 words =	4
21+ words =	5
NO. 1 POINTS:	

NO. 2

Answers:

ROW 1 26, 31, 36

ROW 2 34, 40, 46

ROW 3 L, N, P

ROW 4 8, H

ROW 5 **, +

If you wrote down:	Give yourself:
Zero correct =	0
1–3 correct =	1
4–6 correct =	2
7–9 correct =	3
10–12 correct =	4
13 correct =	5
NO. 2 POINTS:	

NO. 3

Here are all the phrases that you might have remembered after you read the story:

Mike Brown	Small children
Wife	Signing the lease
Judy	Went to
Children's	Favorite restaurant
Shoe store	Jimmy's
A location	Celebrate
Center of town	Lunch
Clarkston	Had worked
Basement-level site	13 years
Oak Street	"If the Shoe Fits"
Too dark	Nearby city
Thursday	Hartsville
Mission Street	Decided
Street level	Play area
Large windows	Front of the store
Sidewalk	Large bin
Storage area	Dress-up clothes
Rear	Brown's Shoes
Playground	
Across the street	
Always filled	
Parents	

If you wrote down:	Give yourself:
Zero phrases =	0
1–8 phrases =	1
9–15 phrases =	2
16–23 phrases =	3
24–32 phrases =	4
33–40 phrases =	5
NO. 3 POINTS:	

NO. 4

Answers:

ROW **1** 28, 53, 104, 486

ROW **2** 27, 320, 24, 11.5

ROW **3** 12, 29, 63, 3

ROW **4** 44, 41, 24, 192

ROW **5** 15, 42, 25, 225

ROW **6** 8, 66, 3, 7

ROW **7** 21, 135, 17, 465

ROW **8** 87, 6, 8, 53

ROW **9** 61, 221, 9, 80

ROW **10** 75, 37, 72, 12

ROW **11** 37, 72, 126, 4560

ROW **12** 34, 16, 18, 368

ROW **13** 47, 48

If you got:	Give yourself:
Zero correct =	0
1–3 correct =	1
4–6 correct =	2
7–9 correct =	3
10–12 correct =	4
13+ correct =	5
NO. 4 POINTS:	

NO. 5

Remembering that list wasn't easy. Here's how to score yourself.

If you remembered:	Give yourself:
Zero words =	0
1–4 words =	1
5–8 words =	2
9–12 words =	3
13–16 words =	4
17–20 words =	5
NO. 5 POINTS:	

NO. 6

Refer to the phrases from No. 3.

If you remembered:	Give yourself:
Zero phrases =	0
1–8 phrases =	1
9–15 phrases =	2
16–23 phrases =	3
24–32 phrases =	4
33–40 phrases =	5
NO. 6 POINTS:	

ANSWERS TO SECTION 1:
Everyday Brain Skills

NO. 7

Faces and names can, for some, be the hardest thing to remember. How'd you do?

If you remembered:	Give yourself:
Zero names =	0
1-2 names =	1
3-4 names =	2
5-6 names =	3
7-8 names =	4
9 names =	5

NO. 7 POINTS:

NO. 8

Now you were asked to remember that list all over again.

If you remembered:	Give yourself:
Zero words =	0
1-4 words =	1
5-8 words =	2
9-12 words =	3
13-16 words =	4
17-20 words =	5

NO. 8 POINTS:

NO. 9

Here is a list of all the objects pictured.

- RED CABBAGE
- LETTUCE
- RED PEPPER
- CELERY
- TOMATO
- CARROTS
- STRAW-BERRIES
- PINEAPPLE
- CROISSANT
- BAGEL
- TRI-COLORED PASTA
- SLICED LOAF OF BREAD
- SPAGHETTI
- PENNE PASTA
- SALAMI
- HAM
- SAUSAGE
- PITCHER OF MILK
- FRUIT YOGURT
- CHEESE

If you remembered:	Give yourself:
Zero objects =	0
1-4 objects =	1
5-8 objects =	2
9-12 objects =	3
13-16 objects =	4
17-20 objects =	5

NO. 9 POINTS:

NO. 10

Your final question in Part 1 asked you to remember a group of names and faces. Here's how to score yourself.

If you remembered:	Give yourself:
Zero names =	0
1-2 names =	1
3-4 names =	2
5-6 names =	3
7-8 names =	4
9-10 names =	5

NO. 10 POINTS:

CONT'D

ANSWERS TO SECTION 2:
Diet

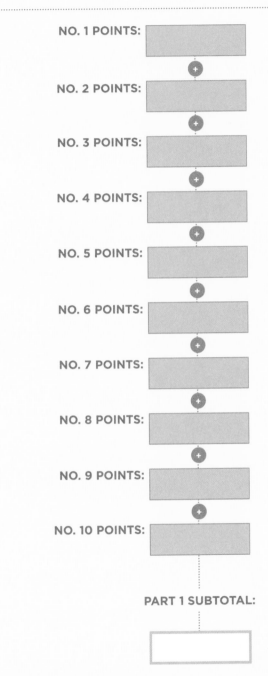

NO. 1 POINTS: [ ]

+

NO. 2 POINTS: [ ]

+

NO. 3 POINTS: [ ]

+

NO. 4 POINTS: [ ]

+

NO. 5 POINTS: [ ]

+

NO. 6 POINTS: [ ]

+

NO. 7 POINTS: [ ]

+

NO. 8 POINTS: [ ]

+

NO. 9 POINTS: [ ]

+

NO. 10 POINTS: [ ]

PART 1 SUBTOTAL:

[ ]

If you answered numbers 1–6:	Give yourself:
never =	1
rarely =	2
sometimes =	3
often =	4
always =	5

If you answered numbers 7–10:	Give yourself:
always =	1
often =	2
sometimes =	3
rarely =	4
never =	5

1 _____   6 _____
2 _____   7 _____
3 _____   8 _____
4 _____   9 _____
5 _____   10 _____

Add up the points you recorded above for questions 1 through 10 for your

PART 2 SUBTOTAL:

[ ]

ANSWERS TO SECTION 3:
Exercise

If you answered numbers 11–20:	Give yourself:
never =	1
rarely =	2
sometimes =	3
often =	4
always =	5

ANSWERS TO SECTION 4:
Memory Fitness, Stress, and Socializing

If you answered numbers 21–26:	Give yourself:
always =	1
often =	2
sometimes =	3
rarely =	4
never =	5

If you answered numbers 27–30:	Give yourself:
never =	1
rarely =	2
sometimes =	3
often =	4
always =	5

11 _____   16 _____

12 _____   17 _____

13 _____   18 _____

14 _____   19 _____

15 _____   20 _____

21 _____   26 _____

22 _____   27 _____

23 _____   28 _____

24 _____   29 _____

25 _____   30 _____

Add up the points you recorded above for questions 11 through 20 for your

PART 3 SUBTOTAL:

Add up the points you recorded above for questions 21 through 30 for your

PART 4 SUBTOTAL:

Total = Your New Brain Q Score

Now that you have taken the Brain Q Quiz a second time, stop for a moment or two to think about your score. How have your results changed compared with your first attempt 4 weeks ago, before you started the Brainpower Game Plan? What were your priorities at the outset? Did you achieve them?

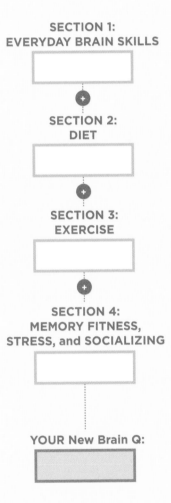

SECTION 1:
EVERYDAY BRAIN SKILLS

+

SECTION 2:
DIET

+

SECTION 3:
EXERCISE

+

SECTION 4:
MEMORY FITNESS,
STRESS, and SOCIALIZING

YOUR New Brain Q:

I HOPE YOUR SCORES IMPROVED IN EVERY SECTION OF THE QUIZ. But if your Brain Q didn't increase as much as you had wanted, consider going back and repeating the part of the plan where you feel you could use the most improvement, whether it's the plan's exercise, diet, or brain-train component. **Think of the book as a resource you can use any time to buff up your brain cells.**

" Moving forward, it's essential to keep caring about your brain."

Make the plan part of your life

As much as possible, try to incorporate the aspects of the Brainpower Game Plan that mattered most to you into your daily life. "This is a jumping-off point for me," says panelist Jane Hess. "I'm ready to do the plan again." If you feel the same, go for it—there's absolutely no reason not to restart the plan if you like. At minimum, however, try to follow the basic principles of the diet and exercise portions, and spend at least a few minutes every day keeping your neurons nimble.

There are limitless ways you can exercise your brain cells, so be on the lookout for new mental workouts. Many panelists told us how much they loved challenging themselves with brain-boosting games every day, and several got their families in on the fun. (Don't forget: you can play a variety of brain fitness games for free at *prevention.com/ braingames.*) Any game that requires you to think, react, recall, or solve problems is acceptable, but playing against the clock is the key to building bigger mental muscles.

Keep practicing those memory strategies too. Your goal should be to make using memory strategies a habit—that is, so engrained that you automatically put them to use for remembering important information without having to think about doing it. And if one strategy doesn't seem to be working for you, go back and review the other strategies you learned about over the past 4 weeks. I know you'll find one that clicks.

Also make a habit of trying new things in order to snap your brain out of its routine. If you devour mystery novels, read some historical fiction instead. Rearrange the living room furniture. Sample a new cuisine—how about Thai food or Spanish tapas? Check out new Web sites—a 2008 study found that surfing the Internet actually stimulates parts of the brain that control your ability to reason and make decisions.

I recommend that you take your mind completely out of its comfort zone and discover an all-new skill or activity once a year—take French lessons, for instance, or learn to play golf. I got this idea from a man attending one of my lectures, who told me that each year he resolves to try something he has never done before. His most recent conquest? Learning to play the guitar.

Don't let your new routine become too routine

In particular, be sure to review the organizational tools you rely on from time to time. It's crucial to rethink the strategies you use to stay on track if you undergo a major life transition and have new information and responsibilities to manage, such as when you move to a new home or start a new job. Or add a new family member, as panelist Diane Cox discovered when she had her fourth child. "We never sat down and regrouped after she came along," says Diane, who credits the Brainpower Game Plan with helping to restore order to her home. "Our routines weren't working anymore because our lifestyle had changed so much. Before we started the plan, we were flying by the seat of our pants. Now there is some method to the madness."

Practice, practice, practice

Remember what the research shows: you need to continue practicing brain skills to keep them sharp. Think of maintaining effective brain skills the way you would keep weight under control. If you have been overeating but cut calories for a month, you will likely lose a few pounds. (And if you lost unwanted weight over the past 4 weeks, pat yourself on the back!) But, as dieters often discover, once you start overeating again, the weight returns.

The same thing is true of the brain skills you have honed over the past month. If you followed the plan closely, your score on the skills portion of the test probably jumped. (Several of our panelists improved their skills score by more than 50%!) However, we know from many studies that the gains people make when they work on brain skills often fade once they stop practicing.

Love your brain

How does it feel to be ahead of the curve? That's right: completing the Brainpower Game Plan makes you a pioneer, undoubtedly the first person on your block to adopt a comprehensive strategy to care for your brain. Moving forward, it's essential to keep caring about your brain. For years, we took brain health for granted, largely because too little was known about the mysterious mental muscle. But more and more each day, scientists are unravelling its secrets—and the secrets of people who stay sharp-witted throughout their lives. Congratulations: you are now well-equipped to be one of them.

SUBSTITUTION GUIDE

While each menu is carefully calibrated, it is possible to substitute one item for another, as long as you follow our substitution guide below. The following foods are interchangeable as long as you adhere to the portion sizes. For instance, if the menu for a given day calls for one whole-grain frozen waffle, I can look under "Grains" to see my options: I can have a toasted English muffin—a personal favorite of mine—instead. Be sure to check the list any time you make a substitution.

GRAINS

- Oatmeal, dry cereal, or pasta, ½ c cooked
- Whole-grain, like brown rice or quinoa, ⅓ c
- Whole-grain crackers, 100 calories
- Whole-grain frozen waffle, 1
- Whole-wheat bread, 1 slice (1 oz or 28 g)
- Whole-wheat English muffin, ½
- Winter squash, 1 c

PROTEIN

- 1% cottage cheese, ¼ c
- Beans, cooked/canned (kidney, black, garbanzo, etc.), ½ c
- Beans, dried ½ c
- Crab, shrimp, lobster, scallops, or clams, 2 oz
- Egg, 1
- Egg substitute, ½ c
- Poultry, fish, or lean meat, 1 oz cooked
- Tofu, 4 oz
- Tuna or wild salmon, ¼ c canned (2 oz, about ½ can)

DAIRY

- Calcium-enriched soy, rice, or almond milk (30% calcium), 8 oz
- Grated Parmesan cheese, ¼ c
- Low-fat cheese, 1 oz
- Nonfat or 1% milk, 1 c (8 oz)
- Nonfat fruit yogurt, 6 oz
- Nonfat or light plain yogurt, 8 oz

FATS

- Butter, margarine, vegetable oil, or creamy salad dressing, 1 tsp
- Grated Parmesan cheese, 2 Tbsp
- Ground flaxseed, 1 ½ Tbsp
- Light dressing, 2 Tbsp
- Light margarine, light mayonnaise, or regular cream cheese, 1 Tbsp
- Light sour cream, 2 Tbsp
- Nut butter, ½ Tbsp
- Nuts (6–7 almonds, 4 walnut halves, 8–10 peanuts, 4–5 cashews, 1–2 Brazil nuts), 1 Tbsp
- Oil and vinegar salad dressing, 1 Tbsp
- Olives, 9 med
- Sunflower, pumpkin, or sesame seeds, 2 tsp

FRUIT

- Dried fruit, 2 Tbsp
- Fresh fruit, 1 sm piece
- Fresh or frozen fruit, ½ c sliced
- Fruit juice, ½ c (4 oz)
- Grapefruit, ½
- Melon, 1 c cubed

VEGETABLES

- Cooked vegetables, ½ c
- Raw leafy vegetables (mixed greens, spinach, romaine lettuce), 1 c

ANSWER KEY FOR BRAINPOWER GAME PLAN

DAY 3: FIND IT

From left:
1st symbol: 12
2nd symbol: 16
3rd symbol: 11

DAY 6: GET THE PICTURE

List of items:
- **LAMPS**
- **CHEST OF DRAWERS**
- **PLANT**
- **LARGE, EMPTY PLANT HOLDER**
- **SMALL, EMPTY PLANT HOLDER**
- **LARGE WINDOW**
- **BLINDS ON LARGE WINDOW**
- **WHITE SOFA**
- **WHITE OTTOMAN**
- **2 STRIPED PILLOWS**
- **GOLD PILLOW**
- **BURGUNDY PILLOW**
- **FLOOR PLANT**
- **COFFEE TABLE**
- **LAMP ON COFFEE TABLE**
- **SMALL VIOLIN**
- **3 SMALL WINDOWS**
- **BOOKSHELF**
- **BOOKS**
- **GLOBE**
- **SMALL PLANT ON BOOKSHELF**
- **SMALL LAMP ON BOOKSHELF**
- **BEIGE CARPET**

DAY 13: HAPPY TRAILS

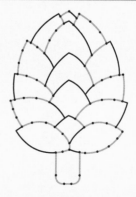

DAY 14: MAZE MYSTERY

DAY 15: REBUS RALLY

- BIG BAD WOLF
- SLOW DOWN
- READ BETWEEN THE LINES
- CLEVER AFTERTHOUGHT
- WARM UP
- EGGS OVER EASY
- KEEP IN TOUCH
- SCOTCH ON THE ROCKS
- CORNER TABLE
- LESSER OF TWO EVILS

DAY 17: HOW SYMBOLIC

Brain training is fun

DAY 19: TRIANGLES

13

DAY 19: RIDDLE ME THIS

Answer: The back man can see the hats worn by the two men in front of him. So, if both of those hats were white, he would know that the hat he wore was black. But, since he doesn't answer, he must see at least one black hat ahead of him. After it becomes apparent to the middle man that the back man can't figure out what he's wearing, he knows that there is at least one black hat worn by himself and the front man. Knowing this, if the middle man saw a white hat in front of him, he'd know that his own hat was black and could answer the question correctly. But, since he doesn't answer, he must see a black hat on the front man. After it becomes apparent to the front man that neither of the men behind him can answer the question, he realizes the middle man saw a black hat in front of him. So he says, correctly, "My hat is black."

DAY 20: LOOK MA— NO VOWELS!

Get in great shape by using the Brain Power Book. Surprise yourself and your friends with your powers of deductive reasoning. Seem familiar? Perhaps you or your kids like to text message.

DAY 21: TEASERS

S, O, N (September, October, and November) are the next in the sequence. The sequence is the first letter of the months of the year.

Mount Everest. It was still the highest in the world even before it was officially discovered.

You don't bury the SURVIVORS!

DAY 21: JIGSAWS

DAY 22: GET THE GROUP

7 groups

DAY 25: TRAIL BLAZER

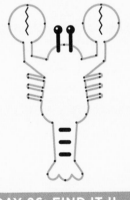

DAY 26: FIND IT II

From left:
19, 6, 12

DAY 28: DECODE THIS

Great job. Your brain is trained.

Adlard, P.A., V.M. Perreau, V. Pop, C.W. Cotman, "Voluntary Exercise Decreases Amyloid Load in a Transgenic Model of Alzheimer's Disease," *Journal of Neuroscience*, 25 (2005):4217–21.

Albert, C.M., C.H. Hennekens, C.J. O'Donnell, U.A. Ajani, V.J. Carey, W.C. Willett, J.N. Ruskin, J.E. Manson, "Fish Consumption and Risk of Sudden Cardiac Death," *JAMA*, 279 (1998):23–28.

Andel, R., M. Crowe, N.L. Pedersen, J. Mortimer, E. Crimmins, B. Johansson, M. Gatz, "Complexity of Work and Risk of Alzheimer's Disease: A Population-Based Study of Swedish Twins," *Journals of Gerontology. Series B, Psychological Sciences and Social Sciences*, 60 (2005):P251–8.

Araujo, J.A., G.M. Landsberg, N.W. Milgram, A. Miolo, "Improvement of Short-Term Memory Performance in Aged Beagles by a Nutraceutical Supplement Containing Phosphatidylserine, Ginkgo Biloba, Vitamin E, and Pyridoxine," *Canadian Veterinary Journal*, 49 (2008):379–85.

Ball, K., D.B. Berch, K.F. Helmers, J.B. Jobe, M.D. Leveck, M. Marsiske, J.N. Morris, G.W. Rebok, D.M. Smith, S.L. Tennstedt, F.W. Unverzagt, S.L. Willis, "Effects of Cognitive Training Interventions with Older Adults: A Randomized Controlled Trial," *JAMA*, 288 (2002):2271–81.

Barranco Quintana, J.L., M.F. Allam, A. Serrano Del Castillo, R. Fernández-Crehuet Navajas, "Alzheimer's Disease and Coffee: A Quantitative Review," *Neurological Research*, 29 (2007):91–5.

Blumenthal, J.A., M.A. Babyak, P.M. Doraiswamy, L. Watkins, B.M. Hoffman, K.A. Barbour, S. Herman, W.E. Craighead, A.L. Brosse, R. Waugh, A. Hinderliter, A. Sherwood, "Exercise and Pharmacotherapy in the Treatment of Major Depressive Disorder," *Psychosomatic Medicine*, 69 (2007):587–96.

Butler, S.M., J.W. Ashford, D.A. Snowdon, "Age, Education, and Changes in the Mini-Mental State Exam Scores of Older Women: Findings from the Nun Study," *Journal of the American Geriatric Society*, 44 (1996):675–81.

Castelli, D.M., C.H. Hillman, S.M. Buck, H.E. Erwin, "Physical Fitness and Academic Achievement in Third- and Fifth-Grade Students," *Journal of Sport and Exercise Psychology*, 29 (2007):239–52.

Cobb, J.L., P.A. Wolf, R. Au, R. White, R.B. D'Agostino, "The Effect of Education on the Incidence of Dementia and Alzheimer's Disease in the Framingham Study," *Neurology*, 45 (1995):1707–12.

Colcombe, S.J., A.F. Kramer, K.I. Erickson, P. Scalf, E. McAuley, N.J. Cohen, A. Webb, G.J. Jerome, D.X. Marquez, and S. Elavsky, "Cardiovascular Fitness, Cortical Plasticity, and Aging," *Proceeds of the National Academy of Sciences*, 101 (2004):3316–21.

Colcombe, S.J., K.I. Erickson, P.E. Scalf, J.S. Kim, R. Prakash, E. McAuley, S. Elavsky, D.X. Marquez, L. Hu, and A.F. Kramer, "Aerobic Exercise Training Increases Brain Volume in Aging Humans," *Journals of Gerontology. Series A, Biological Sciences and Medical Sciences*, 61 (2006):1166–70.

Conklin, S.M., S.B. Manuck, J.K. Yao, J.D. Flory, J.R. Hibbeln, M.F. Muldoon, "High Omega-6 and Low Omega-3 Fatty Acids Are Associated with Depressive Symptoms and Neuroticism, *Psychosomatic Medicine*, 69 (2007):932–4.

Costa, M.S., P.H. Botton, S. Mioranzza, D.O. Souza, L.O. Porciúncula, "Caffeine Prevents Age-Associated Recognition Memory Decline and Changes Brain-Derived Neurotrophic Factor and Tirosine Kinase Receptor (TrkB) Content in Mice," *Neuroscience*, 153 (2008):1071–8.

Crooks, V.C., J. Lubben, D.B. Petitti, D. Little, V. Chiu, "Social Network, Cognitive Function, and Dementia Incidence Among Elderly Women," *American Journal of Public Health*, 98 (2008):1221–7.

Davis, C.L., P.D. Tomporowski, C.A. Boyle, J.L. Waller, P.H. Miller, J.A. Naglieri, M. Gregoski, "Effects of Aerobic Exercise on Overweight Children's Cognitive Functioning: A Randomized Controlled Trial," *Research Quarterly for Exercise and Sport*, 78 (2007):510–9.

den Heijer, T., M.I. Geerlings, F.E. Hoebeek, A. Hofman, P.J. Koudstaal, M.M.B. Breteler, "Use of Hippocampal and Amygdalar Volumes on Magnetic Resonance Imaging to Predict Dementia in Cognitively Intact Elderly People," *Archives of General Psychiatry*, 63 (2006):57–62.

Dodge, H.H., T. Zitzelberger, B.S. Oken, D. Howieson, J. Kaye, "A Randomized Placebo-Controlled Trial of Ginkgo Biloba for the Prevention of Cognitive Decline," *Neurology*, 70 (2008):1809–17.

Dullemeijer, C., J. Durga, I.A. Brouwer, O. van de Rest, F.J. Kok, R.J. Brummer, M.P. van Boxtel, P. Verhoef, "n 3 Fatty Acid Proportions in Plasma and Cognitive Performance in Older Adults," *American Journal of Clinical Nutrition*, 86 (2007):1479–85.

Ertel, K.A., M.M. Glymour, L.F. Berkman, "Effects of Social Integration on Preserving Memory Function in a Nationally Representative U.S. Elderly Population," *American Journal of Public Health*, 98 (2008):1215–20.

Ferris, L.T., J.S. Williams, C.L. Shen, "The Effect of Acute Exercise on Serum Brain-Derived Neurotrophic Factor Levels and Cognitive Function," *Medicine & Science in Sports & Exercise*, 39 (2007): 728–34.

Fratiglioni, L., H.X. Wang, K. Ericsson, M. Maytan, B. Winblad, "Influence of Social Network on Occurrence of Dementia: A Community-Based Longitudinal Study," *Lancet*, 355 (2000):1315–9.

Gómez-Pinilla, F., "Brain Foods: The Effects of Nutrients on Brain Function," *Nature Reviews Neuroscience*, 9 (2008):568–78.

Gruber-Baldini, A.L., K.W. Schaie, S.L. Willis, "Similarity in Married Couples: A Longitudinal Study of Mental Abilities and Rigidity-Flexibility," *Journal of Personality and Social Psychology*, 69 (1995):191–203.

He, K., E.B. Rimm, A. Merchant, B.A. Rosner, M.J. Stampfer, W.C. Willett, A. Ascherio, "Fish Consumption and Risk of Stroke in Men," *JAMA*, 288 (2002):3130–6.

Hillman, C.H., K.I. Erickson, A.F. Kramer, "Be Smart, Exercise Your Heart: Exercise Effects on Brain and Cognition," *Nature Reviews Neuroscience*, 9 (2008):58–65.

Holderbach R., K. Clark, J.L. Moreau, J. Bischofberger, C. Normann, "Enhanced Long-term Synaptic Depression in an Animal Model of Depression," *Biological Psychiatry*, 62 (2007):92–100.

Jaeggi, S.M., M. Buschkuehl, J. Jonides, W.J. Perrig, "Improving Fluid Intelligence with Training on Working Memory," *Proceeds of the National Academy of Sciences*, 105 (2008):6829–33.

Kabat-Zinn, Jon, *Wherever You Go, There You Are*, Hyperion, New York, 2005.

Kang, J.H., A. Ascherio, F. Grodstein, "Fruit and Vegetable Consumption and Cognitive Decline in Aging Women," *Annals of Neurology*, 57 (2005):713–20.

Kapaki, E., "Alcoholic Dementia: Myth or Reality?" *Annals of General Psychiatry*, 5 (Supplement 1) (2006):S57.

Larson, E.B., L. Wang, J.D. Bowen, W.C. McCormick, L. Teri, P. Crane, W. Kukull, "Exercise Is Associated with Reduced Risk for Incident Dementia Among Persons 65 Years of Age and Older," *Annals of Internal Medicine*, 144 (2006):73–81.

Lee, I.M., K.M. Rexrode, N.R. Cook, J.E. Manson, J.E. Buring, "Physical Activity and Coronary Heart Disease in Women: Is 'No Pain, No Gain' Passé?" *JAMA*, 285 (2001):1447–54.

Letenneur, L., C. Proust-Lima, A. Le Gouge, J.F. Dartigues, P. Barberger-Gateau, "Flavonoid Intake and Cognitive Decline Over a 10-Year Period," *American Journal of Epidemiology*, 165 (2007): 1364–71.

Luo, L., Y.M. Huang, "Effect of Resveratrol on the Cognitive Ability of Alzheimer's Mice," *Zhong Nan Da Xue Xue Bao Yi Xue Ban*, 31 (2006):566–9.

Malouf, R., E.J. Grimley, "Folic Acid with or without Vitamin B12 for the Prevention and Treatment of Healthy Elderly and Demented People," Cochrane Database of Systematic Reviews, www.cochrane.org/ reviews/en/ab004514.html, accessed February 11, 2009.

Morris, M.C., D.A. Evans, C.C. Tangney, J.L. Bienias, R.S. Wilson, "Associations of Vegetable and Fruit Consumption with Age-Related Cognitive Change," *Neurology*, 67 (2006):1370–76.

Morris, M.C., D.A. Evans, J.L. Bienias, C.C. Tangney, D.A. Bennett, N. Aggarwal, R.S. Wilson, P.A. Scherr, "Dietary Intake of Antioxidant Nutrients and the Risk of Incident Alzheimer Disease in a Biracial Community Study," *JAMA*, 287 (2002):3230–37.

Morris, M.C., D.A. Evans, J.L. Bienias, C.C. Tangney, D.A. Bennett, N. Aggarwal, J. Schneider, R.S. Wilson, "Dietary Fats and the Risk of Incident Alzheimer Disease," *Archives of Neurology*, 60 (2003): 194–200.

Mukamal, K.J., L.H. Kuller, A.L. Fitzpatrick, W.T. Longstreth, M.A. Mittleman, David S. Siscovick, "Prospective Study of Alcohol Consumption and Risk of Dementia in Older Adults," *JAMA*, 289 (2003):1405–13.

Netz, Y., R. Tomer, S. Axelrad, E. Argov, O. Inbar, "The Effect of a Single Aerobic Training Session on Cognitive Flexibility in Late Middle-aged Adults," *International Journal of Sports Medicine*, 28 (2007):82–7. *New England Journal of Medicine*, 352 (2005):245–53.

Ng, T.P., P.C. Chiam, T. Lee, H.C. Chua, L. Lim, E.H. Kua, "Curry Consumption and Cognitive Function in the Elderly," *American Journal of Epidemiology*, 164 (2006):898–906.

Otto, M.W., T.S. Church, L.L. Craft, T.L. Greer, J.A. Smits, M.H. Trivedi, "Exercise for Mood and Anxiety Disorders," *Journal of Clinical Psychiatry*, 68 (2007):669–76.

Qiu, C., A. Karp, E. von Strauss, B. Winblad, L. Fratiglioni, T. Bellander, "Lifetime Principal Occupation and Risk of Alzheimer's Disease in the Kungsholmen Project," *American Journal of Indian Medicine*, 43 (2003):204–11.

Rajanikant, G.K., D. Zemke, M. Kassab, A. Majid, "The Therapeutic Potential of Statins in Neurological Disorders," *Current Medicinal Chemistry*, 14 (2007):103–12.

Ratey, J., *Spark, The Revolutionary New Science of Exercise and the Brain*, Little, Brown and Company, New York, 2008.

Ravaglia, G., P. Forti, A. Lucicesare, N. Pisacane, E. Rietti, M. Bianchin, E. Dalmonte, "Physical Activity and Dementia Risk in the Elderly: Findings from a Prospective Italian Study, *Neurology*, 70 (2008):1786–94.

Ritchie, K., I. Carrière, A. de Mendonca, F. Portet, J.F. Dartigues, O. Rouaud, P. Barberger-Gateau, M.L. Ancelin, "The Neuroprotective Effects of Caffeine: A Prospective Population Study (the Three City Study)," *Neurology*, 69 (2007):536–45.

Rosenberg, I.H., "Rethinking Brain Food," *American Journal of Clinical Nutrition*, 86 (2007):1259–60.

Sapolsky, R.M., "Glucocorticoid Toxicity in the Hippocampus: Reversal by Supplementation with Brain Fuels," *Journal of Neuroscience*, 6 (1986):2240–44.

Scarmeas, N., Y. Stern, R. Mayeux, J.A. Luchsinger, "Mediterranean Diet, Alzheimer Disease, and Vascular Mediation," *Archives of Neurology*, 63 (2006):1709–17.

Schmidt, K.S., J.L. Gallo, C. Ferri, T. Giovannetti, N. Sestito, D.J. Libon, P.S. Schmidt, "The Neuropsychological Profile of Alcohol-Related Dementia Suggests Cortical and Subcortical Pathology," *Dementia and Geriatric Cognitive Disorders*, 20 (2005):286–91.

Solfrizzi, V., A. Colacicco, A. D'Introno, C. Capurso, F. Torres, C. Rizzo, A. Capurso, F. Panza, "Dietary Intake of Unsaturated Fatty Acids and Age-Related Cognitive Decline: A 8.5-Year Follow-up of the Italian Longitudinal Study on Aging," *Neurobiology of Aging*, 27 (2006):1694–1704.

Solomon, P.R., F. Adams, A. Silver, J. Zimmer, R. DeVeaux, "Ginkgo for Memory Enhancement: A Randomized Controlled Trial," *JAMA*, 288 (2002):835–40.

Spence, J.D., "Preventing Dementia by Treating Hypertension and Preventing Stroke," *Hypertension*, 44 (2004):20.

Stampfer, M.J., J.H. Kang, J. Chen, R. Cherry, F. Grodstein, "Effects of Moderate Alcohol Consumption on Cognitive Function in Women," *New England Journal of Medicine*, 352 (2005):245–53.

Stern, Y., B. Gurland, T.K. Tatemichi, M.X. Tang, D. Wilder, R. Mayeux, "Influence of Education and Occupation on the Incidence of Alzheimer's Disease," *JAMA*, 271 (1994):1004–10.

Suhr, J.A., J. Hall, S.M. Patterson, R.T. Niinistö, "The Relation of Hydration Status to Cognitive Performance in Healthy Older Adults," *International Journal of Psychophysiology*, 53 (2004):121–5.

Verghese, J., A. LeValley, C. Derby, G. Kuslansky, M. Katz, C. Hall, H. Buschke, R.B. Lipton, "Leisure Activities and the Risk of Amnestic Mild Cognitive Impairment in the Elderly," *Neurology*, 66 (2006):821–27.

Verghese, J., R.B. Lipton, M.J. Katz, C.B. Hall, C.A. Derby, G. Kuslansky, A.F. Ambrose, M. Sliwinski, H. Buschke, "Leisure Activities and the Risk of Dementia in the Elderly," *New England Journal of Medicine*, 348 (2003):2508–16.

Weuve, J., J.H. Kang, J.E. Manson, M. M.B. Breteler, J.H. Ware, F. Grodstein, "Physical Activity, Including Walking, and Cognitive Function in Older Women," *JAMA*, 292 (2004):1454–61.

Whitmer, R.A., D.R. Gustafson, E. Barrett-Connor, M.N. Haan, E.P. Gunderson, K. Yaffe, "Central Obesity and Increased Risk of Dementia More Than Three Decades Later," *Neurology*, 30 (2008):1057–64.

Willis, S.L., S.L. Tennstedt, M. Marsiske, K. Ball, J. Elias, K.M. Koepke, J.N. Morris, G.W. Rebok, F.W. Unverzagt, A.M. Stoddard, E. Wright, "Long-term Effects of Cognitive Training on Everyday Functional Outcomes in Older Adults," *JAMA*, 296 (2006):2805–14.

Wilson, R.S., K.R. Krueger, S.E. Arnold, J.A. Schneider, J.F. Kelly, L.L. Barnes, Y. Tang, D.A. Bennett, "Loneliness and Risk of Alzheimer Disease," *Archives of General Psychiatry*, 64 (2007):234–40.

Wilson, R.S., P.A. Scherr, J.A. Schneider, Y. Tang, D.A. Bennett, "Relation of Cognitive Activity to Risk of Developing Alzheimer Disease," *Neurology*, 69 (2007):1911–20.

Yokoo, E.M., J.G. Valente, L. Grattan, S.L. Schmidt, I. Platt, E.K. Silbergeld, "Low Level Methylmercury Exposure Affects Neuropsychological Function in Adults," *Environmental Health*, 2 (2003):8.

A

Abdominal fat
  brain and, 44, 46
  dementia and, 44
Aerobic exercise, 70, 74, 99
ALA. See Alpha-linolenic acid
Alcohol
  abuse, 60, 62
  brain and, 62
  dementia and, 60, 62
  HDL cholesterol and, 58
  moderation in, 60, 62
  red wine, 62
  studies, 60, 62
  women and, 62
Alcohol-related dementia (ARD), 62
Alpha-linolenic acid (ALA), 48–49
Alzheimer's disease. See also Cognitive
  disease; Dementia
  amnestic mild cognitive impairment
    as precursor, 87
  brain in, 40
  brain training as defense against, 80
  caffeine and, 63
  curcumin and, 51
  defined, 12
  diet and, 42
  exercise for preventing, 70
  fish cutting risks for, 46
  hypertension and, 43
  Mediterranean diet and, 56–57
  resveratrol and, 62
  statin drugs and, 57–58
  trans fats and, 57
  vitamin E and, 51
American Heart Association, 49
American Journal of Clinical Nutrition, 53
American Journal of Epidemiology, 91
Amnestic mild cognitive impairment, 87
Amyloid, 70
Amyloid plaques, 51
Antioxidants
  amping up brainpower, 50–53
  in artichokes, 53
  in avocados, 51
  in berries, 53
  in cloves, 53
  in coffee, 53
  in curry, 51–53
  in dark chocolate, 51
  in nuts, 51
  in oils, 51
  in seeds, 51
  in top ten foods, 53
  in vegetables, 50–51
Anxiety, 76
Archives of Neurology, 57
ARD. See Alcohol-related dementia
Arteries, 40, 56–57, 88
Artichokes, 53
Attention, 82
Avocados, 51, 56
Axons, 39

B

BDNF. See Brain-Derived Neurotropic
  Factor
Berries, 53
Beta-amyloid, 40
Blood glucose. See Blood sugar
Blood sugar
  carbohydrates and, 59
  drops in, 58–59
  exercise and, 70
  fiber and, 59
  keeping stable, 58–59
  meals for controlling, 59
  protein and, 59
Blumenthal, James A., 77
BMI. See Body mass index
Body mass index (BMI), 46
Brain
  abdominal fat and, 44, 46
  alcohol and, 62
  in Alzheimer's disease, 40
  atrophy, with dementia, 73
  brain fog, 11
  brain fuzz, 55
  diet and, 42–43
  eating well and, 42–43
  exercising cells, 262
  loving, 263
  makeup, 39–40
  nurturing, 241
  size of, 73
Brain attacks, 47
Brain cramps, 82, 101. See also Memory
Brain games, 11, 84–85, 87. See also Brain
  training
  in Brainpower Game Plan Week
    1, 109, 113, 117, 122–123, 125,
    130–131, *131*, *134*, 134–135
  in Brainpower Game Plan Week
    2, 143, *148*, 148–149, 151, 155,
    160–161, 164–165, *168*, 168–169
  in Brainpower Game Plan Week 3,
    177, 182–183, 185, 190–191, *194*,
    194–195, 197, 202–203, *203*
  in Brainpower Game Plan Week 4,
    212–213, *213*, 215, 219, *224*, 225,
    228–229, 231, 236–237
  role of, 80–81
  strategies in, 101
  studies, 80
Brain health, 6–7, 14
  exercise and, 66–67
  long-term, 46–48
  overweight and, 43–44
  salt and, 64–65
  taking for granted, 263
  water and, 65
Brain Q. See also Intelligence quotient
  defined, 14
  fish boosting, 47
Brain Q Quiz
  for brain skills, 16–25, *21–23*, *25*,
    242–251, *247–249*, *251*
  diet in, 26, 252

exercise in, 27, 253
  for memory fitness / stress /
    socializing, 28, 254
  online, 15
  overview / tools needed, 14–15, 241
  scores, 13, 30–35, 256–261
Brain skills, 82
  in Brain Q Quiz, 16–25, *21–23*, *25*,
    242–251, *247–249*, *251*
  improving, 263
  maintaining, 263
  practicing, 263
Brain training, 11, 84–85, 87. See also
  Brain games
  as Alzheimer's disease defense, 80
  benefits, 80–81
  against clock, 84, 262
  daily practice, 82–84
  diet and, 11
  exercise and, 11
  filling cognitive reserve, 81
  learning as, 87–88
  meditation as, 92–93
  mindfulness as, 92–93
  novelty in, 81
  play in, 85, 87
  practicing, 80–81
  role of, 80
  socializing in, 81, 88–90
  strategies in, 84–85
  studies, 82–83
  with video games, 84
  work as, 90–92
Brain-derived neurotropic factor (BDNF),
  40, 47
  exercise boosting, 75–76
  neurons and, 75
Brainpower
  antioxidants amping up, 50–53
  defined, 6
  exercise boosting, 75–76
  foods and, 98
  spouses sharing, 89
Brainpower Game Plan
  answer key, 264–265
  components, 97–101
  development of, 6–7
  diet in, 98
  exercise in, 99–100
  getting started, 97–101
  incorporating in daily life, 262–263
  proof of, 12–13
  science behind, 11–12
  success secrets, 78–79
  success stories, 29, 41, 45, 52, 61, 69,
    86, 255
  test panel, 12–13
Brainpower Game Plan Week 1
  brain games in, 109, 113, 117, 122–123,
    125, 130–131, *131*, *134*, 134–135
  eating well in, 108, 112, 116, 120, 124,
    128, 132
  exercise in, 110–111, *110–111*, 114–115,
    114–115, 118–119, 119, 121, 126–127,
    126–127, 129, 133
  groceries for, 106
  meals for, 107

■ CREDITS AND ACKNOWLEDGMENTS

PHOTOGRAPHY CREDITS

All photography by Patrik Rytikangas, except: 21: top row, from left: © Daniela Stallinger, © iStockphoto.com/Neustockimages, © iStockphoto.com/Carme Balcells; middle row, from left: © Hilmar, © Daniela Stallinger, © iStockphoto.com/Yuri Arcurs; bottom row, from left: © iStockphoto.com/Digital Savant LLC, © iStockphoto.com/Yuri Arcurs, © iStockphoto.com/Kemter; 23: © iStockphoto.com/dem10; 131: © iStockphoto.com/Kevin Miller; 148: Krasnaya Collection/Superstock; 190 (bottom): from *The Little Giant Book of Optical Illusions* © 1995 by Keith Kay. Used with permission from Sterling Co., Inc.; 247: top row, from left: © iStockphoto.com/Digital Savant LLC, © iStockphoto.com/Avid Creative, Inc., © iStockphoto.com/Digital Savant LLC; middle row, from left: © iStockphoto.com/Andresr, © iStockphoto.com/Aurelio, © iStockphoto.com/Yuri Arcurs; bottom row, from left: © iStockphoto.com/Yuri Arcurs, © iStockphoto.com/Francis Black, © iStockphoto.com/MBPHOTO; 249: © iStockphoto.com/Morgan Lane Photography.

Play Brain Games, 177 (Rebus Rally): © Brain Teaser World; 195 (Riddle Me This): © 2007-2008 www.free-puzzles.net; 202 (Teasers): © 2007-2008 www.free-puzzles.net.

Designed by:
Cooper Graphic Design
www.coopergraphicdesign.com

Illustrations © Headcase Design
www.headcasedesign.com

This book was produced by:
Melcher Media, Inc.
124 West 13th Street
New York, NY 10011
www.melcher.com

Publisher: Charles Melcher
Associate Publisher: Bonnie Eldon
Editor in Chief: Duncan Bock
Senior Editor and Project Manager: Holly Rothman
Associate Editor: Shoshana Thaler
Editorial Assistant: Coco Joly
Production Director: Kurt Andrews
Art Director: Jessi Rymill
Production Assistant: Daniel del Valle

ACKNOWLEDGMENTS

From *Prevention*: We would like to thank the whole team at Melcher Media, as well as Stephanie Clarke, Sue Fleming, Tim Gower, Willow Jarosh, the whole team at Rodale books, everyone on the test panel, Danielle Kosecki, who coordinated the test panel, and the team at *Prevention.com* (including Nicola), for first raising our awareness that brain fitness was a hot topic, for proving that the *Prevention* readers wanted brain games, and for winning a Gold Award for the brain-fitness category page.

From Cynthia R. Green: Thank you to my co-authors, Liz Vaccariello and Leah McLaughlin at *Prevention*, Susan Berg at Rodale, and the rest of the folks at *Prevention* and Rodale, for the opportunity to be part of this team. Your commitment to providing cutting-edge health advice in a way that is smart, accessible, and fun is awe-inspiring. Thank you as well to Andrew Gelman, who in a spontaneous moment saw the possibilities of this connection, and Linda Loewenthal, who helped make it official. Much gratitude to Tim Gower, wordsmith extraordinaire, who managed to take many hours of working together researching, discussing, absorbing, and even rambling about all things brain health and make it all so easy to understand and pleasurable to read. Thank you as well to Sue Fleming, who created the wonderfully creative and fun fitness plan, and Willow Jarosh and Stephanie Clarke, who came up with so many amazing ways to eat brain healthy every day. Thanks to each and every one of the test panel members for volunteering your time and energy, and for being such an invaluable part of making the Brainpower Game Plan so terrific. Danielle Kosecki of *Prevention* did a tremendous job keeping the test panel process on track and on time, always with a great sense of humor and patience. And where do I even begin to thank Holly Rothman, Shoshana Thaler, Jessi Rymill, Bonnie Eldon, and the entire Melcher Media team? Thank you for overseeing this journey with such aplomb, for creating a book we are all so proud to be part of, and for being such a pleasure to work with in the process. To my parents, Susan and Ronald Green, my in-laws, Beverly Jablons and Nick Jablons, my siblings, and dear friends, my gratitude for all your support throughout not only this project but all others. You guys are truly the best. Finally, I give my deepest thanks and endless love to Hannah, Jonah, Zachary, and especially Josh, with whom I am very blessed to share the simple gift of everyday memories.

From Melcher Media: We would like to thank Lori Baird, David E. Brown, Chris Hampton, Kate Johnson, Nancy King, Lauren Nathan, Lia Ronnen, Patrik Rytikangas, Tony Serge, Lindsey Stanberry, Alex Tart, Anna Thorngate, Amanda Valente, Susan Van Horn, Jon Vermilyea, Anna Wahrman, Carl Williamson, and Megan Worman. A big thank-you to Terry Gower for helping us with the number-crunching. Finally, thank you to Michele Cooper at Cooper Graphic Design, who wove our book into a seamless whole, and to Paul Kepple and Scotty Reifsnyder, for providing the whimsical illustrations.